Bicycling Cuba

Bicycling Cuba

50 Days of Detailed Rides
from Havana to Pinar del Río and the Oriente

Wally and Barbara Smith

Backcountry Guides · Woodstock, Vermont

Library of Congress Cataloging-in-Publication Data
Smith, Wally, 1943
Bicycling Cuba : 50 days of detailed rides from Havana
to Pinar del Rio and The Oriente / Wally and Barbara Smith
p. cm.
Includes index.
ISBN 0-88150-553-6
1. Bicycle touring—Cuba—Guidebooks.
2. Bicycle trails—Cuba—Guidebooks.
3. Cuba—Guidebooks. I. Smith, Barbara. II. Title.

GV1046.C9 S65 2002
796.6'4'097291—dc21
2002066616

Cover and interior design by Corin Hirsch
Interior photographs by the authors
Maps by Paul Woodward, © 2002 The Countryman Press
Cover photograph by AFP Photo/Corbis

Published by Backcountry Guides
An imprint of The Countryman Press, P.O. Box 748, Woodstock, VT 05091
Distributed by W.W. Norton & Company, Inc., 500 Fifth Avenue, New York, NY 10110

Printed in the United States of America

10 9 8 7 6 5 4 3 2 1

To the many Cubans who welcomed us into their lives,
and to Gus, who always welcomed us back home.

Table of Rides

RIDE	NAME	DISTANCE	DURATION
I. IN AND OUT OF HAVANA			
1	Havana to Las Terrazas & Soroa	86–96 km	1–2 days
2	Havana to Viñales via the North Road	182 km	2–3 days
3	Havana to Playas del Este & Matanzas	95 km	1–2 days
4	Getting to and from Víazul Bus Terminal	5 km	$\frac{1}{2}$ hour
II. PINAR DEL RIO			
5	Soroa to San Diego de los Baños Loop	123 km	2 days
6	Viñales to San Diego de los Baños Loop	125 km	2–3 days
7	Viñales–Cayo Jutías Loop	136 km	2–3 days
8	The Far West Tour	339 km	5–6+ days
9	Viñales to Puerto Esperanza	50 km	1 day
9	Viñales to Valle Ancón	29 km	$\frac{1}{2}$ day
9	Viñales to Gran Caverna de San Tómas	40 km	1 day
9	Viñales to La Resbalosa	30 km	$\frac{1}{2}$ day
III. CENTRAL CUBA			
10	Cienfuegos–Pasacaballo Loop	39 km	1–2 days
11	Central Cuba Tour	350 km	5+ days
11	Santa Clara–Remedios Loop Option	108 km	2 days
12	Santa Clara to Trinidad over the Sierra del Escambray	144 km	2–3 days
13	Trinidad–Ancón Loop	37–57 km	1 day
14	Cienfuegos to Playa Girón	89 km	1 day
IV. THE ORIENTE			
15	Santiago de Cuba to Siboney and Bacanao	31 km	1 day
16	Santiago de Cuba to El Cobre	35 km	1 day
16	Santiago de Cuba to El Cristo	35 km	1 day
16	Santiago de Cuba to Castillo El Morro	25 km	1 day
17	South Coast Loop	500 km	5+ days
18	Holguín Miradores	29 km	1 day
19	Holguín to Gibara	66 km	1–2 days
20	The Far East Tour	561 km	8+ days
V. CONNECTING THE REGIONS OF CUBA			
21	Cycling Cuba's Great Plains	400 km	4+ days
22	Playa Girón to Matanzas City	152 km	2 days

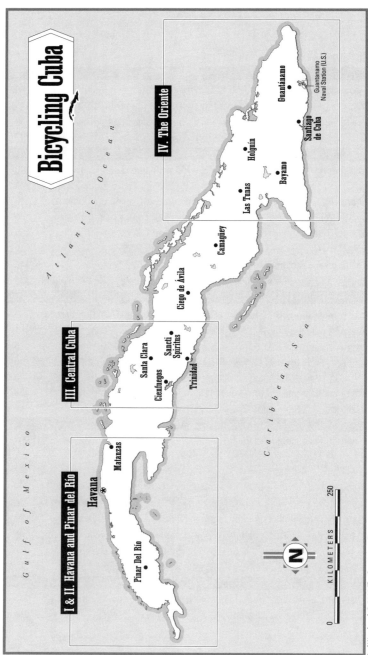

Bicycling Cuba

Gulf of Mexico

Atlantic Ocean

Caribbean Sea

I & II. Havana and Pinar del Río

Havana

Matanzas

Pinar Del Río

III. Central Cuba

Santa Clara

Cienfuegos

Sancti Spíritus

Trinidad

Ciego de Ávila

Camagüey

IV. The Oriente

Las Tunas

Holguín

Bayamo

Guantánamo

Santiago de Cuba

Guantánamo
Naval Station (U.S.)

N

0   KILOMETERS   250

Paul Woodward, © 2002 The Countryman Press

Contents

List of Maps

Acknowledgments

Before we submitted the manuscript for this book, experienced cyclists from many countries contacted us through our web site, www.bicyclingcuba.com. Several of them agreed to use drafts of the manuscript in their own cycling tours of Cuba and to provide feedback upon their return. We appreciate the encouragement and the many helpful comments they sent us. They are the "correspondents" to whom we occasionally refer in the text.

Here in Vermont, we want to thank Larry, Dawn, and everyone else at Bike Vermont for their friendship and encouragement. The hundreds of Bike Vermont guests whom we have met on tours also contributed to this book without realizing it; they showed us how much average cyclists like ourselves can achieve and how adventurous and resilient we can all become. We also want to thank Miriam Newman and her daughter Mary, our neighbors in Strafford. Miriam read the manuscript and made many helpful suggestions and corrections. Mary diligently snacked her way from one end of Cuba to the other during her junior year at the University of Havana, becoming a well qualified contributor to our "Cycling Gourmet's Guide to Cuban Street Food" sidebar on page 36. And we want to thank the good folks at The Countryman Press for making this book a reality.

Above all, we are grateful to the many people in Cuba who welcomed us into their homes and taught us about their wonderful country. We cannot begin to list them all, but we want to give special thanks to Tony and Ara in Viñales, Raúl and Magaly in Havana, and Rubi, Hebert, Virginia, and Rafael in Santiago de Cuba.

Introduction

In the course of writing this book, we discovered that bicycle touring in Cuba produces the unforeseen side effects of melancholy and sleeplessness—melancholy because we missed the island and the kind people who befriended us and sleeplessness because we lay awake at night planning our next trip.

If you have never visited Cuba, you will be astonished by its sheer size, diversity, and beauty. The distance by road from one end of Cuba to the other is about the same as from Montreal to Halifax in Canada, or from Chicago to Washington, D.C., in the United States—about 1,250 km! There are hundreds of kilometers of flat or gently rolling lowlands, lofty mountain chains, and countless tropical beaches. During most of the year, the climate is ideal for cycling, and the scenery is stunning.

There are more reasons to tour in Cuba than scenery and climate. Cycling is the ideal way to learn about a country and its people, and there are few places more worthy of knowing than Cuba. The people are renowned for their warmth, hospitality, and sense of fun. Just as the colors of the Cuban people cover the spectrum from the fairest blonde of northern Europe to the darkest hue of Africa, so their music, art, and dance are a unique harmony of European and African cultures.

The last hundred years of Cuban history have been a continuous, often inspiring, struggle for independence; and since the 1950s Cuba has been the

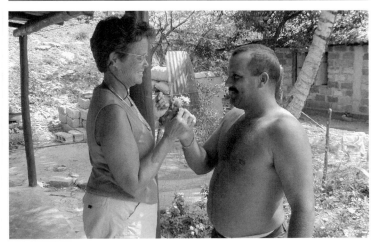

Welcome back from a friend in Soroa.

site of a revolutionary social and political experiment. There is a great deal to learn from Cuba's history, from the revolution's admirable achievements, and from the country's problems as well.

Cuba is uniquely friendly to cyclists because of the role that bicycles played during a decade of difficulties. From the early 1960s to the early 1990s, Cuba escaped the worst effects of a punishing U.S. embargo through preferential trade agreements with the Soviet Union and the Warsaw Pact nations. Then, with the collapse of the Soviet Union, aid and trade ended, oil shipments ceased, lights dimmed, transport ground to a halt, and the economy went into a free fall. In the 1990s, Cubans endured what was called the *Special Period,* a time of genuine hardship from which the country is still emerging. When gasoline was unavailable during the Special Period, Cubans turned to bicycles. Hundreds of thousands of clunky but nearly indestructible bikes, the ubiquitous Flying Pigeons, were imported from China, and Cuba soon had its own bike factory. Within a few years, millions of Cubans were traveling on two wheels. Driven by necessity, it was perhaps the fastest, most thoroughgoing transformation in the transportation system of any country in the world.

In the new millennium, the economy is improving, and more cars and trucks are on the road. Still, millions of Cubans continue to ride bicycles, and even the small minority who drive today depended on bikes yesterday. As a result, motorists accept the right of cyclists to share the road, and they are remarkably courteous. In 8,000 km of cycling in Cuba, we never felt threatened by a hostile motorist; on the contrary, we were impressed by the patience of Cuban drivers who typically stayed well behind until they could pass us safely.

There are thousands of kilometers of lightly traveled, paved roads in Cuba, and while the condition of pavement in rural areas is not always perfect, it is good enough for enjoyable cycle touring. Because bicycling is important for many Cubans, there are conveniences for cyclists including designated bike lanes on major roads, *parqueos* where bicycles can be left safely for pennies, and *poncheras,* small businesses that fix flats and do minor repairs. If you travel by automobile or tour bus, you are cut off from the people by glass walls of wealth; but when you ride a bike, just as Cubans do, human contacts are natural and easy. Cycling is without a doubt the best way to see Cuba.

We hope this book will make it easier for you to experience Cuba on your bike. When we began riding in Cuba, there were no cycling guides, and the available maps were often inaccurate. On many a day's ride we did not know how soon we would find food and water or where we would spend the night. We were often lost, or worried that we might be lost.

Today a reasonably good, complete set of maps is available in Cuba, but it omits essential information about road conditions, grades, and availability of food, water, and accommodations. There are plenty of general guidebooks on the market, but their route directions are designed for motorists. They are not detailed and precise enough for cyclists. (It is no problem if a motorist overshoots a turn by a few kilometers and has to drive back. If this happens to a cyclist, it can turn a pleasant ride into a near disaster—especially if the extra riding means arriving after dark or needlessly climbing difficult hills.)

We give detailed descriptions of routes and landmarks that will help you ride in Cuba with confidence. We provide specifics on the availability of food and bottled water, and we often recommend accommodations. Also, we try hard to let you know what the experience of cycling in Cuba is really like.

We do not attempt to duplicate the immense amount of information that is available in the general guidebooks. We concentrate on the special needs of cyclists. For information on visas and travel arrangements, health, detailed restaurant and accommodation guides, tourist attractions, and many other topics, you should read a general guidebook as well. Our two favorites are *Cuba Handbook* by Christopher Baker and *The Rough Guide to Cuba* by Fiona McAuslan and Matthew Norman. Both are available in many bookstores and from online booksellers.

Even in six months and 8,000 km of cycling, we could not come close to trying every promising bicycle route in Cuba. The routes necessarily reflect our own values and preferences. For example, we usually choose diverse terrain over flat country. Most of the routes are rural. They may begin and end in cities, but we concentrate on getting you safely out of these cities and into the countryside. Unless you are used to it, cycling in urban traffic is neither enjoyable nor safe. Some of the routes and suggestions involve city cycling, but we advise that you do most of your downtown sight-seeing on foot.

Many of the routes take you off the beaten path, some on roads that do not even appear on maps, but this is not a mountain biking book. The roads

Unique Bicycles in Cuba

When we lived in Africa, we saw bicycles that had been modified for all sorts of practical uses, but Cuban cyclists show inventiveness that we have not witnessed elsewhere. The owners of some bici-taxis add sidecars for carrying single passengers, while others stretch the frames to create recumbents. Our favorite was the old bike frame that had been transformed into a car for the comfort of paying passengers. Cuban streets are also full of special-purpose designs: utility trikes for carrying goods, hand-pedaled bikes for the disabled, even tandems—all homemade of scavenged parts.

Cubans find ways to carry things on their bikes that are as ingenious as the designs. In Bayamo we saw a cyclist with a passenger on the rear rack who was, in turn, pulling a backwards wheelbarrow loaded with goods. We have seen cyclists or their passengers carrying building supplies, an entire banana tree, bales of hay, gigantic wedding cakes, and ladders. Cyclists with live, trussed pigs and other livestock strapped to their racks were almost commonplace. Sometimes animals pull the cyclists.

It is astonishing to see how many passengers Cuban cyclists sometimes carry. We often saw three people on a bike— the cyclist, a smaller person or child on the crossbar, and a third person on the rear rack. It was more unusual to see four, typically a family group, with dad driving, a son or daughter on the crossbar, and mom in back carrying a baby or small child. Of course, the most remarkable contraptions and arrangements of people always rolled by when we did not have a camera ready.

A horse-drawn bike

While it is fun for a visiting cyclist to see the clever ways that Cubans modify and use their bikes, it is sometimes discouraging. There are occasions when you are laboring up a hill on your multi-speed, high-tech rig that cost a thousand dollars or more, and a Cuban pulls up beside you, smiling, on his old, 60-pound, single-speed Chinese bike—with a friend on board.

are all paved, though the quality of the pavement varies. Furthermore, we do not include routes where it is necessary to carry camping gear or sleep on the beach—though you certainly can if you like.

We have tried to find the very best routes in Cuba for the touring cyclist, not for the endurance athlete. Most of the rides in this book should be a pleasure for any experienced, reasonably fit rider. When routes are particularly difficult, we give ample warning.

Because most visitors will fly into Havana, Part I of this book deals with arriving in the capital and then leaving it. Two routes lead to Pinar del Río Province, and one goes to the beaches east of Havana, as far as Matanzas City. We also include a few suggestions for rides in Havana, but try them only if you are comfortable in urban traffic.

The next three parts concentrate on regions of Cuba that offer superb cycling: Pinar del Río Province in the west; the area of central Cuba roughly bounded by Santa Clara, Remedios, and Sancti Spiritus in the north and by Cienfuegos and Trinidad in the south; and the Oriente (eastern) provinces of Holguín, Granma, Santiago de Cuba, and Guantánamo. In each part there are a few single-day excursions based on popular destinations, and also more ambitious, multi-day tours.

If you are thinking of cycling from Havana all the way to central Cuba or the Oriente, there is a section at the end of the book that contains suggestions—and perhaps a surprise—for long-distance cyclists who want to connect the three principal cycling regions, perhaps to complete a tour of Cuba from one end to the other.

We should explain two omissions: We do not include Isla de La Juventud because cycling opportunities are limited, especially when weighed against the time and trouble of getting there. More significantly, we do not include routes near Varadero and some of the other heavily pro-

Rating the Routes

After many years of leading bicycle tours in Vermont, Wally has become wary of rating routes according to simple categories like *easy* or *intermediate*. Cyclists have different expectations. He would sometimes say that a ride was easy, only to learn too late that his discouraged guests had done all their cycling in Florida or Manitoba and had never climbed a real hill. Even the easiest route may have difficult sections, and vice versa. And rides can be more or less challenging for so many different reasons—hills, distance, complex directions, headwinds. Therefore, instead of using a simple rating system, we try to describe each route in sufficient detail so you will have a good idea of what to expect—which aspects are difficult and which are not—and will be able to choose rides accordingly.

This could be any good beach resort in the world.

moted beach resorts of Cuba. It is possible to have a great time and get a wonderful tan at Varadero, but visiting there does nothing to acquaint you with Cuba—you might as well be at any good beach resort in the world. In fact, most Cubans are deliberately excluded from resorts like Varadero, Santa Lucía, and Cayo Coco.

Although we have deliberately omitted some popular beach resorts, we love sun, sand, surf, and warm water as much as anyone. Our routes take you to beaches that are smaller and closer to excellent cycling country. Guardalavaca and nearby resorts on the north coast of Holguín Province, Playa Ancón on the south coast near Trinidad, and many pocket beaches along the routes are all delightful.

For meeting warm-hearted, welcoming people, enjoying their great art and music, riding through splendid scenery, and sunning on dazzling beaches washed by warm, clear seas, Cuba can't be beat. And you will find it immensely worthwhile to learn about Cuba's valiant independence struggles and revolutionary efforts to build a new society. Before you pack your panniers and rush to the airport, we will deal with a number of practical matters and try to anticipate some of your questions.

Getting Started

When and Where to Go

There is little temperature variation between winter and summer in Cuba.

Except in the high mountains, it is warm or hot all the time. In general, there is more rain and humidity from May through October than from November to April. During the wet months, the mornings are typically bright and warm, with clouds building up and rain falling late in the afternoon. Only occasionally does it rain all day—most often in September and October. If you aren't on a bike, it is possible to have a great time during any season.

Conditions during the rainier months are harder on cyclists. When extra humidity is added to Cuba's heat, cycling can become an ordeal. Also, if you are caught out in the rain repeatedly, the wet eventually works its way into your panniers, threatening to make your clothes rank with mildew and turn books and papers into a soggy mess. Riding on slick roads or in heavy downpours can be dangerous. If possible, plan your cycling trip between mid-November and April.

There are significant differences among the dry months. In late November and December there is little rain, but the grasslands are still green and the countryside tends to be more lush than in April, when some parts of Cuba have had no rain for many weeks. On the other hand, days grow noticeably longer as spring approaches. An extra hour or more of daylight can be handy when you are cycle touring.

If it is impossible for you to visit Cuba during the winter months, go anyway. Cycling in Cuba during the summer, though less than ideal, is better than not cycling there at all.

Each of the main cycling regions covered in this book has its own special appeal. For people with limited time, and for those whose highest priority is to ride in quiet, scenic, unspoiled rural areas, Pinar del Río can't be beat. We were able to find more short loop rides here than elsewhere, and this region is the most accessible from Havana.

The great attractions for the cyclist in central Cuba are the antique towns of Trinidad and Remedios, the beach at Ancón, Cienfuegos (the Pearl of the South), and the lively city of Santa Clara with its grand monument to Che Guevara. Riding between towns is pleasant, sometimes very beautiful, but it is the destinations that appeal most strongly to us. Except for the climb over the Sierra del Escambray, which is optional, the rides in central Cuba are the easiest in this book.

The Oriente is where the history of Cuba's revolutions is most strongly in evidence, and Santiago de Cuba is a must for lovers of Cuba's traditional music. The cycling in the east is probably the most spectacular on the island, but it is also the most challenging. Some days are long because of the distance between accommodations. The rides around Holguín are fine for

Racing an approaching storm in Pinar del Río

anyone, but the two longer loops in the Oriente are best for experienced touring cyclists.

Cycling Independently Versus Organized Tours

If you have cycle touring experience, if you have the skills needed to handle basic repairs and to maintain your bike, and if you are reasonably fit, then you should be able to ride the routes in this book on your own.

However, if you have never ridden a loaded bike or if you or a companion can't fix a flat and do not want to learn, then you should consider riding with an organized group. On a group cycle tour, a van or truck will carry your gear (and you, if necessary), and experienced guides will help with bicycle repairs.

The number of companies and organizations offering bicycle tours in Cuba is growing at an astonishing rate. Be cautious in selecting a tour company. Three good organizations are suggested in the appendix.

We have met several groups of cyclists in Cuba who organized their own tours. It is possible to hire a driver and a van or truck to haul luggage and provide support for tired riders. A group of 4 to 12 friends could manage this nicely, using this book as an aide in route planning.

Tips on Travel Agencies

It is easy to book flights using any of the travel agencies listed in general guidebooks. From North America, we have had excellent service from Nina

An organized tour of Swiss cyclists

Goldman of Heritage Travel in Montreal. Call 1-877-485-6004, extension 244, or e-mail ninagoldman@hotmail.com. Cuba is Nina's specialty, and she knows the country well.

Even using a good agent, it is difficult for independent travelers to make certain kinds of advance arrangements from outside Cuba. Suppose you want air tickets plus a hotel room for your first couple of nights in Havana. Most travel agencies in Canada, for example, would probably be unable to book the room. They rely on wholesalers, and they normally sell either air-only tickets or complete package tours, nothing in between. Even if your travel agent is willing to make individual arrangements for you, it may be impossible to book a room through a wholesaler for less than three nights at a top hotel.

Independent travelers to Cuba have other alternatives. One is CubaLinda.com, the first Internet travel agency based in Havana. CubaLinda.com can help you design your own package of accommodations, transportation, and activities—as much or as little as you wish to book in advance. In some locations, CubaLinda.com can arrange homestays in *casas particulares*.

Also, CubaLinda.com has services of special interest to cyclists. They rent quality bicycles for independent touring—though with a hefty $250 security deposit required. They can also arrange vans or trucks, with or without drivers, for small groups of cyclists who would like to organize their own supported tours. Check the CubaLinda.com web site and send specific questions by e-mail to the attention of Marisela Colejo. Whenever we have done so, we have received helpful replies within 24 hours.

MacQueen's Bicycle Tours of Prince Edward Island, Canada, operates a travel agency that offers more individualized and diverse services than typical travel agencies. This is possible because MacQueen's has full-time representatives in Cuba who deal directly with hotel chains and state tourism organizations. MacQueen's is also the most experienced operator of bicycle tours in Cuba. Check www.macqueens.com or call 1-800-WOW-CUBA.

Once you are on the ground in Cuba, additional resources are available. We have used Rumbos, a diversified state company that operates restaurants, guided tours, and travel agencies in major cities. Rumbos can help you book rooms and arrange ground transport. Infotur is another helpful Cuban travel organization with offices in and near Havana. There are tourism offices in major hotels around the country. Even if you are not staying in one of these hotels, you are welcome to use the services. In smaller hotels, the front desk will often help with arrangements at your next destination.

Bringing Your Bike to Cuba

It is no more difficult or expensive to bring your bike to Cuba than to any other overseas destination. Costs and regulations vary considerably depending upon your point of departure and the airline on which you fly. Some airlines charge extra, typically $50 to $75, for your bike. Others simply count the bike against your weight allowance. This can be the best deal if the weight allowance is sufficiently generous. Charter airlines flying to Cuba from Canada generally carry bikes for free, outside the modest weight allowance.

Most airlines require that your bike be in a box. At press time, Cubana, the national airline of Cuba, was the only exception among the airlines flying from North America and Central America.

The appendix contains information (effective at press time) on the policies of the major airlines flying to Cuba from North America. There are also suggestions in the appendix for boxing your bike. You should check with your travel agent for current policies before actually purchasing your ticket. If you are handling reservations yourself, call your airline before booking the flight. If possible, get the information from the airline in writing.

Rental Bikes

Bicycles are available for rent in Cuba at major tourist resorts. Also, if you stay in a private home, your host can often arrange a bike rental for you. However, the bikes that are available are almost always heavy, poorly maintained, and lacking in basic accessories like water bottles and racks. Most often they are single-speed Chinese clunkers. Though Cubans go everywhere on them, they don't do it for pleasure. These bikes are suitable only for short day rides. CubaLinda.com is the only commercial source of quality rentals that we have found.

If you go to Cuba without a bike and plan on renting one at a resort for short rides, be sure to bring a light backpack or fanny pack so that you can carry water and food. Also, bring your own wrench, screwdriver, and lubricant. You may find that the seat on your bike is too low or too high, or the gears (if any) will not shift, simply because the rental company does not have tools or lubricants to maintain bikes properly.

Several of the shorter rides around Viñales, Trinidad, and the major cities can easily be done on rental bikes. All the longer routes require better quality bikes set up for touring.

What Kind of Bike Is Best?

You can do all the routes in this book on many different types of bicycles. In fact, it is easier to specify the two common categories of bikes that should *not* be used for touring in Cuba: Ultra-light road bikes with thin tires and narrow-range gearing would be difficult to use on many of these rides. Also, the cheap bikes sold in department stores should not be used in Cuba. Besides being heavy and difficult to ride, they are not reliable enough for use in a country where spares are almost nonexistent.

During our rides in Cuba, we have used inexpensive mountain bikes, a classic touring bike, and BikeE semi-recumbents. Good quality hybrid bikes designed for touring—what many Europeans call "trekking bikes"—are excellent.

More important than the type of bike you ride is the way you set it up. If you ride a road or touring bike, be sure it has a triple crankset and a wide range of gears. The best riding in Cuba is not on the plains but in the hills and mountains. If you are pedaling in the afternoon heat with baggage on board, you will want the lowest gears you can get.

Be sure your bike has sturdy wheels, preferably 36-hole with 14-gauge spokes, and quality tires. We have had great luck over the years with Avocet Cross tires, but similar designs of good quality should be fine. We don't recommend tires narrower than 32 mm.

A comfortable saddle is essential, and a shock-absorbing seatpost is a good idea, though not necessary. The reason for these suggestions is the condition of roads in Cuba. Though all the routes in this book are paved, the quality of pavement varies. Your posterior will thank you for making your bike as comfortable as possible.

If you ride a mountain bike, you will *not* need tires with aggressive tread

European trekking bikes—a good choice for Cuba

for routes in this book. Save weight and make your work easier by mounting tires that carry higher air pressure and have a tread pattern that rolls smoothly. If you use a mountain bike for touring, consider adding bar ends. It is important to change hand positions frequently. The same point applies to hybrids.

What to Bring

Cycling Accessories

No matter what type of bike you bring to Cuba, be sure to provide enough carrying capacity for water as well as gear. If you can mount cages for three water bottles, great. If not, use a Camelbak or the equivalent for extra water.

For rides lasting more than a day, you will need a sturdy rear rack and panniers. Your bike will handle best if you use a low-rider front rack as well, with smaller panniers than those in the rear. Ideally, you should carry about 60 to 70 percent of the total weight in the rear and 30 to 40 percent in the front. We like to tour with roomy handlebar bags as well. They are the most convenient way to carry a camera, sunglasses, sunscreen, and other small items that we use frequently. Select a bag that has a plastic sleeve on top for directions.

Even if you customarily ride at home only in daylight, you never know when you might be out on the road at dusk. We recommend LED flashers and a headlamp. A bike mirror will also add to your safety, whether mounted on your handlebar, helmet, or eyeglasses. Be sure to get accustomed to it before your trip. Padded cycling gloves are a necessity; they help prevent

A sidewalk bike shop with as large a selection of parts as you are likely to see

soreness and numbness on longer rides. And, though there is little crime in Cuba, bicycles are occasionally stolen, so bring a sturdy cable lock.

We like to tour with cycle computers. They are not absolutely necessary for following the route directions, but we enjoy keeping track of the distances we travel. If you decide to use a cycle computer, consider a wireless model. Packing and unpacking bikes and loading them aboard planes and buses increase the probability of tearing the delicate wires on regular models.

In Cuba, pedestrians and even horses, goats, and cows sometimes wander around in congested streets. It is a good idea to have an old-fashioned bicycle bell or horn mounted on your handlebars. Fun, too!

Tools and Spares

Selecting tools and spares for riding in Cuba requires more thought than for riding in many other countries. There are virtually no bike shops as we know them in North America and Europe, and most spares are difficult or impossible to find. You must be more self-sufficient than usual, but don't go overboard and carry too much.

To keep things in perspective, you should know that every town has *poncheras,* where people specialize in fixing flats and are usually versatile

A *ponchera* fixes flats and much more.

bike mechanics. Cubans keep bikes running with the same ingenuity that they use on their old American cars.

We decide what to carry based on the frequency of various types of emergency repairs and maintenance tasks. The single most frequent mishap is flat tires. Next in frequency are chain and spoke problems. A discussion and a list of the tools and spares needed to fix these problems, together with items for routine bike maintenance, appear in the appendix.

If you decide to cycle on your own in Cuba and you have never fixed a flat, repaired a chain, or replaced a spoke, learn and practice these skills before you go. Bicycle repair is not rocket science, after all. There are plenty of books on the market, and a few of the best are listed in the appendix. It is a good idea to ask a knowledgeable friend to teach you, or better yet, persuade the knowledgeable friend to go along!

Clothing and Personal Items

For folks who like lists, there is a complete one in the appendix that includes all the clothing and personal items that we bring on cycle tours in Cuba. In addition to the list, there are a few other packing tips. Here, because needs and tastes are so different, we will simply give some general advice and add a few specific suggestions.

"Pack light. Leave behind half of what you decided to bring along. You will still have more than you really need." How many times we have heard this advice, given this advice, and then failed to follow it ourselves! But it really is true. Especially in a tropical country like Cuba, where informal dress is the rule, you can get by with less than you think.

Bring clothes that are appropriate for a tropical climate. We recommend travel shorts and slacks of supplex nylon or similar material. They wash easily and dry in no time. Do not bother with denim jeans or cotton sweats; they are far too heavy and bulky for cycle touring.

Wear cycling clothing when you ride. Cycling shorts give you padding and protection from chafing; cycling jerseys are more comfortable than cotton in a wide range of temperatures, and they wash and dry in a jiffy. If you are one of those folks (like Barbara a few years ago) who hates being seen in lycra, try to get over it. Cubans—especially women—have a peculiar fondness for colorful lycra, and no one will pay attention to cycling clothes except perhaps to admire them. Otherwise buy baggy mountain biking shorts with padded inserts.

Don't bother with bulky sweaters, even if you plan to spend time in the mountains where it can be cool at night. A long-sleeved polypro layering garment is all you need, together with a lightweight windbreaker or well-ventilated rain jacket.

Consider leaving your shoes at home. We ride with clipless pedals, as do many experienced cyclists, and we use Shimano's SPD Sandals. Similar SPD compatible sandals are made by Lake. They are not easy to find, but they are remarkably comfortable and work well both on and off the bike. We each bring a second pair of sturdy leather sandals to wear in the evenings and for long walks. We also bring socks in case our feet get sunburned or sore—but only one or two pairs each, and we hardly ever wear them. Why deal with smelly shoes and washing socks in the tropics?

Where to Stay

Casas particulares

When we travel in Cuba, we stay most often in *casas particulares. Casa particular* simply means private house, but tourists use the term for homes that are licensed to take in guests. Staying in a *casa* is much like staying in a B&B in England, Canada, or the U.S., except that dinner as well as breakfast is usually offered. Food in *casas particulares* is much better and more plentiful than in most hotels. Also, you get to know families by staying in their homes, and this is one of the greatest rewards of traveling in Cuba.

Joaquín and Olga operate a great *casa particular* in La Boca, near Trinidad.

Casas may not always be as comfortable in some respects as better hotels. Mattresses often sag, and pillows sometimes feel as though they were stuffed with knotted rags. Nearly all *casas* claim to have *agua caliente,* hot water, but this usually means that the showerhead is equipped with a frightening electrical device from Brazil that is supposed to heat the water. Temperatures can be erratic, and sometimes you may get a mild shock when adjusting the taps. Fortunately the current in these devices is low enough that you will not be fatally electrocuted in the shower!

Despite such drawbacks, we usually choose *casas* for the warm hospitality and good food. Also, *casas particulares* are very economical. Outside Havana and the Playas del Este, a comfortable room for two usually costs $15 or $20. With breakfast and dinner, the total is usually less than $40 for two people.

You can choose a *casa* from among those mentioned in this book or listed in the general guides. Moon's *Cuba Handbook* and *The Rough Guide to Cuba* have listings for tourist destinations. *Casas particulares* can also be found on the Internet. On the road, you can ask other travelers for the names of good places where they have stayed. (Nearly all *casa* owners have printed cards to give away; it is a good idea to collect them and exchange them with fellow travelers.)

When you pedal into a new town, young men will ask you repeatedly if

Electric showerheads can provide a shocking experience.

you want a *casa* or *una habitación,* a room. They are hoping to lead you to a *casa particular* because they will be entitled to a commission from the owner. If you don't already know of a place and time is short, you might as well accept their help. It will cost you a few extra dollars or cut into the *casa* owner's earnings, but this sometimes beats wandering around an unfamiliar town when you are tired and ready for a rest.

Most licensed *casas* display a small blue triangle on or near the front door. If a *casa* displays a *rent room* sign, it is licensed as well. When you check in, licensed operators are supposed to record your passport number and other information on a form that is submitted to the government, just as hotels do.

Operators of legal *casas particulares* are required to pay high license fees every month, whether they have guests or not. Some Cuban families try to rent rooms to tourists without a license. If you stay in an unlicensed *casa,* you are not breaking the law, but the family is doing so and could be fined heavily if caught. You could be evicted in the middle of the night.

We try to avoid unlicensed *casas* because we don't like the fact that unlicensed operators shirk the fees while others pay their share. Despite hard times, Cuba has continued to provide free education and health care and to subsidize theaters, parks, athletic facilities, and other amenities that enrich people's lives. This is expensive for a poor country, and it is an important reason that tourism revenue—including license fees from *casas*—is badly needed.

In some small towns there are no licensed *casas particulares* simply because there is not enough tourist traffic to support them. These are the only places where we have reluctantly stayed in unlicensed *casas.* (We can't list the names and addresses of families running unlicensed *casas,* for obvious reasons. However, you will have little difficulty finding them. In fact, most often they will find you.) Note: *Casas particulares* are forbidden in Varadero, Guardalavaca, and a few other resort areas because government has invested so heavily in the hotels there.

This emblem shows that a *casa particular* is licensed to take guests.

Hotels

Cuba's hotel chains are all run by state corporations, sometimes with foreign partners. The largest chain of moderately priced tourist hotels is Horizontes. Their hotels are nearly always adequate; and outside Havana, the rooms are usually less than $50 per couple with breakfast included. Often, however, these hotels are drab, and the food is rarely good.

Another large budget hotel chain is Islazul, and their hotels are usually cheaper. You may read that Islazul hotels are geared for domestic tourism—not up to international hotel standards—and not desirable for tourists. There is some truth to this, but we have stayed in Islazul hotels that are quite acceptable, with staff that speak English and are eager to attract international guests. In fact, two of our favorite Cuban hotels are run by Islazul—Hotel Royalton in Bayamo and Hotel El Mirador in San Diego de los Baños.

Hotels run by Gran Caribe, Gaviota, and Cubanacán tend to be more upscale, though we have stayed in a couple of Cubanacán places that were no better than mediocre Islazul hotels. Many foreign groups like Superclubs (Jamaica) and Sol Meliá (Spain) operate luxury hotels and resorts in joint ventures with these Cuban chains.

Most tourist hotels charge higher rates during the busier winter months. Rooms usually have twin beds—the *matrimonial* (with a double bed) is hard to find. The single rate is usually about 30 percent less than the double rate, but you can't always count on this discount. As tourism takes off in Cuba, new hotels are being built and many older ones are being closed or renovated, so prices and conditions change from month to month. Refer to a recent edition of a general guidebook or check hotel web sites, and still be prepared for surprises.

Camping

Although we have enjoyed cycle camping and cooking in the U.S. and Canada, we don't camp in Cuba. Organized campsites with basic amenities like running water and toilets—even pit toilets—are exceedingly rare. Also, while there is now plenty of food in Cuba, there are few lightweight, packaged items that make cooking easier and more convenient for backpackers and cyclists.

In a total of six months and 8,000 km of cycling in Cuba, there were only two occasions when we really wished that we had camping gear: one night in a particularly dreadful motel in central Cuba, and a second time when we shivered through much of the night on a lonely beach because the *campismo* we had counted on was closed for the season. Though it would have been nice to have our tent and sleeping bags on those occasions, we would much rather be uncomfortable one or two nights in a month than carry gear for hundreds or thousands of kilometers when we so rarely need it.

If you are an experienced cycle camper, accustomed to roughing it in undeveloped sites and cooking without convenience foods, you will certainly be able to do so in Cuba. However, if you have this kind of experience, you already own the appropriate equipment and do not need our advice. If you do not have extensive cycle camping experience, Cuba is not the place to start.

Campismos

While campgrounds like those found in North America are rare in Cuba, *campismos* are almost everywhere. These are inexpensive holiday camps where guests stay in small cabañas, usually built of cement blocks. A typical *campismo cabaña* will have single beds or bunk beds for two to six people, a simple chest of drawers, and a tiny bathroom. In the better ones that we recommend, the toilet will usually flush and the shower will have cold water. Be warned, however, that water failures are common, and some bathrooms are *bucket-powered*. That is, a bucket is provided, and you are expected to fill it with water from a tap for washing and for flushing the toilet. This is partly why one of our correspondents described staying in a *campismo* as "just like camping in a concrete tent."

Campismos may have a cafeteria or restaurant serving inexpensive meals. Sometimes the cafeteria will be closed, or the food may be gone; it depends upon when you arrive. Also, the better *campismos* in beach areas may be booked by Cubans on summer weekends and closed in the winter.

There are two government agencies running *campismos* in Cuba. The greater number by far are Campismos Populares. These facilities are meant for domestic tourism, but foreigners are usually accepted. Cubamar operates a smaller group of *campismos*, some of which aspire to be inexpensive international eco-resorts. These *campismos* typically charge dollar rates for tourists and much lower *peso* rates for Cuban citizens, and their accommodations are generally adequate.

If you plan to stay at a *campismo* near a beach area, especially on a weekend, it is prudent to make a reservation. At least check to make sure it will be open when you plan to arrive. Booking offices for Campismos Populares are found in the capital cities of each province, and they can handle reservations at Cubamar *campismos* as well.

Whatever kind of accommodation you choose, a final word about bathrooms is in order. Because Cuban plumbing systems are often in poor shape, you are usually expected *not* to flush toilet paper. A receptacle is provided in the bathroom for the soiled paper. Also, many toilets do not have seats, though this seems to be changing rapidly. As long as the toilet is clean—as it always seems to be in *casas particulares,* in decent hotels, and even in most *campismos*—there should be no problem; just sit a little lower.

Money Matters

Overview of Costs

Some cycle tourists in Cuba feel they are being extravagant if they spend more than $15 per person per day. At the other extreme, Butterfield and Robinson, one of the world's best and most expensive cycle touring companies, now offers a 10-day expedition in Cuba for $4,800 including single supplement, plus airfare. Bring the whole family and invite some friends!

The fairest, most accurate information we can give on costs is based on our own experiences and records. We stay in *casas particulares* most nights, in moderate hotels about 25 percent of the time, and in *campismos* occasionally. We eat breakfasts and dinners in our *casas* or hotels, and we snack, usually for *pesos,* during the day. With lots of bottled water, beer, and soft drinks, the occasional bottle of rum, ferries, buses, and all other miscellaneous expenses, we average about $50 per day for two. We always bring several hundred dollars extra for an unforeseen emergency, which we've never had to use.

Cuban Currencies

U.S. dollars and Cuban *pesos* are both official currencies. The *peso* is available in notes of 1, 3, 5, 10, 20, and 50 *pesos,* and there are 1 and 3 *peso* coins. There are also 1, 2, 5, and 20 *centavo* coins. In late 2001 the *peso* was devalued from 22 per U.S. dollar to 26. You can buy *pesos* in currency exchanges

A typical dollar kiosk

called CADECAS, short for *casas de cambio*. Even though, as a cyclist, you will have more use for *pesos* than the average tourist, you will still do most of your spending in U.S. currency.

There are two sources of confusion with Cuban currencies. First, some places accept payment only in dollars, some accept *pesos*, and some accept *pesos* from Cubans but only dollars from foreign tourists. Nearly all hotels and *casas particulares* require payment in U.S. dollars. So do fast-food chains like El Rápido cafeterias and dollar stores. U.S. coins used to be widely accepted, but in late 2001 the policy changed and only U.S. paper currency is now accepted. U.S. dollars are sometimes called *divisas,* and *pesos* are referred to as *moneda nacional.*

The second source of confusion concerning money in Cuba is the existence of a third, quasi-currency. Cuba has issued special bills and coins that are convertible to U.S. dollars. The convertible bills and coins can be used in Cuba exactly like U.S. money. That is, you can spend convertible currency everywhere that requires dollars; and before you leave, you can exchange it for normal U.S. cash, no questions asked.

It is a good idea to visit a CADECA soon after you arrive in Cuba and change some U.S. dollars to *pesos.* Ask for some convertible bills as well. Look them over so you will see the obvious differences. Convertible coins are shiny metal, while *peso* coins are flat and dull. (The only *peso*-value bill or coin that is sometimes confused with convertible currency is the *Che,* a large, relatively new, three-*peso* coin. They are easily recognizable because they bear a portrait of Cuba's guerilla hero, Che Guevara. Che coins are popular souvenirs, so an *entrepreneur* of the street may try to sell you one for a few dollars. Remember, Che coins are worth only three *pesos*—slightly less than twelve cents.)

Credit Cards Versus Cash

If you are traveling for more than a week or two in Cuba, you will not want to carry all the cash that you will eventually need. Credit cards from Canadian or European banks can be used for cash advances, but not cards issued in the U.S. Banks and tourist hotels will cash traveler's checks for a fee, but they usually refuse to accept those issued by American Express or other U.S. firms.

These options are not quite as safe and convenient as a Transcard International Finance Card. A Transcard is a special debit card. You deposit funds with Transcard's office in Canada. This can easily be done by mail inside Canada; it is better to use a wire transfer from the U.S. and other countries. When you arrive in Cuba, you pick up your Transcard at an office in Havana or another major city. The card can be used to withdraw cash at hundreds of participating banks and CADECAS, and it is accepted for payment at many hotels, restaurants, and stores across Cuba.

When you need cash, you take the Transcard to a bank or a CADECA, show your passport, and pick up your U.S. funds. It is reassuring to know that if your Transcard is lost or stolen while you are in Cuba, you can report it immediately, and arrange to pick up a new card with a new account number. It would be much more difficult, or perhaps impossible, to replace traveler's checks or credit cards in this way.

If you do not have time to make the arrangements in advance, you can take cash to Havana and immediately deposit it at Transcard's main headquarters at Calle 2 #302, between Avenida 1 and Avenida 3 in Miramar. (This is just across the river from Vedado.) You can then pick up your card in 48 hours and use it throughout your travels.

Of course there is a charge for all of this. The exact percentage varies with the amount you deposit in your Transcard account, but 4 to 5 percent is typical. If you consider that there is a fee for cashing traveler's checks and for credit card advances, it is not a bad deal. The Transcard fee is deducted up front when you make your deposit.

Funds can be withdrawn from your Transcard account only in Cuba. If you leave money in the account when you go home, you must return to Cuba to get it! Just remember before you depart to empty your account and bring home any unused funds. For more details, check the Transcard web site at www.transcardinter.com, or call 1-800-724-5685 from anywhere in North America.

Shopping on a Bicycle Tour

For some necessities like bottled water, toothpaste, and soap, you will need to rely on dollar stores. As the name implies, these stores accept payment only in U.S. dollars. They were initially created to serve foreign diplomats and other expatriates in the major cities. After 1993, when Cubans were first allowed to own and spend U.S. dollars, the number of these stores increased dramatically.

Now dollar stores are found almost everywhere, and they sell everything from food and clothing to stereos, televisions, and kitchen appliances. Most of the dollar stores belong to national chains—TRD Caribe, Tiendas Panamericanas, Caracol, and Cubalse are the ones we see most often. There are also dollar kiosks, structures generally made of metal that look like large shipping containers. Goods are sold over a counter, and sometimes the buildings are dressed up with awnings.

When you can buy what you need for *pesos,* you will save a great deal of money. As you ride along, especially when passing through smaller towns, you will often see vendors selling snacks and fruit for *pesos.* This is just what you need. One of the best ways we've found to use *pesos* is to visit *agromercados* (farmer's markets) established by the government or other small markets and roadside stands where farmers sell their produce.

Food, Drink, and Good Health

Finding Enough to Eat

Not too many years ago, in the depths of the Special Period, it was difficult to find enough to eat—for Cubans and visitors alike. The situation is better now. Cubans are not going hungry and neither will you. However, Cuba is still not the best destination for fine dining, and you will probably lose weight during a cycle tour.

In general, the best and most plentiful food is in *casas particulares.* During our rides, we also relied upon the wide variety of snacks sold for *pesos* by vendors at sidewalk stands and house windows. For your dining pleasure, see the sidebar entitled "The Cycling Gourmet's Guide to Cuban Street Food" on page 36. If you have any problems finding food, it will probably be during the day on long rides.

We are always on the lookout for fruit. Sometimes bananas and oranges

A selection of fruit and vegetables is available in *agromercados.*

are for sale at nearly every street corner and crossroad, but it depends upon where you are and the time of year. In larger towns there is always an *agromercado,* and you can usually buy fruit of some kind.

We like to carry cheese and bread. Cuban cheese is generally good, when you can find it. In the cities and larger towns, ask in dollar stores. We have often been surprised to find packets of imported cheese slices in the small convenience stores attached to gas stations. In the countryside, you may be able to buy fresh white farmers cheese.

Every town and neighborhood has an Empresa Cubana del Pan, a government bread store. Often these stores refuse to sell bread to tourists. This is because their responsibility is to provide the bread that Cuban customers are entitled to buy at subsidized prices on their ration cards. Sometimes, however, we have been able to buy loaves of warm bread for *pesos* at these stores. We think it depends on the time of day and upon how much is on hand. It never hurts to ask. Otherwise, many dollar stores sell bread. In the bigger cities there are bakery shops that also sell bread for dollars. Don't expect fancy whole grains—white only is the rule.

If bread is not available, you can buy inexpensive, round crackers—about the size of small pitas—in most dollar stores. Also, small packets of crackers and cookies imported from Argentina are available even in the dollar kiosks. The nutrition they provide is no doubt terrible, but it is good to have a packet or two in your panniers in case things get desperate.

The Cycling Gourmet's Guide to Cuban Street Food

Cycling through Cuba, you will have many opportunities to sample foods sold by entrepreneurs along the streets. Some vendors operate from stands or rolling carts, others from the windows or doors of their houses and apartments. Vendors are usually in the vicinity of parks, squares, or schools.

Trying street food can be fun, it is always cheap, and it is sometimes the only thing you'll find to eat. Note: Vendors often sell out early in the afternoon, sometimes even by noon. If you see something you want, buy it and save it if necessary; it may not be around for long.

Fruit. Nothing is better or healthier on the road than fruit. Although *fruta bomba* (papaya), *piña* (pineapple), *guayaba* (guava), *toronja* (grapefruit), mangoes, and other less familiar fruit are available in *agromercados,* we find the most practical fruit to carry in a pannier are *naranjas* (oranges), *mandarinas* (mandarin oranges), and *plátanos maduros* (ripe yellow bananas). They are often sold from pushcarts in cities and towns, along roadsides, and at farmers' markets.

Peanuts. *Maní* are great street snacks. *Maní tostado y salado* are roasted, salted peanuts sold in white paper cones for a *peso*—our absolute favorite treat, with a cold drink, at the end of the day. *Maní* can be mixed with other ingredients—usually honey or sugar—to form sweets that actually have some nutritional value. *Turrón de maní* (peanuts mixed with honey) and *maní molido* (a peanut and sugar paste like sweetened peanut butter) are both sold in squares.

Meals. *Bocaditos* are sandwiches, usually on small rolls. Typical fillings include *queso* (cheese), *jamón* (ham), *chorizo* (sausage), and *mortadella* (bologna). *Frituras* consist of batter, sometimes containing corn meal and seasonings, dropped in hot oil to create something like crispy fried bread—either salted or powdered with sugar. Unhealthy but often delicious. *Croquetas* are minced meat or fish mixed with and/or coated with bread or bread crumbs, and then fried. In Cuba, *croquetas* usually contain little meat or fish. They are sometimes served in sandwiches—which amounts, essentially, to fried bread inside baked bread. *Tamales* are made of corn and stuffed with meat, usually hot dog meat. They may be called *tamal* if wrapped in corn husks, or ayaca if wrapped in plantain leaves. *Tostones* are thin slices of green plantain, fried in oil and salted, a substitute for those who crave potato chips. *Boniato frito* is sweet potato, sliced and fried, a delicious alternative to *papas fritas* (french fries).

Pizzas. This is Cuba's quintessential street food. Ready-made rounds of dough are baked in ovens fashioned from old metal barrels. Though Cuban street pizzas are nothing like the North American versions, they can be greasily good, depending upon the toppings. These range from a thin, disappointing smear of tomato sauce to more elaborate combinations including *queso* (cheese), *jamón* (ham), *chorizo* (sausage), and *cebolla* (onion). Pizzas usually cost 3 to 10 pesos.

Boxed Lunches. *Cajitas* are little boxes, literally. When you spot *cajitas* for sale from a door or window of a house, you will usually get a complete meal in a small cardboard box for 10 to 25 *pesos*. Some typical ingredients include *congris* (mixed rice and beans), a staple of restaurant food and home cooking; *vianda* (any of several starchy root vegetables including yuca, potato, and *malanga); ensalada* (salad), which usually consists of *col* (shredded cabbage), tomatoes, and sometimes *lechugas* (lettuce) or *pepino* (sliced cucumber); and *cerdo* (pork), usually a cheap cut such as *lomo* (pork shoulder or back) or *bistec* (thinly sliced shoulder steaks). *Fricasé de cerdo* is chunks of pork in tomato sauce. Once in a while we have found chops *ahumado* (smoked) in these inexpensive boxed meals.

Fast Food. Found in cities and larger towns, El Rápido is a chain of fast-food restaurants that deal only in dollars. In addition to the essential fried chicken *(pollo),* El Rápido chains often sell hamburgers, french fries, and ice cream. You can get hot, toasted sandwiches on bread *(pan)* rather than rolls, with generally the same fillings as street *bocaditos. Perros calientes* (hot dogs) are often available. El Rápido chains call them *rápi-perros,* and they resemble hot dogs on steroids, huge things on sub rolls, quickly heated in a microwave. Ugh!

There is also a chain of fast-food places called Pollo, which only sells chicken and french fries, and another called Burgui, Cuba's tribute to McDonald's.

Sweets. All sorts of sweets are sold on the street. Consider sampling some of the following. *Pasteles* or *empanadas* are flaky pastries with guava jam or other sweets inside. *Tartaletas* are small tarts, like miniature pies, also containing some sort of sweet jam. *Rosquitas* or *churros* are sugar-covered doughnuts. *Guayabita* is a firm, sticky jelly made of guava and sugar, sold in large blocks. *Coco* is coconut, the basis for many sweets. Squares made of shredded coconut and sugar are very common in the Oriente. *Cucurucho* is a coconut-based treat found only in eastern Guantánamo Province. Shredded coconut is combined with honey, sugar, and various fruit and nuts into a firm paste that is sold in conical wrappings of banana leaves. A real energy food. *Galletas* are cookies sold in many varieties. *Torticas,* our favorites, are rather like shortbread with a dab of sweet jam in the center. *Helado* (ice cream) can be wonderful. The only excellent brand that is often sold for *pesos* is Coppelia. Other good brands usually sell for dollars only.

Drinks. *Refrescos* are often sold on the street for a *peso* or less. These drinks are like Kool-Aid, mixed with water of unknown origin. Canned *refrescos* are sold in dollar stores for about $.45, and they are much like good North American soft drinks. One brand of bottled cola—Fiesta—is sometimes sold for *pesos.*

Batidos are fruit smoothies made by mixing ice, fruit, sugar, water, powdered milk, and sometimes a pinch of salt in a blender. They are so good that we take our chances and drink them without worrying where the ice came from. *Pru* is a homemade bottled drink made from sugar, plant roots, and even pine needles. The flavor varies widely. *Pru* is boiled before bottling so it is quite safe to drink—though we don't care for it. *Guarapo* is fresh-pressed juice from sugar cane. It can be delicious and provides a quick energy boost. *Limonada* is lemonade, a treat as long as you trust the water. The most commonly sold fruit juices are *piña* (pineapple) and *naranja* (orange), and though they are not often found on the street, you can always find good Tropical brand fruit juice in dollar stores. Beer *(cerveza)* is widely available in Cuba, and rum *(ron)* is plentiful and cheap!

If you carry a supply of zip-lock bags, you will often be able to put together a midday meal for nothing. Sometimes we pack bread or fruit from the breakfast table. Your hosts at *casas particulares* are usually glad to give you some kind of snack, and occasionally they will press food upon you without being asked. At hotels, it is easy to raid the buffet table. Correspondents told us of putting extra beans and rice in zip-lock bags at dinner, then eating them for lunch the next day. When you buy street food, use the plastic bags to store treats for later in the day.

Food and Water Safety

When you are cycling in Cuba, nothing is more important to your health and well-being than water. Afternoon heat, even in the winter months, can be intense, and you will often be doing hard exercise. We each carry three large water bottles. On really long rides we buy extra bottles of water and stuff them in our panniers. A hydration pack is an excellent idea. Camelbak makes several types of this backpack-style water carrier.

Remember that you must drink before you are thirsty—if not, you may already be suffering the ill effects of dehydration. Discipline yourself to take small sips regularly. (Barbara's system: Whenever she sees turkey vultures circling overhead, she imagines they are waiting for her to collapse, and she takes another swallow of water. There are enough turkey vultures in rural Cuba to keep her well-hydrated.)

Besides making certain to drink plenty of water, you must be concerned about its quality. We have met travelers in Cuba who say that they drink tap water everywhere in the country with no ill effects. However, we know Cubans who do not trust their own tap water, and they either boil it or use purifying tablets. In fact, water in most Cuban towns is usually safe, but antiquated systems or the lack of necessary chemicals can cause unpredictable treatment failures. In some places, water may not be treated at all. We play it safe and urge you to do so as well.

We rely heavily on bottled water, but we also carry a water filter called the Pur Hiker. It is compact, reliable, and effective. It costs $60, but you should spend about $20 more for the purifier cartridge that uses iodine resins to kill viruses and charcoal to improve the taste. Boiling water is effective, but fuel is a major expense for Cuban families so we do not ask them to do this for us.

You can get by with bottled water alone if you buy enough of it. Bottled water can be purchased in dollar stores, where it typically sells for 55 to 85 cents per 1.5-liter bottle. It is more expensive in restaurants, bars, and *casas particulares*—usually $1 for 500 mls. In the route directions, we make a point of mentioning the location of dollar stores in all the smaller towns. Remember that many dollar stores open late—usually 9 AM—and some are closed on Sunday or Monday. If you are planning an early start, stock up on water the day before.

Just as you should drink before you are thirsty, you should eat—or at least nibble—before you are hungry. You may have some concerns about the sanitation of the foods sold by vendors from sidewalk stands or from the windows of their homes. If you peer into the kitchens where some of these foods are prepared, do not expect the antiseptic gleam of McDonald's. A certain dinginess is probably the result of years of paint shortages and lack of the abrasive cleansers, not a sign of careless food handling or poor sanitation. Cuba's public health system has stressed education and prevention for decades, and the folks selling food from their homes and stands are probably just as knowledgeable and careful about food as North Americans or Europeans. Many are also licensed and inspected. Unless we see something obviously wrong, we eat and enjoy.

Certainly, if you buy tomatoes or greens at a market or from a roadside vendor, you should wash them before eating them. Avoid street foods with mayonnaise and other ingredients that go bad easily in the heat. You may experience the typical traveler's illness while you are in Cuba, but this can happen even if you exercise every conceivable precaution. We only want to assure you that it is possible to eat the local food without undue anxiety or serious danger to your health. You should take the same commonsense precautions with food that you do at home, and exercise the degree of caution that makes you comfortable.

Cycling Safety

The precepts of safe cycling are no different in Cuba than anywhere else. When Wally leads cycling tours in the U.S. for Bike Vermont, he emphasizes the following points. If you are an experienced cyclist, you already know these things, but take a look at the latter part of this section to learn more about some cycling issues specific to Cuba.

- Stay in cycle lanes if they are provided.
- Ride to the right in traffic but not too close to the shoulder—within a meter is fine.
- If in a group, ride single file and spread out so that cars can get around you.
- Never swerve or turn unpredictably.
- Keep speed under control and use front and rear brakes simultaneously.

• Be constantly aware of road and traffic conditions.

Heat. Unless you are from the southern U.S., you may not have cycled in weather as warm as Cuba's. We have already mentioned the importance of drinking plenty of water. It is also important to take frequent rests in the shade (if you can find any) during the afternoon. If possible, keep your head covered and avoid riding during the hottest time of day—about 12 to 3 PM, depending somewhat on the time of year.

If you have any tendency toward chafing or saddle sores, it may be worse in Cuba's heat. Always wear clean cycling clothes, wash frequently, use talcum powder or creams if it helps, and be prepared to take a day off when necessary.

Road surfaces. Many cyclists who ride in Cuba for the first time are surprised to find that roads are in better condition than they expected. Still, there are more potholes and washouts on Cuban roads, especially in the countryside, than on those in wealthier countries. Note: It is necessary to be aware of the road surface at all times, especially when riding downhill at speed.

Rain. During the dry season in Cuba it may not rain for weeks at a time, and there may be an accumulation of grease and clay on road surfaces. It is not noticeable as long as the weather is dry, but when it starts to rain, the roads can suddenly become very slippery. Be careful and anticipate that your brakes will not work as quickly as usual. If you are caught in a tropical downpour, get off the road. Visibility will be terrible.

Animals. In rural areas, all kinds of animals wander in the roads—especially cattle, pigs, and goats. It is surprising how quickly a cow can get in your way if you are riding fast down a hill. Be on the lookout for animals, slow down when you are near them, and use your bell or horn.

Animals leave deposits on the roads. In wet weather, rain turns these deposits into a slurry that you do not want splashed onto your water bottles. For continuing good health, stuff your water bottles in a pannier, cover them, or buy the kind that has a little cap over the nozzle.

Riding at night. Cubans are on their bikes at all hours of the day and night, and motorists sometimes drive at night without headlights or with only parking lights. The only reason more cyclists are not killed is probably the fact that drivers expect them to be on the roads. Try to avoid night riding, even with lights and reflectors; it is terribly dangerous.

Bicycle helmets. The single most important thing cyclists can do to ensure their own safety is to wear helmets. You may notice in the photographs in this book that we sometimes rode without them in Cuba, for which we have no excuse. Please do as we say, not as we do.

Health Issues

For cycle touring in Cuba or anywhere else, you should know CPR and basic first-aid procedures. Carry a good first-aid kit with the usual assortment of bandages, swabs, safety pins and so on. Based on our own mishaps and minor illnesses, we recommend these additions to the basic kit:

- Betadine swabs or wipes for disinfecting scrapes
- Loperamide HCL (imodium) and packets of rehydration salts in case of severe diarrhea
- Hydrocortisone cream for skin irritations
- Clotrimasole or other anti-fungal cream for treating fungus infections like ringworm
- Diphenhydramine tablets, an antihistamine for stings, itches, and allergies
- Your favorite cold tablets and antacid tablets
- Ibuprofen for reducing pain and fever and also for muscle and joint soreness

Be sure to bring an adequate supply of any medicine you are taking regularly. Because nearly all medicines and first-aid items are in short supply in Cuba, try to bring more than you need and leave behind extras as gifts. Even a few cold tablets or painkillers will be deeply appreciated by most Cubans. (Women should bring products for personal hygiene; sanitary napkins and tampons are not available everywhere, and you may not be able to find the type you prefer.)

Use sunscreen every day, and wear a hat when you are not on the bike. Also be sure to carry mosquito repellent. These insects are not usually a problem during the day, but you may stay in a campismo or casa particular where the windows are not screened, and then they can make you miserable. When swimming in the ocean, be careful not to step on *erizos del mar* (sea urchins). Cubans will suggest all kinds of household remedies for this mishap; but if you pick up a lot of spines, go to a clinic for help.

A treatise on traveler's medicine is beyond our expertise. We carry a compact reference that we recommend highly: *Wilderness and Travel Medicine* by Eric A. Weiss, available in many shops and online bookstores for only $6.95. Buy it, read it, and carry it in your first-aid kit.

Cuba is, in general, a healthy country. It also has an extraordinary public health system, with small clinics throughout even the most remote areas. Doctors and nurses are well trained, even if there are shortages of medicine and equipment. In major cities and tourist areas, special clinics catering to foreigners require payment, usually $25 plus the cost of medicine, but in an emergency, local clinics may treat you for free.

Freedom, Personal Safety, and Security

Freedom

Many North Americans are under the impression that travel in Cuba is heavily restricted and that tourists are only allowed to visit places the government wants them to see. This isn't true. In fact, you can get on your bike (or rent a car for that matter) and go anywhere. The only exceptions, obviously, are military bases, and this kind of restriction applies in any country in the world.

Cuba does not have a free press, and there are restrictions on freedom of expression. This does not mean that you can't have frank discussions with Cuban people. The key is to show respect for their government and political system even though its principles may be different from those to which you are accustomed. If you arrive already confident that you understand Cuba's problems, you will not learn much while you are there.

Personal Safety and the Problem of Theft

Violent crime, especially against tourists, is extremely rare in Cuba. In fact, one of the nicest things about cycling in Cuba is the peace of mind that comes from knowing you are in one of the safest countries in the world.

Theft is another matter. Almost anytime we stop to buy food at a roadside stand, someone gestures by pointing a finger at each eye, indicating that we should watch our bikes. If we stay at a *casa particular* and leave a bike outside the door, we often discover that it is gone a few moments later. Our host has rolled it into the living room rather than take a chance that anything might happen. Once at a resort in Pinar del Río, we hung a few T-shirts to dry in the sun behind our cabaña while we went on an afternoon ride. When we returned at dusk, we noticed an employee sitting in the yard near the back door—he might have been there for hours. He was watching our T-shirts to make sure they were not stolen!

Be careful of your possessions. Do not leave valuable items lying in plain sight in hotel rooms. Remember that a hotel worker who earns $20 per month may define *valuable* differently than you do. Carry your passport and other important documents in a passport case or money belt, and make sure they are locked or hidden away securely when they are not on your person. Make photocopies of your passport, plane ticket, tourist card, and other important documents, and keep them separate from the originals.

Your bicycle may be the single most valuable item that you bring to Cuba, and bike thefts sometimes occur. It is a good idea to bring a bike lock.

Sign for a *parqueo.* Some say "Se cuidan bicis," meaning, roughly, "Bicycles guarded."

Cuba is not full of professional thieves with powerful bolt cutters, so a cable lock of reasonable quality should do.

Locking your bike to a lamp post will not prevent theft of pumps and panniers. If you must leave a loaded bike unattended in a city, find a *parqueo.* These guarded parking areas for bikes and scooters are common in all cities and larger towns. If you are leaving your bike overnight in a *parqueo,* be sure to remove anything that a thief might easily snatch. We once lost our mirrors because we neglected this simple rule. At any hotel, you must make arrangements for your bicycle and gear. If you can, it is best to bring the bike right into your room. Some hotels will not allow you to do this, but it never hurts to ask. Several hotels have offered us the use of a locked storeroom for our bikes.

Topics for U.S. Citizens

Are Americans Welcome in Cuba?

The U.S. has enforced a punishing embargo against Cuba for more than 40 years and has attempted to prevent other nations from trading with Cuba as well. The U.S. supported the invasion at the Bay of Pigs, and since then it has turned a blind eye to the terrorist operations of fanatical Cuban exile groups based in Florida. Under such circumstances, you might think Cubans would be hostile to American visitors.

In fact the opposite is true. Americans are not only allowed to visit Cuba, they are welcomed with special warmth. This may be due to the "ties of singular intimacy," to borrow a phrase from historian Louis Pérez, that have long existed between these two estranged nations. Before the revolution, many middle class Cubans sent their children to the U.S. for their education, and it is still common to meet older Cubans who studied in the States. In the 1940s and 1950s, Cuba and the southern U.S. were so closely connected that department store sales in Miami and New Orleans were regularly advertised in Havana newspapers. Today, millions of Cubans have relatives in the U.S. Cubans watch videos of U.S movies and television shows and listen to U.S. radio stations. The Cuban youth are fans of U.S. musical groups, and baseball is Cuba's favorite sport, by far.

Perhaps even more important is the fact that it seems natural for Cubans to distinguish between the policies of the U.S. government and the feelings of the American people about the policies. Fidel Castro frequently states, and correctly we might add, that the majority of U.S. citizens do not support their own government's harsh treatment of Cuba or are ignorant of it.

Travel Restrictions

At press time, the U.S. restricted travel to Cuba by most American citizens, but not all American citizens. Cuban-born Americans could travel to Cuba legally under certain conditions. Many other individuals—journalists, aid workers, and people involved in professional meetings or educational programs, for example—were licensed to travel there routinely or were eligible for special licenses to go.

For other Americans, the situation was more complicated. At the beginning of 2002, it was illegal under the Trading with the Enemy Act for Americans to spend money in Cuba. That is, it was technically legal to visit Cuba, but illegal to spend money there without a license from the U.S. Department of Treasury. If you were an American, if you went cycling in Cuba, and if you bought even a single cup of coffee, then you would probably be breaking the law and could be subject to a fine.

In fact, tens of thousands of Americans were going to Cuba without licenses every year. They usually did this by traveling via a third country such as Mexico or Canada. Cuban immigration officials sometimes cooperated with such travelers by stamping tourist cards instead of passports. In any event, such travelers were normally able to return to the U.S. from Canada or Mexico without showing their passports or admitting they had been to Cuba.

Unlicensed American travelers who openly admitted visiting Cuba, as

Plaza Martí on the Malecon, with the U.S. Interests Section framed by the arches.

Plaza Martí

On the Malecón, Havana's waterfront esplanade, in front of the U.S. Interests Section (USIS), is Plaza Martí. This concrete plaza is perhaps a couple of hundred meters long. At one end is a statue of José Martí, Cuba's national hero, carrying a child in his arms. At the other end, directly in front of the USIS, a large stage has been erected. Steel towers and arches looming above the plaza support lights and loudspeakers. Here, protests are frequently held. In fact, Cubans jokingly call this place the Protestadia, the Stadium for Protests. (It was an exceedingly busy place during the Elian Gonzales affair in 2000.)

On the base of one of the steel towers that line the plaza is an array of brass plaques bearing the names of heroes to Cubans: Marx, Engels, and Lenin, Che Guevara, and dozens of leaders and martyrs of Cuba's struggles for independence. Beside Plaza Martí, facing the USIS, is the famous billboard depicting a Cuban saying to Uncle Sam, "Mr. Imperialist, we have absolutely no fear of you." If there is any place in the world that is the focus of symbolic, hostile confrontation between Cuba and the U.S., this is it.

But there is a surprising irony here. If you walk across the square to the tower directly opposite the one bearing names of Cuba's heroes, you will see an array of similar plaques honoring North Americans: Jane Addams, social worker; Nat Turner, rebel slave; Abraham Lincoln, emancipator of slaves; and Martin Luther King, fighter for civil rights. Others include Benjamin Spock, Ralph Waldo Emerson, Mark Twain, Walt Whitman, Ernest Hemingway, Helen Keller, Henry Wadsworth Longfellow, Thomas Edison, Linus Pauling, Frank Lloyd Wright, Frederick Douglas, the Martyrs of Haymarket Square, Clara Barton, Harriet Tubman, Malcolm X, and many more. We find it strangely moving that Cubans honor so many of the same historic figures that Americans do. It saddens and angers us that U.S. law treats Cuba as an enemy state, and U.S. citizens are prevented from spending money in Cuba by the same legislation that outlawed trade with Nazi Germany in World War II.

Barbara shows the flag before an anti-blockade sign near Guantanamo.

we did, were liable to be fined. However, the law granted the right to a hearing before actually paying a fine. At press time, no hearings had been held, and there was a large backlog of cases. It appeared that even if you were subject to a fine, you might never have to pay it. Our personal policy was never to tell an outright lie to a customs or immigration official. We would rather take the chance of being forced, someday, to pay a fine.

At press time, former President Jimmy Carter had recently visited Cuba—the first U.S. president to do so in more than 70 years. He called for an end to the embargo and the travel restrictions. Almost immediately, President Bush played to Florida's Cuban-American voters with even tougher rhetoric than usual, but he made no substantial changes in policy. A bipartisan coalition in Congress hoped to force changes in Cuba policy whether President Bush agreed or not, possibly by attaching amendments to vital spending bills. It was impossible to predict what the next few months would bring. If you are interested in visiting Cuba, you must check current regulations and enforcement policies. If restrictions are still in place, be sure to find out what the consequences might be if you were to violate them.

You can get the latest regulations by checking with the U.S. Department of Treasury, but a more complete, intelligible picture of the situation is provided by non-governmental organizations that have expertise on U.S.-Cuban policies. See the appendix for a list of organizations and web sites.

Finding Your Way Around—On and Off Your Bike

Maps and Route Directions

The maps and route directions in this book should be sufficient for a cycle tour in Cuba. However, if you do any exploring on your own, you will almost certainly want additional maps.

The best choice for the cycle tourist is *Guía de Carreteras* (Road Guide) published by Directorio Turístico de Cuba. It contains 23 maps that, together, cover all of Cuba in good detail, plus distance charts, a Havana city map, and an index for locating every town in Cuba. All of this comes in a compact folder that fits easily in a handlebar bag. It costs $6 and is worth every penny.

The *Guía de Carreteras* is sold at Havana's José Martí airport, at least in the daytime when shops are open. You can also buy it from Tienda de Navegantes at #115 Calle Mercaderes in Havana Vieja, half a block from the Hotel Ambos Mundos. The *Guía* is sold at Infotur offices in Havana, and outside of Havana you may find it at car rental agencies.

The provincial maps included in general guidebooks contain too little detail to be of use to cyclists. However, the guidebooks recommended in the appendix contain detailed maps of the central areas of most Cuban cities, and they can be helpful when you are downtown.

If you were to do all the rides in this book, you might notice a few places where our directions do not agree with available published maps. Whenever the reality we observed from our bikes did not agree with maps, we always rode over the problem area again, and again if necessary. In general, if there is any confusion, you should follow our printed directions. More than likely, the map is inaccurate. There are mistakes even in the *Guía de Carreteras*. But it is also possible that the mistake is ours. If you suspect we goofed, ask people for directions. (See the sidebar entitled How to Ask Directions When You Don't Speak Spanish on page 48.) If you are willing to send us corrections or suggestions when you get home, an address for this purpose is included in the appendix.

In cities you will not often see signposts with street names. Instead, street names often appear on the sides of buildings or sometimes on low, freestanding cornerstones. In the countryside and on highways, directional signs have a way of disappearing just when you need them most.

There are a few terms that come up repeatedly in the route directions. One is *municipio* (municipal area). Cuba is divided into 169 *municipios*, roughly equivalent to counties in Canada and the U.S. The names of the *municipios* are normally the same as their principal town or city—the county seat. You may see a welcome sign that says BIENVENIDOS A CONTRA-MAESTRA and believe that you are entering town. Then you may be puzzled as you ride kilometer after kilometer, passing through little villages with other names, and there is no further sign of Contramaestra. The explanation is that the welcome sign referred to the large *municipio*, not the town.

We use boulevard to refer specifically to broad avenues divided by grassy medians, typically with benches and trees for shade. We do not use boulevard for major streets where traffic lanes are separated merely by stone dividers or speed bumps. An *entronque* is a connecting road or junction. Entronque Pilón, for example, is an intersection from which a main road leads to Pilón.

Kilometers and Cycle Computers

In Cuba all maps and road signs are in kilometers, and so is this book. U.S. readers who plan to cycle in Cuba might as well begin making the adjustment right away. It is easy to start thinking in kilometers. A kilometer equals 0.625 miles, so distances are more impressive when expressed in kilometers. A 50-km ride is the same as a 31-mile ride. It just sounds longer.

How to Ask Directions When You Don't Speak Spanish

We spoke no Spanish when we first visited Cuba so we had to develop a simple system for asking directions when we were lost.

Don't simply say *"Por favor* (please), Viñales?" while looking helplessly confused. Your new Cuban acquaintance will think you are asking "How do I get to Viñales?" (as indeed you are). He will reply with a torrent of helpful directions in Spanish—rapid-fire, nearly unintelligible Cuban Spanish—and you will not understand a single word.

Instead, first point in what might be the right direction, say *"Por favor,* Viñales?" and look helplessly confused. Now your interlocutor will think you are asking "Is this the way to Viñales?" and he will probably answer with a simple *sí* (yes) or *no* (no). This you can understand. If the answer is *sí,* you are on your way. If it is *no,* point in some other direction and watch your interlocutor.

There is another possibility. Your would-be informant may look as confused as you are, or he may smile and nod. The problem, most likely, is that you are badly mispronouncing the word Viñales, and he has no idea what you are asking. In this situation, write Viñales on a slip of paper or pull out this book and show him the word. Be sure to keep pointing here and there so that you will get a similar, non-verbal response. Honestly, we have been reduced to this device more than once.

When you are beginning to pick up more Spanish, you may want to expand your questioning capabilities with some phrases and possible responses. See "Spanish for Cyclists" in the appendix.

If you are a typical touring cyclist pedaling a lightly loaded bike on an easy route, you will probably average something close to 20 km per hour in the saddle. That means you can ride 40 or 50 km between breakfast and lunch. In hilly country or with strong headwinds and a heavy load, you may be hard pressed to average 12 or 14 km per hour, and you may want to stop more often. Depending on conditions, a moderate day ride might be anywhere from about 60 km (37 miles) to 100 km (62 miles), which is the approximate range of distances for rides in this book Most of the rides in Pinar del Río and central Cuba are closer to 60 km per day than 100 km.

To measure distances for the routes, we carefully calibrated two cycle computers, using the *roll-out* method to measure the circumferences of our wheels. If you do the same thing, your readings will probably agree with ours within about 1 percent. However, even a 1 percent variation translates into significant discrepancies over the course of a ride. If you use a cycle computer, don't be surprised if your readings differ from those in the book by several tenths after an hour or two of riding, and by a few kilometers before the day is over. Do not focus on accumulated kilometers but on the distance from each landmark or from one turn to the next.

Cycle computers can be handy, but they are not necessary for following the route directions in this book. You will quickly get a feel for the time it takes to ride various distances. If a turn is coming up in 0.1 km, it is only 100 meters away, about the length of a football field. If it is 1 to 2 km away, it will take you a few minutes to get there; and if it is 20 or 30 km away, you will not be there for an hour or two. We try to give landmarks or other identifying clues before each turn as well as at the turn itself. Also, we usually mention another landmark that comes up soon after the turn so you will know that you are, indeed, on the right road.

When You Don't Want to Cycle—Trains, Buses, and More

Suppose you fly into Havana for a two-week vacation and want to cycle in the Oriente. You don't have time to bike all the way to Santiago de Cuba and back; you need alternate transportation. The possibilities are air, taxis, trucks, trains, and buses. We favor buses.

It is easy to get a connecting flight from Havana to Santiago or to other major cities. Try to book your connecting flight when you buy your ticket to Cuba. The drawback is cost; this is the most expensive way to go. It is sometimes possible to hire a taxi to haul you and your bike over long distances. Even with tough negotiating and a *private* (illegal) taxi, this could cost almost as much as air travel. Trucks are the cheapest alternative by far. You usually pay in *pesos*. Unfortunately, trucks are also the most dangerous, unreliable, slow, noisy, and uncomfortable way to travel long distances. We do not recommend them.

Most cyclists in Cuba have relied upon trains. Two correspondents have complained of not being able to carry unboxed bikes on board or of being charged more for their bikes than for passenger tickets! If a train does not have a special baggage car, it may not carry bikes at all. Sometimes trains are the only option, however, and some trains may carry bikes for free. It is unpredictable.

Until recently, bus travel was not a viable option for visiting cyclists. Throughout the 1990s, buses were invariably packed, it often took days or weeks to get a seat, and they would not carry bikes anyway. This is still true of buses run by ASTRO, the national interprovincial company. However, in the late 1990s a small bus line named Víazul was launched to cater to tourists.

Víazul uses big Mercedes or Volvo buses complete with bathrooms, air-conditioning, and *in-flight* movies on the longer runs. They are reliable, and in our experience, always depart and arrive on time. Most important for cyclists, these buses have capacious luggage compartments where bicycles can be stowed easily and safely. Even with all these advantages, Víazul's overnight run from Havana all the way to Santiago de Cuba cost $51 in 2002, half the price of an air ticket. Víazul buses cost less than many trains when you add the railroad's extra charge for your bike. (When you check your under-coach baggage, Víazul may or may not ask something extra for your bike, but we have never been charged more than $3 per bike. If you are not charged anything, you might tip the baggage handler to encourage extra care.)

You will not experience the *real* Cuba aboard a Víazul bus; only tourists and affluent Cubans use them. However, there will be plenty of time for the real Cuba once you are on your bike. We highly recommend these comfortable and reliable buses.

You can find directions for cycling to the Víazul terminal in Havana in Part I. In other cities, you can buy tickets and board Víazul buses at the regular interprovincial terminals that are also used by ASTRO buses. Víazul schedules and prices are on the web at www.Víazul.cu.

Other Matters

Communications
By the beginning of 2002, using the telephone and the Internet in Cuba had become easier than ever before. Riding around the country in 2001, we were

amazed by the number of crews that we saw repairing and upgrading telephone lines.

Empresa de Telecomunicaciones de Cuba (ETECSA) has sold a prepaid telephone card for several years. Now, the high-tech telephones that accept these cards are readily available in every city and large town. The prepaid card is sold at ETECSA offices and at many hotels. When you pop the card into the telephone's slot, a digital readout tells you how much credit remains on the card. There is even a printed list of national and international codes right on the telephone. You simply dial the code, follow it with the number you want, and you're done. This is a convenience used more by travelers than by Cubans because the cards are sold only for U.S. dollars, starting at $5. There are still many pay phones that take *pesos* for domestic calls.

Progress on Internet access has been just as remarkable. ETECSA has scattered glass-enclosed kiosks offering Internet service in major cities, and Internet service is available in many regular ETECSA offices as well. Again, a prepaid card is sold. For $5 (U.S.) you can buy a card for e-mail only; for $15 you get five hours of unrestricted Internet access. You just sit down at the computer (possibly waiting a while for someone else to finish) and type in the identification codes on your card. ETECSA's server tracks the time remaining on your account. During our last two-month trip to Cuba, we sent and received lots of e-mail, and we occasionally checked the news on www.CNN.com, but we never used up our five hours.

If you can't find an ETECSA office or kiosk with Internet service, you can still send e-mail from many post offices, and better tourist hotels usually provide more expensive e-mail service or web access. If not, they can sometimes direct you to an educational organization where you can use the web. Suffice to say, whenever we really wanted to send or receive e-mail in 2001, we were able to do so. This was not the case even a year before.

Jineteros

Jinetero translates loosely as hustler, understood in the broadest sense. For example, a young man will approach unbidden and offer to lead you to a *casa particular* or a *paladar* (private restaurant). The owner will pay him a commission, usually a percentage, for bringing a new customer. Female hustlers are *jineteras*. Most *jineteros* and *jiniteras* perform legitimate services, but others peddle something less savory like counterfeit cigars or paid sex. What they have in common is that they want U.S. dollars, and their activities are not licensed or approved by government. We think of them as *entrepreneurs* of the street.

With tourism booming and many Cubans underemployed, *jineteros* have become more prevalent and persistent. They can be mighty irritating. But here is an important anecdote: We had cycled to Guardalavaca, a beach resort in Holguín Province, and we were looking at the crafts in an outdoor market near the tourist hotels. This is exactly the kind of place where *jineteros* hang out to ply their trade. A young man approached Wally and asked, in English, "May I talk with you for a minute?" Typical. *Jineteros* always know a little English. Instantly, Wally was on the defensive, almost growling his response. But the man was not asking for anything at all. He explained that he had seen us riding a couple of days earlier with both Cuban and American flags flying from our bikes. He had wanted to stop and talk to us then, but he was on a bus. That evening, he told his family about our flags and us. He was glad to have found us again, he said, because seeing the Cuban and American flags flown together meant a great deal to him and his family. They knew it was a gesture of friendship, and they only wanted to thank us. Well!

So one problem is that *jineteros* give visitors the impression that Cubans only want their money. Because of *jineteros*, some visitors even become apprehensive whenever a Cuban approaches them.

Another problem is that *jineteros* themselves get a bum rap. Some are con artists, but most provide a real service. When we arrived in Manzanillo for the first time, a young man offered to show us a *casa*. We were tired and it was getting dark, so we agreed. He led us on his own bike through a couple of kilometers of tangled streets. When we arrived at the *casa*, which was a large second-floor apartment, he ran up to make sure there was a room available. Then he helped the owner lug our bikes and gear upstairs. We never would have found the place without his help, and he earned the commission that he surely received.

Cuba's Dual Economy

Jineterismo (if there is such a word) is a symptom of what may be Cuba's most serious economic problem. Most imported goods, some foods, and virtually all luxury items can be purchased only with U.S. dollars, and the exchange value of the dollar is over 20 times that of the *peso*—26-to-1 at the beginning of 2002.

Virtually all Cuban workers are paid in *pesos*, and the salaries that professionals receive—teachers, engineers, doctors—are roughly equivalent to $15 to $30 U.S. dollars per month. Nonprofessionals earn even less. The *peso* goes a very long way in Cuba. Still, families can't live in even modest comfort unless they subsidize *peso* salaries with U.S. dollars.

How do Cubans get U.S. dollars? The easiest way is to have relatives in the U.S. or other countries who send gifts. Hundreds of millions of dollars flow into the island economy this way every year. In fact, Cubans sometimes say *"Hay que tener fe"* (you must have faith). *Fe* means faith, but here it is shorthand for *familiares en el extranjero*—relatives abroad!

The other important source of dollars is tourism. Although waiters, tour guides, and taxi drivers receive their official salaries in *pesos,* they are frequently tipped in U.S. dollars. A waiter in a good restaurant or resort can make more in tips in one night than a doctor or teacher earns in a month!

This situation has terrible implications for the future. Teachers, to take one example, sometimes quit to find work as tour guides or taxi drivers. Several teachers have told us that they hate abandoning their students, but they need to earn more for their families. We have met a doctor running a *casa particular* and a psychologist working in a car rental agency. In the long run, or perhaps even the short run, Cuba can't stand to lose its professionals to the tourism industry.

Also, the dollar-peso problem increases disparities between well-off Cubans and the less fortunate in a society that has worked for decades to achieve greater economic equality. When you stay in a *casa particular,* for example, you are supporting a family that is already well-off by Cuban standards, if only because they have a nice home with one or more extra rooms. You and other guests pay in dollars, so they are earning far more than most Cubans, even after paying high license fees. Because of the dollar-*peso* problem, the rich get richer and the poor get poorer.

In practice, there are innumerable ways that U.S. dollars find their way into the pockets of people who do not work in tourism or rent rooms or have relatives in Miami. In many *casas particulares,* for example, other people besides your host may help in one way or another. An older lady—perhaps a grandmother or an aunt—may do your laundry. A young woman—perhaps a niece or cousin—may appear in the mornings to mop and dust. What is happening is that the owners of the *casa* are paying relatives to help out—either sharing your dollars with them, or at least paying more *pesos* than would be possible if you were not there.

Jineteros are part of the process by which dollars filter through the economy. When a young man earns $5 for leading you to a *casa particular,* he will probably stop at a market and bring home food or some treat that he and his family would otherwise have been unable to buy. Of the $20 to $30 that you might pay the owners of the *casa particular* for a room and meals, $5 has just been distributed to another Cuban family.

These informal arrangements are not a long-term solution to the dollar-*peso* problem. We are not economists and have no idea how it can be solved or what the future holds.

The Question

The question people ask us most often about cycling in Cuba is "What is it like?" They aren't asking about the road conditions or the tap water. They are asking a harder question about people, living conditions, and politics.

It is almost a cliché to say how friendly and welcoming Cuban people are, but it is less often said how well educated and informed they are. We read a comment somewhere that Cuba is a *Third World* country inhabited by First World people. There may have been a touch of condescension in the comment, but the intent was correct. The literacy rate equals or surpasses developed countries, and Cuba's system of free education churns out huge numbers of doctors, teachers, engineers, and other professionals. The problem is that the stunted economy does not provide enough rewarding work to match the capabilities of the people.

Cuba's public health system is also excellent. Despite chronic shortages of medicine and equipment, key health statistics—infant mortality rates and life expectancy—match or surpass those of developed nations.

There is much poverty in Cuba. You will see homes and public buildings that are unpainted or poorly maintained, shortages of some ordinary foods and consumer goods, and people forced to mend old clothes and struggle in many ways to get by on meager salaries. However, in the real Third World, poverty often means that people do not have homes at all. They watch helplessly as babies die of malnutrition and curable diseases, children have no opportunity for education and a better life, and people live without basic sanitation and medical care—they have no hope. This degree of poverty does not exist in Cuba.

Compared with nearby Caribbean nations Cuba is doing fairly well, but Cubans compare themselves with North Americans. Someone who can't find a good job or even a tire for his bicycle is not comforted by the fact that Jamaicans or Haitians are worse off. Young people, especially, ache for greater opportunities and for the consumer goods enjoyed by North Americans. But widespread dissatisfaction does not imply widespread opposition to the government. The objective situation and the feelings of individual people are too complex for most generalizations.

We got to know a family in which both the parents and their two sons were exceptionally talented, well-educated professionals. The mother said to us, "We know that our sons, with their education and ability, could live better in another country, but this is our revolution. We know there are

The billboard says "Solidarity and love can do everything."

problems, but we want to make it work." Just down the street lived another family of professionals in similar economic circumstances. The father said one day, "I'm too old to leave here now, but my greatest hope for my son is that he will get out of this terrible country."

If there is a fair generalization about the conditions and the politics of Cuba, it is this: As a visitor, you can see what you expect or want to see. If you come to Cuba looking for evidence of a police state, inefficient bureaucracy, and dissatisfied people, you can find it. If you look for evidence of a uniquely idealistic society in which people have a strong sense of community, respect their government, and are trying to solve problems without sacrificing the achievements of their revolution, you can find that too.

Let's ride!

Part I:
Havana

If your image of Havana comes from the film *Buena Vista Social Club*, be prepared for surprises. While much of the city is still as dilapidated as it appears in the movie, many areas are being spruced up, and there is a bustling energy in the air. Historical buildings are being restored and new ones are under construction here and there. The Malecón, Havana's incomparable waterfront esplanade, appeared almost deserted in the film, but in 2001 it reminded us more of New York City's West Side Drive years ago, though with more swimmers, sunbathers, strollers, musicians, and lovers.

We have become accustomed to life in rural Vermont, and when we first visited Havana, we were put off by its size. With a population over 2 million, it is the largest city in the Caribbean. In time, however, we came to enjoy its historical buildings, leafy parks, and lively crowds. If you can manage it, you should plan to begin or end your trip with at least a couple of nights in Havana. Don't miss this lovely old city.

Arriving in Havana. If you fly to Havana, you will arrive at José Martí International Airport, about 25 km from the heart of the city. It is possible to jump on your bike and ride, either into the city or away from it, but we advise against it.

Cycling into Havana means riding on busy, multilane roads with fast traffic through largely industrial areas. We have done it twice but will not do

Havana's malecón, with El Morro on the left

it again. It is stressful during the day and downright dangerous at night, especially if you are tired from a long journey. Two cyclists with bikes and gear can hire a taxi from the airport to Vedado or Havana Vieja for about $15–20, a worthwhile investment.

Cycling in the city. We can't in good conscience recommend that everyone go sight-seeing in Havana by bike. Yes, many locals still use bikes every day, but there are more cars, trucks, and buses zooming around than there were in the 1990s. Speed bumps on the Malecón used to prevent motorists from driving in the cycling lane, but the bumps are gone now. On other busy streets in the city, parked cars and trucks often block the cycling lane—if there is one—forcing you to pull into traffic. Cycling in Havana would be more dangerous were it not for the fact that motorists are accustomed to sharing the road.

We regret to predict that as Cuba's economy strengthens, conditions for cycling in downtown Havana are likely to get worse. Still, many people enjoy bicycling in New York City, Toronto, and other great cities. There are several rides in Havana that we like, and if you are an experienced urban rider, you may enjoy them too.

❶ A first possibility is simply cruising up and down the Malecón. Carry a guidebook, stop at the great monuments, and take your time. Be especially careful at the east end, near the mouth of the harbor, where the Malecón, the Prado, Avenida del Puerto, the ramp for the harbor tunnel, and a couple of other streets and avenues all join in a confusing tangle.

❷ You can ride south from the Malecón on the Prado to see Parque Central, the Capitolio, and the Teatro Nacional de Cuba, then head back north and turn right to visit the Palacio Presidencial, home of the Museo de la Revolución, and the Granma Memorial. If you want to visit the museum, find a *parqueo* for your bike.

❸ Farther west on the Malecón in Vedado, you can ride south on Paseo, a lovely but very busy boulevard, to see the Plaza de la Revolución

Refurbishing a building in Havana Vieja

and the huge memorial to José Martí. (This is the first couple of kilometers of Ride 1, Havana to Las Terrazas and Soroa.)

4 You should enjoy following the first 5 km of Ride 2, Havana to Viñales via the North Road, to visit Miramar and see how Cuba's elite lived in the bad old Batista days. Miramar is laid out in a simple grid, so it is easy to explore without getting lost.

5 The Jardín Botánico Nacional, about 25 km from downtown, makes

Castillo El Morro guards the entrance to Havana Harbor.

a great all-day outing. There are 35 km of paved trails in the huge garden, and you are allowed to tour them on your bike. Birding in the garden is great. Just across the street, you will find Expo Cuba, and you can explore Parque Lenin on the way out or back. See the standard guidebooks for details on these attractions. You can cycle to the Jardín Botánico Nacional by following the directions for Ride 1, Havana to Las Terrazas and Soroa, as far as km 7.8. Instead of going north on Calle 100 to the Autopista, go south on 100. Follow signs to Parque Lenin and Expo Cuba. Some of this ride is on the same busy roads that we advised against using when you arrived at the airport. Only do this ride when you are rested and have become accustomed to Havana traffic.

6 You can visit El Cristo de Casablanca and Castillo El Morro. Both can be seen across the harbor from Havana. El Cristo is the huge white statue of Christ on a hilltop *mirador* (lookout) with wonderful views of the city. Cross the harbor on the little ferry, following directions for Ride 3, Havana to Playas del Este and Matanzas. At km 0.2, instead of bearing right, continue steeply uphill to the left around the little park. After a switchback, the road climbs to El Cristo.

It is possible to reach Castillo El Morro by continuing past the El Cristo *mirador,* but you will be less likely to get lost if you ride back down the hill and follow the directions for Ride 3, Havana to Playas del Este and Matanzas, as far as km 4.7. Turn left instead of right on Avenida 15. Keep going until you reach a sports complex and the huge Estadio Panamericano. The crossroad here is Vía Monumental; a left will take you to El Morro.

Leaving Havana. When you are ready to leave Havana, the closest great cycling region is Pinar del Río Province. You can use three main roads heading west: the Autopista; the Carretera Central; or the Mariel Highway leading to the Carretera Circuito del Norte, which we will simply call the North Road. These routes can be combined in various ways. We have tried them all. We give directions for the two routes we like best: from Havana to Las Terrazas and Soroa via a combination of the Autopista, Carretera Central, and scenic back roads; and from Havana all the way to Viñales via the Mariel highway and the North Road.

Some cyclists may want to visit great beaches that are not far to the east of Havana. The third route in this section goes to the Playas del Este, Playa Jibacoa, and as far east as the city of Matanzas.

Many cyclists, either to save time or to avoid urban riding, may choose to leave the city by public transport. As we said in the introduction, the best public transport option is a Víazul bus, whether you are headed to Pinar del Río or to the east. The final route in this section consists of directions for finding the Víazul bus terminal in a section of Vedado that is somewhat off the beaten path.

(There is no Víazul bus or any other regularly scheduled public transportation to Soroa and Las Terrazas. If your heart is set on going there and you do not want to cycle from Havana, you should be able to hire a cab for two people with bikes for under $50. Alternatively, take the Víazul bus to Viñales and use the routes in Part II, Pinar del Río, for riding back to Soroa and Las Terrazas.)

❶ Havana to Las Terrazas and Soroa
86 or 96 km, 1 or 2 days

Soroa and Las Terrazas, only 17 km apart, are the first likely stops in Pinar del Río Province, and they are worthy destinations in their own right. These centers of eco-tourism are set in high valleys at the eastern edge of the Sierra del Rosario, near the border of Havana Province. Both are part of a UNESCO-designated biosphere reserve of 25,000 protected hectares (65,000 acres). Though the area is only 250 meters above sea level, the air is fresh and nights are often cool and invigorating.

Las Terrazas is a compact, handsomely designed community for workers employed in reforestation projects and in tourism, and also for artists and craftsmen whose studios and galleries are open to the public. Nearby attractions include the partially restored ruins of a 19th-century coffee estate, diverse restaurants in pretty settings, and a superb freshwater

The right lane on the Autopista is reserved for tractors, horse carts, and cyclists.

swimming hole. Las Terrazas also has Hotel Moka, one of the country's finest.

In Soroa, hiking trails lead to a waterfall, ruins of coffee estates, and to a mountaintop *mirador* with spectacular views in every direction. The mixed woodlands around Soroa are excellent for birding walks, and the *orquideario* (orchid garden) is worth a visit. On 35,000 square meters of steep hillside, 700 species of orchids are grown, along with other ornamentals, amid limestone formations, palms, and towering semi-deciduous trees draped in vines. Only a few orchids bloom in winter, but the gardens are marvelous even then.

The standard, two-day route takes you first to Las Terrazas. The distance is either 71 or 79 km from Havana, depending on where you choose to spend the night. The second day's ride is only 17 or 25 km. This allows plenty of time to enjoy the Las Terrazas complex.

Alternatively, you may ride directly to Soroa in a single day, using a variation of the standard route that is 86 km, the One-Day Autopista Option (see page 73). From a base in Soroa, you can explore the nearby attractions of Las Terrazas, or you can travel farther west toward San Diego de los Baños.

We love riding on quiet country roads, but for 15 km (or more if you choose), this route follows the Autopista, the closest thing in Cuba to a U.S.

interstate or the Trans-Canada Highway. Why would we recommend such a route? Because, surprisingly, the Autopista is one of Cuba's safest roads for cyclists.

Traffic is lighter than on other major roads around Havana, and the Autopista is wide—six lanes with a center median and full-width, paved shoulders. Perhaps even more important, the Autopista makes provisions for cyclists. The right lane is reserved for cyclists, as well as for pedestrians, hitchhikers, horse carts, ox carts, tractors—and we have even seen a man in a wheelchair tooling along on this highway! Once outside Havana, the Autopista traverses scenic countryside.

The trickiest part of the ride is getting through Havana to the Autopista, but we have given detailed directions for an easy way to do this. You should read the directions with care, stopping occasionally to review them as you ride.

Once you are on the Autopista, the going is easy. However, the Autopista can become boring after a while, and there are only two rest areas/snack bars between Havana and the turn for Las Terrazas, nearly 50 km. Therefore, for the sake of variety, the standard route leaves the Autopista after getting well outside Havana. The route follows the Carretera Central long enough for you to see smaller Cuban towns and have lunch or a snack. Then the last part of the route uses quiet, rural roads with wonderful views.

Alternatively, if you have plenty of food and energy and want to go directly to Soroa, you can save time by staying on the Autopista for an additional 40 or 50 km. If the wind is behind you, it is fast and easy—until the last few hilly kilometers.

For the first three-quarters of the route, the terrain is flat to rolling. Hard climbing occurs between Las Terrazas and Soroa, or between the Autopista and Soroa if you choose the One-Day Autopista Option.

At the end of the route directions for Day 2, we describe a little-used road that connects the Soroa-Las Terrazas area with the Carretera Circuito del Norte. We cleverly call it the North Road Connection. This road is useful if you want to loop back to Havana along the coast.

Food

On the standard route, food is no problem. Cold drinks and snacks or light lunches are available at several places mentioned in the directions including an El Parador rest area on the Autopista; an El Rápido cafeteria, Coppelia ice cream shop, and other options in Bauta; another El Rápido cafeteria, plus other options in Guanajay; and several choices in Las

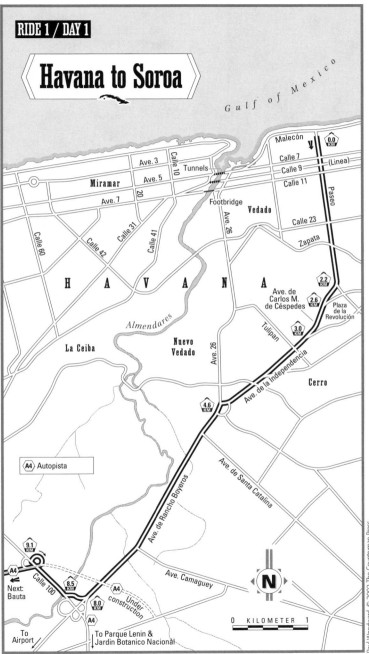

RIDE 1 / DAY 1

Havana to Soroa

Gulf of Mexico

Malecón
0.0 KM

Calle 7
Calle 9 — (Linea)
Calle 11

Ave. 3
Calle 10 — Tunnels
Ave. 5
Miramar
Ave. 7
20

Footbridge

Paseo

Vedado

Ave. 26

Calle 23

Calle 60
Calle 42
Calle 31
Calle 41

Zapata

H A V A N A

Ave. de
Carlos M.
de Céspedes
2.2 KM

2.6 KM
Plaza
de la
Revolución

Almendares

Nuevo
Vedado

Tulipan
3.0 KM

La Ceiba

Ave. 26

Ave. de la Independencia

Cerro

4.6 KM

A4 Autopista

Ave. de Santa Catalina

Ave. de Rancho Boyeros

9.1 KM

A4
Next:
Bauta

Calle 100
8.5 KM
A4
8.0 KM
Under
construction

Ave. Camaguey

N

A4

To
Airport

To Parque Lenin &
Jardin Botanico Nacional

0   KILOMETER   1

Paul Woodward, © 2002 The Countryman Press

The lobby at Hotel la Moka in Las Terrazas

Terrazas. Note: It is a fairly long haul from Guanajay to Las Terrazas, so be sure to top off your water bottles and pick up something to nibble before you leave this town.

If you plan to use the One-Day Autopista Option to Soroa, you should pack some bread or crackers and cheese, fruit, or other snacks, and lots of water. After the El Parador rest area on the Autopista, the next place for drinks and snacks will be at La Chorrera, 49 km later. You may, however, see men along the side of the Autopista selling farmers cheese and *guayaba*.

Lodging

There are three good choices for spending the night in or near Las Terrazas. Villa Juanita is 4 km east of the entrance to Las Terrazas and was first licensed as a *casa particular* in 2001. Juanita and her family are friendly hosts, and they offer two rooms upstairs with an entrance separate from the family quarters downstairs. The guest rooms share a bath and a dining area with balconies at either end. Meals are available, and a refrigerator is stocked with mineral water, soft drinks, and beer that you pay for on an honor system. Total cost at Villa Juanita for a couple, dinner and breakfast included, runs $35 to $40, depending on your food choices and how much you deplete the contents of the refrigerator.

A beautiful pool set among the hills at Villa Soroa

A second possibility is a new *casa particular* just across the street from Villa Juanita. It was not open when we were last there, but correspondents who cycled through in the spring of 2002 assure us that it is very attractive.

Hotel Moka is a casually elegant, small hotel in a beautiful setting. Its design is so thoughtfully integrated with its natural surroundings that a tree grows right through the handsome lobby. The cost for two with breakfast, dinner, and drinks should be close to $150. If you intend to stay at Hotel Moka, make arrangements with a travel agent before you leave Havana. Even if you do not stay there, stop for a cool drink some afternoon when you are in the area.

In Soroa, you can stay at the hotel Villa Soroa or at *casas particulares* in a village 2 km downhill from the hotel. Villa Soroa is our favorite accommodation on this ride. Blocks of small, air-conditioned *cabañas* with comfortable beds and immaculate, modern bathrooms are scattered on rolling lawns beneath shade trees. They are arranged around a beautiful swimming pool. The food improved dramatically between 2000 and 2001; now we can honestly say it is pretty good, and this is high praise for a Horizontes hotel. Live traditional music in the dining room was also added in 2001. Villa Soroa costs about $50 per night for a couple, with a relatively good buffet breakfast included. It is increasingly popular, so you should make reservations in advance and check current rates.

Sunday afternoon crowds relax on Havana's malecón.

Villa Virginia and Casa Pepe are *casas particulares* located 2 km south (and very much downhill) from Villa Soroa. We heard good things about Villa Virginia from German cyclists who stayed there, but one of our correspondents objected to paying $25 for the room. We have no firsthand reports about Casa Pepe.

There are also three *campismos* along the route, one off the Autopista near Soroa, another in Las Terrazas, and a third that is 2 km north of Villa Soroa. All are noted in the directions.

Day 1: Havana to Las Terrazas (71 km)

The route begins at the foot of Paseo in front of the Meliá Cohiba Hotel. It is just off the Malecón.

0.0 Ride south on Paseo, with the Malecón and the sea behind you. Note mansions along the route, most of which are now headquarters of organizations and government agencies.

2.2 Turn right onto the connector for Avenida Céspedes, following signs to Aeropuerto and Ciudad Deportiva. (The Teatro Nacional de Cuba is across Paseo on your left just as you make the turn.)

2.6 Merge with *Avenida Céspedes*, a one-way, three-lane road coming from the left. At a traffic light just ahead, the designated bike lane abruptly switches from the right, where you normally ride, to the left lane. It is safest to pull over and wait for the light to stop traffic. Then walk your bike to the correct lane.

A typical El Rápido cafeteria, this one in Guanajay

3.0 Merge with *Avenida de la Independencia*. You are now on a huge, 12-lane boulevard, 6 lanes in each direction. Stay in the bike lane!

3.3 Continue straight at the intersection with Tulipán. This is the turn for the Víazul bus depot. It comes just after the headquarters of the Policía Nacional Revolucionaria (PNR) and the Ministry of Transport, both on the right.

4.4 Carefully cross traffic lanes when the designated bike lane switches to the right and exits from the main avenue. You will now be riding parallel to Avenida de la Independencia.

4.6 Continue straight after a busy traffic circle. Independencia becomes Avenida de Rancho Boyeros. Soon four lanes in each direction will narrow to three, with the right lane still designated for bicycles.

7.8 Cross railroad tracks with care. Notice a sign on the right saying *boyeros*. Watch for the next turn.

8.0 Turn right onto the connector for Calle 100, following signs for Expo Cuba and *Este-Oeste*.

8.5 Merge with Calle 100. Continue straight on Calle 100 for less than 1 km.

9.1 Turn right onto an entrance ramp just *after* you cross a bridge over the Autopista.

9.7 Merge onto the Autopista proper. Stay in the right lane but *do* *not* take the immediate exit to Parque Lenin. Now that you are riding on Cuba's equivalent of an interstate highway, you will quickly relax with the realization that it is less crowded and much safer than the roads in Havana.

18.0 Watch for El Parador, a rest stop with fast food on the far side of the Autopista. You can safely get off your bike, check traffic, and walk across for cold drinks and sandwiches.

25.2 Exit for Bauta and turn left at the top of the ramp; do not bear right toward Baracoa. (Here, Baracoa refers to a beach on the north coast of Havana Province, not the city in the Oriente.) If you are following the One-Day Autopista Option, do not take this exit.

29.0 Go straight at the point of a narrow triangular park; do not bear left. Across the park to the left there is an El Rápido cafeteria for cold drinks and sandwiches.

30.5 Turn right onto the Carretera Central. This turn comes after another park on the right and a Coppelia ice cream shop.

33.9 Pass through decorative gates welcoming travelers to the *municipio* of Caimito.

36.9 A sign on the right says CONSEJO POPULAR CAIMITO. In less than 1 km, there is a TRD Caribe dollar store on the left, and in another 200 meters, just as you are leaving town, there is an El Rápido cafeteria on the right.

44.2 A sign says WELCOME TO GUANAJAY.

46.4 Turn right, following a group of signs for the Autopista, Mariel, and Pinar del Río. If you continue straight, you will be going the wrong way on a one-way street.

46.5 Take the next left, following signs to the Autopista, Artemisa, Candaleria, and Pinar del Río.

47.2 The main square of Guanajay is on the left. A soft ice cream stand, a *peso* restaurant, and an El Rápido restaurant are located here, a good spot for a break. Then continue riding with the square to your left and the Teatro Vicente Moro on your right.

47.4 Turn left about 200 meters past the square. This turn is immediately after a small, modern movie theater on the right. When you have made the turn, you will see a rotary ahead.

47.6 Continue straight through the rotary on the Carretera Central.

49.5 Turn right at a crossroad. About 150 meters before this turn, there is a sign that indicates to continue straight to Artemisa and turn left to Ceiba del Agua. There is a large, thatched cafeteria on the left at this crossroad but no sign to indicate where the right goes.

51.7 Continue straight, passing beneath an Autopista bridge. In 4 or 5 km, you will enjoy unobstructed views to the right over rolling green farmland dotted with lakes and Royal Palms that continue all the way to the ocean in the north.

57.9 Enter La Sierra, a village that amounts to no more than a row of small houses.

60.5 Be careful on a 1-km downhill because the road surface is rough with occasional potholes.

62.7 Ride through the small town of El Rancho. There will be a *peso* store on the left. After you leave town, watch out for a section of road that has particularly bad potholes.

65.0 Begin another long downhill over rough pavement—and be prepared to bear left in 1 km. This downhill begins shortly after a yellow sign and small lane on the right for Establo Cimiento Fabrile El Rancho.

65.9 Bear left at the fork; do not continue downhill to the right.

67.3 Pass the community of El Mirador (the Lookout) on the left.

68.5 Turn right at the T-intersection. There is a sign before this turn indicating a left turn to Cayajabos and the Autopista, but nothing to indicate where the right goes.

70.2 Watch for a painted cement sign on the left for the Julio Antonio Mella cooperative. It signals that another turn is coming up.

70.4 Turn left. There is a concrete block structure here, on top of which rests a large water tank. Proceed through the small village of El Establo.

71.2 Villa Juanita is on the left. This is a two-story home with a prominent sign. There is another *casa particular* on the right. This is a two-story home with a prominent sign. (If you are continuing to Hotel Moka, follow the route directions for Day 2.)

Day 2: Las Terrazas to Soroa (25 km)

0.0 Turn left toward Las Terrazas as you leave Villa Juanita.

4.3 Enter the Las Terrazas complex. You will have to pay $2 per person at the toll gate. (Save your receipt; it may be checked later.) You can buy a map of Las Terrazas for $1. There is a road to the right at the entrance to Las Terrazas that leads to Cafetal Buenavista, the ruin of a 19th-century French coffee estate, now partially restored. There is an elegant restaurant, and the views are great. If you choose to visit by bike, expect a difficult, twisting climb of more than 1 km—and a screaming downhill on your return to the main road.

6.2 Pass the entrance on the right to Centro de Investigaciones Ecológicas.

6.9 A road on the right goes to the Las Terrazas administration center and to Rancho Curujey, a thatched bar and restaurant overlooking a small pond.

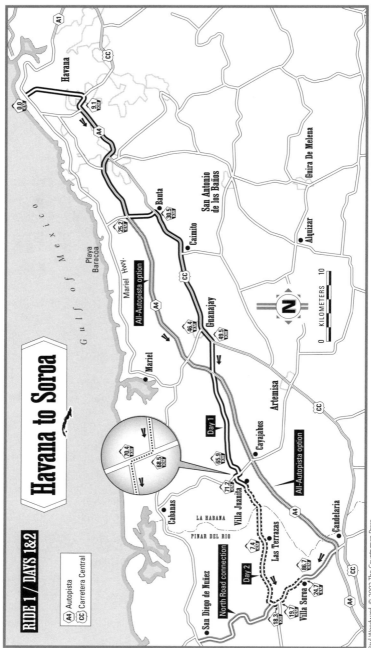

RIDE 1 / DAYS 1&2

Havana to Soroa

A4 Autopista
CC Carretera Central

Gulf of Mexico

Havana

Playa Baracoa

Mariel

Cabanas

Mariel Hwy.

All-Autopista option

San Diego de Nuñez

North Road connection

Villa Soroa

Las Terrazas

LA HABANA
PINAR DEL RIO

Villa Juanita

Cayajabos

Artemisa

Candelaria

All-Autopista option

Guanajay

San Antonio
de los Baños

Caimito

Bauta

Alquizar

Guira De Melena

A1

CC

0.0 KM/M
9.1 KM/M

25.2 KM/M
30.5 KM/M

46.4 KM/M
49.5 KM/M

65.9 KM/M
68.5 KM/M
70.4 KM/M
71.2 KM/M

7.4 KM/M

86.7 KM/M
24.7 KM/M

18.3 KM/M
19 KM/M

Day 1

Day 2

N

KILOMETERS
0   10

Paul Woodward, © 2002 The Countryman Press

7.0 Continue straight, passing a road on the left to Campismo El Taburete. (When we were in Las Terrazas in 2000 and 2001, this *campismo* was open, but there was no water.)

7.4 Turn left to visit Las Terrazas, the Hotel Moka, and Baños de San Juan—surely some of the best swimming holes in Cuba. (By going straight instead, you will be heading directly for Soroa.) After your visit, ride back to the main road and turn left toward Soroa.

10.5 Pass a turn on the left for Hacienda Unión. If you turn here to visit Hacienda Unión, you will be on a rough but passable dirt lane that leads to a restaurant in the style of a small, rural farm home. Simple *criollo* meals—the

Visiting Las Terrazas

If you turn left at km 7.4, you will soon cross a bridge over Lago San Juan. The main buildings of Las Terrazas are straight ahead. Hotel Moka is on the hillside behind them, nearly hidden by trees. Baños de San Juan are 3 km beyond Hotel Moka.

Ride toward Las Terrazas, and bear left immediately after the bridge, heading toward the main buildings. The road will pass under these buildings. Galleries and workshops as well as apartments are located here. Be sure to ask for Lester Campa's studio. We love his fabulously intricate landscape paintings even though we can't begin to afford them. We also enjoy the nearby *serigraph* (silk-screening) workshop, where there are items that fit our limited budget. Take the time to explore Las Terrazas on foot.

Baños de San Juan, surely one of the nicest swimming holes in Cuba.

Continuing beyond the main buildings of Las Terrazas, you will soon reach a right turn to Hotel Moka. This paved driveway twists and climbs 0.8 km through shady woods to the hotel entrance.

To reach Baños de San Juan, continue straight, instead of turning right up the hotel driveway. Stay well to the right on this well-paved, narrow lane. At a toll house on the left in less than 3 km, you may be asked to show the receipt you were given when you paid your entry fee to Las Terrazas.

The parking area for Baños de San Juan is just ahead. There may be a guard who offers to watch your bikes, but you should still chain them to the heavy wooden rails around the thatched picnic shelter. Be sure to take valuables with you. Follow the stone pathway and cross the footbridge. The pathway continues along the riverbank, leading to delightful swimming holes. There is also a small, thatched bar and a cafeteria for lunch. Toilets and changing rooms are available. This is a fine place to rest in the shade, dive into the deep, natural pool, and sit under a small waterfall. We have spent more hours here than at any other place in Las Terrazas.

The North Road Connection

If you were to turn right instead of left when leaving Las Terrazas at km 18.3, you would be on a quiet, unnamed road that reaches the Carretera Circuito del Norte (the North Road) near the little village of San Diego de Núñez, just to the east of Bahía Honda. This connection is useful if you would like to loop back to Havana.

It is 24 km to the North Road, mostly downhill or level, with only a couple of moderate climbs. The road passes first through wooded hills with dense, luxuriant foliage. About two-thirds of the way along, the countryside becomes more open, and you may catch occasional glimpses of the coast far ahead.

The condition of the road is good for several kilometers, but then the pavement is badly broken with yawning potholes. We had no difficulty riding it, but watch the road surface at all times. The road passes two army bases and a tiny village with no services.

After riding just over 22 km, you must turn left, following the sign to Bahía Honda and Cabañas. You will ride through the village of San Diego de Núñez. (In the *Guía de Carreteras,* it appears that there is a road branching to the northeast here, a slightly shorter connection if you are headed to Havana. Though this road may have once existed in the mind of a planner in Havana, it was never built.) You will reach the North Road 2 km after San Diego de Núñez, at km 94.9 of Ride 2, Havana to Viñales via the North Road. Turn right for Havana or left for Bahía Honda.

traditional country cooking of Cuba, including pork, beans and rice, salad, and fried bananas—are served on the shady porch for about $6 or $7. The setting is enjoyable, with farm animals wandering in the yard. You can also visit the ruins of an adjoining coffee plantation, which are being developed as gardens. Then return to the main road, turn left, and continue toward Soroa.

12.6 Exit through a tollgate. A gatekeeper will probably ask for the receipt you were given when you entered Las Terrazas. Continue straight toward Soroa. (The dirt road on the left leads through shady woods to a thatched restaurant and a pleasant swimming hole, both about 1.2 km from the start.) Continuing toward Soroa on the main road, you will ride over rolling terrain punctuated by a few short but very steep hills.

18.3 Turn left just after passing an older tollgate, no longer used in 2002. After more climbing, the terrain is rolling again for about 1 km, when the last difficult climb before Soroa begins. (The right at 18.3 is the North Road Connection.)

19.7 Bear left; do not take the road to the right with the yield sign. (The road to the right is part of the loop to San Diego de los Baños. It doesn't appear on most maps—but here it is!)

19.9 Start a long downhill. Ride under control.

22.8 Pass the entrance to Campismo La Caridad on the right. This is a very basic *campismo*.

24.7 Turn right at the entrance to Villa Soroa. It does not look attractive from the road, but wait until you are inside. Enjoy the pool! If you prefer to stay in a *casa particular,* Villa Virginia and Casa Pepe are about 2 km past this point, downhill in the village. Casa Pepe comes first, on the right; Villa Virginia is another 0.5 km farther on the left.

One-Day Autopista Option (86 km)

If you wish to ride from Havana directly to Soroa, saving Las Terrazas for another day or for your return trip, stay on the Autopista at km 25.2 of Day 1, rather than exiting for Bauta. Ride another 41 km on the Autopista to km 66.5 and then use the following route directions.

66.5 Reach a rest area on the right with a thatched snack bar. This is the first place for refreshments and rest rooms in nearly 50 km, so you will enjoy stopping. There is a sign here for Campismo La Chorrera. This Cubamar *campismo* is up a lane behind the rest area. It has a basic cafeteria, a water slide into a swimming hole, and small cabins. Four French cyclists told us they stayed here and found it buggy and uncomfortable but cheap.

67.8 Continue past a right turn with a sign for Las Terrazas and Hotel Moka. (If you took this turn, the toll gate at the entrance to Las Terrazas would be to the left at a T-intersection in about 4 hilly km. You would be at km 75.5 of the standard route.)

78.9 Turn into a Cupet gas station on the right, where you'll find a snack bar, a convenience store, and rest rooms. Each time we have stopped here, there has been delicious ice cream available. The exit ramp to Soroa is an asphalt lane at the back of the gas station. Ride on this lane past small homes on the right.

Visiting Soroa

While you are in Soroa, be sure to visit the *orquideario.* The entrance is on a road to the right just past the entry to Villa Soroa. Ask to see orchid prints by resident artist José Bocourt. For lunch, try the Castillo de Las Nubes, a long uphill trudge past the entrance to the *orquideario,* but worth the walk (or ride) for the view. Another lunch option is El Salto, a touristy alfresco restaurant shortly past the entrance to Villa Soroa on the left. This restaurant is near the trail to El Salto Cascades, a pretty waterfall. (There is a charge for using the path to the waterfall, but it is waived for hotel guests.) Another rough path, starting near the parking area, leads to the *mirador,* a lookout with a fabulous, 360-degree view. There are many other trails in the area, including some to the ruins of old coffee plantations. A booklet about the trails is available from the front desk at Villa Soroa.

Two Great Guides

At the *orquideario* in Soroa, you may be lucky enough to meet José (Joel) Bocourt, a guide who is often assigned to English-speaking groups. José knows not only the orchids, but all the other plants, trees, and birds that can be seen in these wonderful gardens. He is more than a guide, however. José is an artist of international stature.

When he was only 16 year old, José began working in the gardens as a laborer. He enjoyed drawing pictures of the flowers in his spare time. The manager of the gardens noticed José's sketches, thought he had talent, and eventually arranged for José to study botanical illustration in Mexico.

Now José is back at the gardens. He has learned enough English to work as a guide, but when he is not busy with visitors, he can be found working in his studio in the orquideario. His drawings have been published abroad and are on permanent exhibition at a museum in Spain.

Artist Joel Bocourt does lovely watercolors of the orchids at Soroa.

The reason we remember him so vividly—besides the lovely set of his orchid prints that we bought for only $20—was his open-hearted declaration of happiness. When we talked to José, he told us how delighted he was with his wife and new baby, with his work among the flowers, with his art, and with his life.

At the Villa Soroa, we engaged a guide named Alberto Fernández to lead us on a birding walk. He had been an English major in university, and he spoke our language flawlessly, but he was a self-taught naturalist. Walking quietly through the woods of Soroa, Alberto would listen for a bird and then imitate its call. Over and over, he carried on dialogues with birds, locating them and even luring them nearer. Then he would try to help us spot the birds in the tangles of greenery, sometimes successfully and sometimes not.

Alberto gave detailed answers to our numerous questions about the trees, bushes and flowers that interested us. He was a remarkable teacher. During our hours in the woods, he also answered questions about Cuba. He spoke about his country with as much love and insight as he did about nature. When you get to Soroa, look him up!

Guide Alberto Fernández leads bird and nature walks.

79.7 Merge with the road to Soroa. You are now heading directly toward the mountains.

82.6 Pass Villa Virginia on the right as you are going down a hill.

83.2 Pass Casa Pepe, another *casa particular,* on the left. Shortly after this, begin the first of two difficult climbs. These hills will make you glad that Villa Soroa has a great swimming pool! (At the top of the first climb after Casa Pepe, there is an entrance on the left to a small military resort called, confusingly enough, Villa Soroa. If you pull in by mistake, don't worry, you will not be shot. The public hotel is 1 km farther in the tourism complex, after a restaurant on the right and the orchid gardens on the left; it has a wide entrance and big sign, so you can't miss it.)

85.5 Enter the Soroa tourism complex.

85.9 Continue straight past a left turn to the orchid gardens and the Castle in the Clouds, a former mansion that how houses a restaurant (open for lunch only in 2002).

86.0 Turn left into Villa Soroa.

❷ Havana to Viñales via the North Road

182 km, 2 or 3 days

Viñales, about 180 km west of Havana and 80 km beyond Soroa, is both a small town and a lush valley of picturesque tobacco farms called *vegas.* From the level valley floor erupt *mogotes*—giant humped formations faced with pitted limestone cliffs and capped with greenery. The effect is stunning, and Viñales is a photographer's paradise, surely one of the most beautiful places in Cuba. The little town is built around a handsome square, and two of the nearby hotels command astonishing views.

We have ridden this 182-km route twice and enjoyed it both times. It leaves Havana via the Malecón and Miramar. After Mariel, the North Road rolls through small villages and farming areas, and there are many places along the route with grand views of the sea to the north and the mountains to the south. The farther you ride into Pinar del Río, the rougher and hillier the route gets, but there are only a few truly difficult climbs, mostly after La Palma.

Food

There are considerable distances between towns, so be sure to carry plenty of water, and stop at every dollar store along the route for more. It is a good idea to buy fruit in Havana the day before you leave. Bread, cheese, and many other foods are available at the supermarkets at km 8.6 or 11.8.

Hotel Los Jazmines outside Viñales

You can picnic along the way. As on any long ride in Cuba, try to start early; and if you ride in the heat of the afternoon, be sure to stop frequently in the shade and have a drink, even if you do not feel that you need it.

There are several dollar stores along the route, and tasty roadside snacks are available here and there, especially in La Palma. These possibilities are noted in the route directions. If you stay at a *casa particular* in Cabañas, Bahía Honda, or La Mulata, a reasonably good dinner and breakfast should be available. Once you reach Viñales, there is no shortage of places to eat, including the three hotels in or very near town, a few restaurants described in general guidebooks, and many *casas particulares*.

Lodging

The main drawback of this route is relative scarcity of licensed accommodations before Viñales. The first possibility after Havana is Villa Cocomar. (Before 2000 it was called Villa El Salado.) In 2001, only a handful of drab rooms were being rented to the general public, but they were adequate.

There is a licensed *casa particular* just across the highway from the entrance to Villa Cocomar called Casa Silvio, which has two clean rooms for $15 per room per night. Villa Cocomar and Casa Silvio are only about 30 km from the start of the route, but staying at one of these places can be a good strategy for a jump on the next day's long ride.

Guidebooks mention a *peso* hotel in Mariel called Motel La Puntilla. Mariel's main attraction is Cuba's biggest cement factory; and because it is not far from either Havana or Villa Cocomar, we have never had reason to stop there. There is private, unlicensed accommodation in Cabañas (km 70) on the border between Havana Province and Pinar del Río Province.

To divide this route into two days of reasonable length, Bahía Honda is the best place to stay. There is a motel north of town called Motel Punta de Piedra. We have been there twice to enjoy the view and have a beer with friends who live nearby, but we have never stayed in the rooms. Seven Americans from Minnesota were not so lucky. They spent the night at Motel Punta de Piedra in early 2001, and they told us it was the worst place they stayed in Cuba—noisy, dirty, and smelly. However, they survived it, and more recently, two correspondents stayed there and commented only on the wonderful view. This place will do in a pinch, and it may be improving. Make sure you have mosquito repellent.

There is also an unlicensed but adequate *casa particular* in Bahía Honda. Suffice to say that within minutes after you arrive in Bahía Honda on your bike, you probably will be asked if you want a room.

About 25 km past Bahía Honda, guidebooks mention Motel La Mulata just outside the village of the same name. The motel is now closed to foreigners, but there are a few unlicensed *casas particulares* in town.

Another possibility is Hotel Cayo Levisa. This place is relatively expensive, sometimes full, and accessible only by ferry. On the other hand, Cayo Levisa is said to have one of the best beaches in Pinar del Río, and there is an international dive center. You might consider it if you are interested in scuba diving but don't want to ride all the way to Playa María la Gorda. Make advance reservations for Cayo Levisa.

There are three Campismos Populares on the north coast before the turn to Viñales. We tried one of them, Campismo Playa San Pedro, and discovered that it is open only in the summer, when you will probably not be cycling. We ended up sleeping outdoors on a concrete patio in February. Chilly and uncomfortable! Campismo Herradura is closer to Havana, and it is almost certainly closed except in the summer months. Campismo La Altura, after Bahía Honda, is open throughout the year. However, it is far off the paved road, and local Cubans have told us that it is a poor accommodation, rife with mosquitoes. We have not checked it out and can't recommend it. In summary, *campismos* on this route are not promising.

Once you reach Viñales, the shortage of good accommodations is over. There are scores of *casas particulares* in town, many of them on side streets near the pretty central plaza. We are particularly fond of Casa La Esquinita, run by Aracelys Fernández and her genial husband Tony. Ara is a superb cook, and her meals are made even better by ingredients that come fresh from her large garden. Casa La Esquinita is on Rafael Trejo, No. 18, between Grajales and Pérez, just one block off Salvador Cisneros, the main street of town.

There are also three Horizontes hotels close to Viñales. We have visited and recommend Hotel La Ermita and Hotel Los Jazmines. Meals may be average Horizontes fare, but the extraordinarily beautiful settings of these two hotels more than make up for any culinary deficiencies. Note: La Ermita and Los Jazmines are heavily booked by tour groups. If you want to try one of them, make a reservation several days in advance. If you stay in a *casa particular*, be sure to visit the hotels to enjoy the spectacular views—especially at sunset. You can have a drink and use the pools as well.

A final possibility for accommodations near Viñales is Campismo Dos Hermanos. Rooms at this attractive Cubamar *campismo* were $12 per couple, or $15 including breakfast, in early 2001. Later that year there was a price increase at Cubamar *campismos,* so expect to pay somewhat more. The restaurant serves pork and chicken dinners for $5 or $6. There was noisy music around the small swimming pool on both afternoons when we visited, but the manager promised that it is quiet at night. This *campismo* is popular with both Cubans and foreign tourists.

Despite the fact that lodging between Havana and Viñales is not ideal on this route, it is a beautiful and rewarding ride. If you are flexible about where you stay and up for the challenge of rather long distances, we recommend it highly.

Day 1: Havana to Bahía Honda (101 km)

You will leave Havana by riding west on the Malecón, starting at the bottom of La Rampa (Calle 23) in Vedalo. The landmark Hotel Nacional with its waterfall is at the corner, and the Hotel Habana Libre, the city's biggest, is just a few blocks up La Rampa. The Malecón dives beneath Río Almendares into a tunnel, emerging as Avenida 5 in the suburb of Miramar. Eventually, Avenida 5 becomes the road to Mariel, so in theory this part of the route should be a straight shot with no turns. In reality, bicycles are not allowed in the tunnel, and they are forbidden on Avenida 5 in Miramar. Therefore it is necessary to cross Río Almendares on a small bridge for cyclists and pedestrians and then use roads parallel to Avenida 5 until it is legal to ride there.

0.0 Ride west on the Malecón from the bottom of La Rampa, with the sea on your right.

0.7 Ride past Plaza Martí on the left, a place where demonstrations are frequently held. The U.S. Interests Section, formerly the embassy, is the modern building just past the plaza.

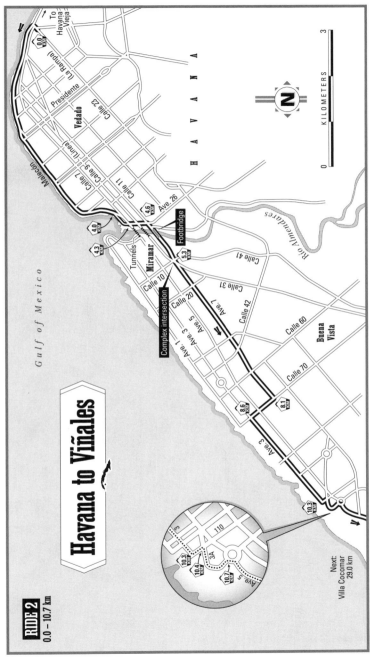

RIDE 2
0.0 – 10.7 km

Havana to Viñales

Gulf of Mexico

To Havana Vieja

0.0 KM

(La Rampa)

Presidente

Vedado

Calle 23

Malecón

Calle 7 (Línea)

Calle 9 (Línea)

Calle 11

Ave. 26

4.6 KM

4.0 KM

4.3 KM

Footbridge

Tunnels

Miramar

Calle 10

5.3 KM

Calle 41

Calle 31

Calle 20

Ave. 5

Ave. 3

Ave. 7

Calle 42

Río Almendares

Calle 60

Calle 70

Buena Vista

Ave. 1

Complex intersection

8.6 KM

8.1 KM

H A V A N A

N

KILOMETERS

0   3

10.3 KM

10.3 KM

10.4 KM

10.7 KM

3A

110

3

Ave. 5

Next:
Villa Cocomar
29.0 km

Paul Woodward, © 2002 The Countryman Press

1.9 Ride past a handsome equestrian statue on the left. It honors Calixto García, one of Cuba's most important generals during the wars of independence against Spain.

3.5 Follow the Malecón as it makes a sweeping turn to the left. Immediately after the turn, there is a set of traffic lights. You will be exiting from the Malecón in another 0.5 km.

4.0 Turn right onto a small lane, leaving the Malecón. There is an old

Latin American School of Medical Sciences

A sprawling complex of buildings, once a naval academy, now houses the Latin American School of Medical Sciences. Established in 1999, this school provides free medical training for over three thousand young people from abroad. Most come from Latin American nations, but others are from Africa and Asia. After two years of training here, students are placed in one of Cuba's regular medical schools for four more years of free education. In return, they must agree to return to their home countries and work among the poor.

Cuba is able to offer such a program because it has a surplus both of physicians and of training facilities. In 2001 the country had over 67,000 medical doctors for a population of 11 million. That makes it possible to have a small clinic, offering primary care and preventive services, for every 120 families, plus a system of polyclinics and referral hospitals for serious illnesses.

There are 21 medical schools in Cuba graduating two thousand new physicians every year, more than needed to maintain Cuba's health system. Every year Cuba sends thousands of doctors to work in the poorest regions of Africa, Asia, and Central America. The excess of training capacity makes it possible to accommodate foreign students from the Latin American School of Medical Sciences.

Cuban medical training stresses primary care and community medicine. There is also a clear ideological component that traces back to Che Guevara's concept of the revolutionary physician—one who not only cares for patients but also works to understand and change social and economic conditions that threaten their health. In a speech at the Latin American School of Medical Sciences in 2001, Fidel Castro said that the medical profession must develop a new culture, one in which health care is not a commodity to be bought and sold. "Doctors," he said, "are being trained to fulfill a sacrosanct mission, like missionaries, giving their services in remote and comfortless areas."

In 2000, a delegation of African-American congressmen from the U.S. visited Cuba and met with Castro. One of them mentioned that there were large areas in his Mississippi district that did not have a single physician. Castro responded with an offer of 250 full scholarships for students—primarily members of racial and ethnic minorities—from impoverished areas in the U.S. The places have not all been taken, but at press time there were over 30 Americans at the Latin American School of Medical Sciences, and more were on the way.

fort and a café on the right at this turn. Immediately after making the turn, you will pass the upscale 1835 Restaurant on the right.

4.3 Follow the lane as it curves to the left and crosses a bridge over the Malecón. **Bear right immediately after this bridge**.

4.5 Cross another bridge over the entrance to a second tunnel under Río Almendares.

4.6 Turn right at a four-way intersection onto Calle 11. There is a yield sign on the right just before this turn. After making the turn, look for a sign to Punta de Hierro—*solo cyclos,* indicating a small pedestrian bridge just one block ahead.

4.8 Cross Punta de Hierro. The bridge surface is a metal grating so ride carefully or walk your bike.

4.9 Continue straight after the bridge. You are now in Miramar on Avenida 7.

5.3 Reach a complex intersection where Avenida 7 crosses Calle 31, a busy, multilane road. There are traffic lights here. Be careful and walk your bike across Calle 31; then ride to the left, and bear right, still on Avenida 7. This is a gradual right; *do not* make the immediate right onto Calle 10. You will continue along Avenida 7 for almost 3 km. Here in Miramar, you are riding through what was once Havana's poshest suburb. Some of the fine old homes are still in private hands, but many have become embassies or the offices of corporations and government agencies. Note: Avenida 5, a handsome boulevard, is one block to the right. We have ridden our bikes on Avenida 5 several times, but every time we have eventually been stopped by a policeman and politely told to use one of the parallel avenues.

8.1 Turn right where Avenida 7 ends in a T-intersection with Calle 70.

8.5 Continue straight across Avenida 5.

8.6 Turn left at the major crossroad onto Avenida 3. You will immediately begin passing a row of high-rise tourist hotels on the right, the Tritón, then the Neptuno, and finally the Meliá Habana, the newest of the lot. (Note: If you ride to the right on Avenida 3 for 100 meters, you will come to the entrance of Supermercado 70, a supermarket that may have the biggest selection of food in Havana. This is a worthwhile stop if it is open when you go by; on Saturdays it does not open until 10 AM.)

10.3 Continue on Avenida 3 as it makes a 90-degree turn to the left. To the right, a short dirt lane ends at the water.

10.4 Turn right, following the arrow. Straight ahead, the street is one-way in the wrong direction.

10.6 Turn left onto a wide, unmarked, three-lane road at the end of Avenida 3. For safety's sake, use the far right lane.

10.7 Turn right at a large rotary, and then immediately bear right. You are now on Avenida 5, a broad boulevard, and it is now legal to ride bikes.

11.2 A sign on the median says to continue straight ahead to Pinar del Río and PABEXPO, an exhibit hall for trade shows. At this spot, on the far side of Avenida 5, there is a collection of fast-food restaurants.

11.4 Enter a busy rotary and follow the signs to PABEXPO and Mariel, continuing on Avenida 5.

11.8 On your right is Centro Comercio Náutico, a shopping center, where you can buy food for picnicking, including bread and cheese.

13.5 Follow Avenida 5 as it curves to the right after a busy intersection.

15.5 Pass the entrance to Marina Hemingway on the right. Marina Hemingway is a center for international yachting. Notice that across the street, staring directly in the face of this bastion of the upper bourgeoisie, is the Escuela Superior del Partido, that is, the training school of the Communist Party.

17.5 Approach a dangerous curve with care, and bear left following a sign to Mariel. Do not go straight to Santa Fe. (Santa Fe is one of the places where the *organopónico* movement started, a people's revolution in agriculture. See the sidebar entitled Alphabet Soup, page 104.)

22.0 Cross Río Santa Ana. You are now leaving the limits of the Havana metropolitan area. On the right is the Escuela Latinoamerica de Ciencias Médicas, the Latin American School of Medical Sciences.

29.0 The entrance to Villa Cocomar is on the right where a sign says PLAYA EL SALADO. Also look for Casa Silvio, a *casa particular,* on the left.

38.5 Note fields of *henequen,* also called *sisal,* on both sides of the road. Tough fibers in the leaves of this plant are dried and woven into rope and twine. Since the introduction of synthetics, this has become a marginal crop.

44.2 Turn left at the T-intersection, which comes just after a succession of small billboards paying tribute to local heroes. After making the turn, you will pass a huge cement plant on the left.

47.0 Turn left at another T-intersection. You are in Mariel, and there are a dollar store and a cafeteria at this turn. The busiest part of Mariel is to the right.

51.5 Turn right. There is a large billboard here saying ZONA FRANCA, MARIEL S.A, 19 KM, and a very small *peso* kiosk to the right. You will soon climb into the little town of Orlando Nodarse. There are no services.

57.7 Pass a faded sign to Campismo Herradura on the right. Soon enter the small town of Quiebra Hacia. There is a *peso* café on the left.

A typical stretch of the North Road

67.2 Cross a dangerous set of railroad tracks. It is absolutely necessary to walk your bike across these tracks because of their extreme angle, the height of the rails, and the sandy surface between them. You are entering the small town of Sandino. There are no services.

69.8 Turn left at a T-intersection in Cabañas. There is a dollar store with cold drinks and snacks, and there is a pleasant town square. There are unlicensed *casas particulares* in town, and if you hang around for a while, you will probably be offered a room.

69.9 Turn right, just after the sign indicating that it is 32 km to Bahía Honda. This is the first turn after the dollar store.

71.4 Enter the *municipio* of Bahía Honda, not the town itself, which is still 30 km ahead. But congratulations! You have made it to Pinar del Río Province. From now on, the road will gradually become hillier, narrower, and sometimes rougher, but sweeping views and great downhills will more than repay you for the challenge.

74.0 Bear left at a fork. The sign for the road to the right says NO ENTRY, MILITARY ZONE.

86.5 Pass a right turn with a sign for Campismo Popular Playa San Pedro. It is open only in summer.

94.9 Continue straight but make note of an inconspicuous left turn. Though unmarked, this road on the left, which we are calling the North

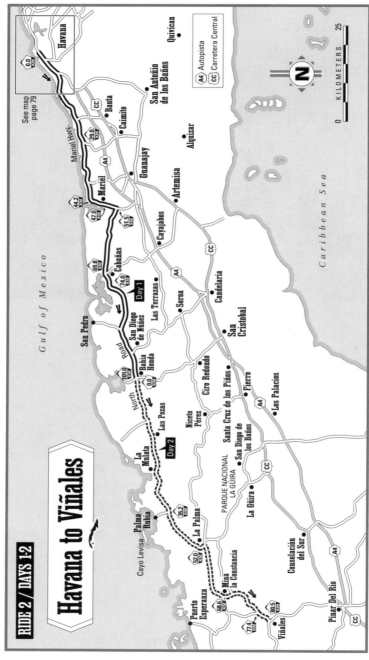

RIDE 2 / DAYS 1-2

Havana to Viñales

Gulf of Mexico

Caribbean Sea

Havana

See map page 79

Mariel Hwy.

0.0 KM

Bauta
CC
Caimito
San Antonio de los Baños

29.0 KM

A4

Mariel

44.2 KM
47.0 KM
51.5 KM

Guanajay
Artemisa
Cayajabos
Alquízar

Cabañas
69.8 KM
24.0 KM
Day 1
Las Terrazas
Soroa
CC
Candelaria

A4

San Pedro

North Road
San Diego de Núñez

101.0 KM
Bahía Honda
0.0 KM

San Cristóbal

Ciro Redondo
Santa Cruz de los Pinos
Pierro
Los Palacios
A4

Las Pozas
Niceto Pérez

La Mulata
Day 2

PARQUE NACIONAL
LA GÜIRA
San Diego de los Baños
La Güira
CC

Cayo Levisa

Palma Rubia

36.2 KM
La Palma

52.0 KM
Consolación del Sur
A4

Puerto Esperanza
68.6 KM
Mina la Constancia
80.5 KM

77.4 KM
Viñales

Pinar Del Río
CC

N

A4 Autopista
CC Carretera Central

0   KILOMETERS   25

Quivicán

Paul Woodward, © 2002 The Countryman Press

Road Connection, is the road to San Diego de Núñez. It is preceded on the right by a large iron structure used for offloading sugar cane from carts and trucks. At the turn itself, there is a small bus shelter.

101.0 In the center of Bahía Honda, there is a TRD Caribe dollar store on the left and a small park on the right. There is another dollar store on the other side of the park, though the sign is not noticeable from the road. It is much better stocked than the TRD Caribe. There is an unlicensed *casa* in Bahía Honda. Motel Punta de Piedra is 3 km north of town. You can reach it by turning right at the first street after the park.

Day 2: Bahía Honda to Viñales (81 km)

0.0. From Bahía Honda, continue west on the North Road.

10.4 Pass a sign on the right for Campismo Popular Playa Altura. The *campismo* is 12 km by rough road from this point and we can't recommend it.

14.5 Ride through the pretty little town of Las Pozas; note a monument set back from the road on the left. It commemorates heroes from the wars of independence against Spain.

25.5 Enter La Mulata. There is a dollar kiosk on the right where you can get water or soft drinks. There are good but unlicensed *casas particulares* nearby.

35.2 Pass the right to Hotel Cayo Levisa. The ferry departs from Palma Rubia, 3 km down this road.

50.5 Pass a fading sign on the right for La Palma. Quite soon, look on left for a vendor with *frituras, galletas,* and *turrón de maní.* Not much farther on the right, a pillared building with shady front steps houses a TRD Caribe dollar store. Across the street, there are two vendors, one selling *guarapo,* the other offering *peso* pizzas.

52.0 Turn right at a crossroad about 100 meters after the dollar store. (There is a small park on the left. Look around for a stand with a blender on it; you may find a *batido.)*

52.1 Bear left at a small monument surrounded by low white walls. This monument commemorates eight local men who were killed on the same day in December 1958 by Batista forces. After the monument, there is a long, moderately difficult hill, and there will be more hills to come. If you are riding in the afternoon, take advantage of patches of shade, stopping frequently and sipping water even if you don't feel the need. Soon you will be riding past tobacco fields and thatched buildings in which tobacco leaves are partially cured. You may also notice plots of low-growing plants with very large, arrow-shaped leaves. This is *malanga,* a root crop, tasty

19th-century church on the Main Square in Viñales

when fried like potato chips (crisps). You may spot occasional coffee bushes along the side of the road as well. Pinar del Río truly is Cuba's garden province. In 1 km along this stretch of road, we noticed coffee, *malanga*, yuca, a mango tree, sweet potatoes, a citrus orchard, banana trees, and coconut palms!

68.6 Turn left at the top of a long, gradual hill. The small collection of houses at this turn is called Mina la Constancia. This settlement and the road to the left appear in *Guía de Carreteras* but not on most other maps. It is possible to reach Viñales by continuing straight at this spot and then turning left in another 3 km. However, turning here at Mina la Constancia will give you a quieter, easier, more scenic ride, and it is also somewhat shorter.

72.9 Continue straight, passing a turn on the left to República de Chile.

77.4 Turn left at the T-intersection. This is the main road into Viñales.

80.0 Bear right as you pass a Cupet gas station on the left. This gas station also has a convenience store with cold drinks and fast food. You are now on Calle Salvador Cisneros, the main street of Viñales.

80.5 Reach the Viñales town square on the right.

Education in Cuba

In a Viñales Schoolyard. One Friday morning in Viñales, we asked the host at our *casa particular* if we could visit the school where she taught second grade. She gladly agreed.

We cycled across town together, and when we arrived at school we saw that many parents had come with their children. They were there for the Friday morning assembly. Children took turns on an outdoor stage reading passages from José Martí, reciting poetry, and making brief speeches. Patriotism and self-discipline were the themes. As former teachers, we were impressed by the behavior of the children and by the good-natured, professional manner of the faculty.

All over Cuba you will see schools of every size and condition, from the humblest one-room country schools to large urban institutions, sometimes dilapidated but always with a freshly whitewashed bust of José Martí and a Cuban flag by the front door. You will also see students everywhere, neatly dressed in their school uniforms.

When we returned home in December 2001, we were not terribly surprised to read in *The New York Times* that Cuban elementary schools are doing an extraordinary job. *The Times* reported on a United Nations study of Latin American education. "The performance of Cuban third and fourth graders in math and language so dramatically outstripped that of

Children and teacher in a Viñales schoolyard.

other nations that the United Nations agency administering the test returned to Cuba and tested students again." The results were confirmed. In fact, the performance of the *lowest fourth* of Cuban school children was above the average for the rest of Latin America.

Morning Television. In another *casa particular,* someone in the family had quickly vacated their room to accommodate us. There was a small television near the bed. We didn't notice that it was attached to a timer.

At 6 the next morning, we were awakened by the sounds of French being spoken in our bedroom. The television had come on, and a French class was underway on Cuba's *University for All.* This is a new channel on Cuban television offering university-level classes all day long. Everyone we spoke to about it was enthusiastic and many people are watching regularly.

Cubans can't seem to get enough education. In fact, commitment to education was evident from the very beginning of the revolution, when rebels established schools in the Sierra Maestra. Less than a year after the victory, government announced a plan to wipe out illiteracy. In 1960, over a hundred thousand volunteer teachers were recruited, most of them young high school students. Armed only with books and gas lanterns, the volunteers entered the most remote areas, teaching peasants of all ages to read and write.

Some of the young teachers were terrorized and at least one was killed by counterrevolutionaries who knew that the literacy brigades were helping solidify Fidel Castro's support among the peasantry. But the campaign succeeded anyway. Practically overnight, Cuba's literacy rate rose to 97 percent, and it has stayed there ever since.

❸ Havana to Playas del Este and Matanzas

95 km, 1 or 2 days

The following route goes all the way to Matanzas City, about 95 km east of Havana. (You may notice that distance charts say 105 km for Havana to Matanzas. We save kilometers by taking a ferry across Havana Harbor and using the Vía Blanca rather than the Autopista and Carretera Central.) We describe this as a one-day ride, but there are several beaches along the route, any one of which is worth a stay—and the beaches are the best reason for doing the ride

Most of the way, the route follows the north shore highway, the Vía Blanca. The advantage of using the Vía Blanca rather than roads farther to the south is the abundance of beaches and options for accommodations along the way. On the Vía Blanca the terrain is easy at first, but there are rolling hills to the east. Headwinds along the coast may be a challenge as well.

Leaving Havana, you must cope with the fact that bicycles are not allowed in the tunnel under the harbor. The two best ways to reach the Vía Blanca are the Cyclobus, a conventional bus that has been emptied of seats in order to carry cyclists through the tunnel, and the *lanchita*, a little ferry that chugs across the harbor every 20 minutes or so. We have tried both and prefer the ferry. Once you make your way to the Vía Blanca, the route is straightforward all the way to Matanzas.

Only 18 km from Havana, the Playas del Este begin. These beaches are popular with locals and European visitors as well. The two most important centers are Santa María del Mar and Guanabo. Santa María del Mar has more hotels and is oriented toward international tourism, while Guanabo is popular with Cubans, as well as visitors, and has more *casas particulares*.

Our favorite beach in this region is Playa Jibacoa, about 30 km beyond the Playas del Este, still an easy day's ride from Havana. Choices of accommodations range from simple *campismos* to a brand-new, five star Superclub hotel.

After Jibacoa, the route returns to the Vía Blanca and passes one of Cuba's great sights—the valley of Río Bacunayagua, spanned by Cuba's high-

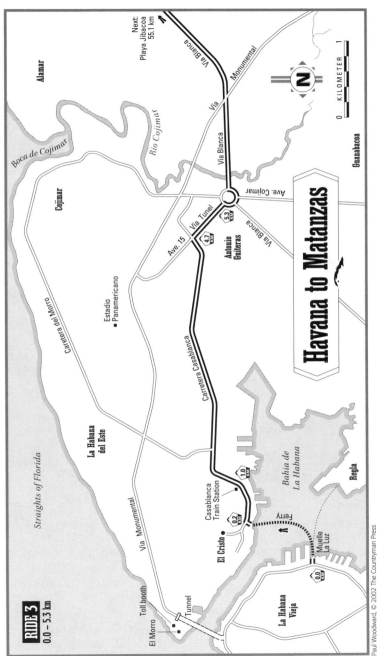

RIDE 3
0.0 – 5.3 km

Havana to Matanzas

Paul Woodward, © 2002 The Countryman Press

North coast near Playa Jibacoa.

est bridge. Shortly before Matanzas, the route turns south to Valle de Yumurí, a pretty area with a comfortable hotel. It is possible to reach Matanzas by continuing straight on the Vía Blanca, but riding through Yumurí is more enjoyable.

From anywhere along this route, you can cycle back to Havana in a single day. If you go all the way to Matanzas City, continue on Calle 83 past the Hotel Louvre and then follow signs to Havana and the Vía Blanca. Alternatively, you can return to Havana on the daily Víazul bus from Matanzas. If you aim to ride farther east than Matanzas, be sure to read the section on connecting the regions of Cuba.

Food

There are cafeterias noted in the directions just a few kilometers outside Havana, but they are so close to the start that you probably will not want to stop. There are numerous options for food if you get off the Vía Blanca at Playa Santa María or Guanabo. Continuing toward Jibacoa or beyond, you can buy sandwiches and cold drinks at a seaside snack bar at km 30 or a restaurant with views of the ocean that is 5 km farther.

Around Playa Jibacoa, there are adequate meals at the Islazul hotel, and there is a small dollar store. The restaurant at Campismo El Abra was dreadful when we stayed there. Still farther along the way, just off the Vía

Blanca, there is a snack bar with sandwiches, good cookies, drinks, and coffee at Mirador de Bacunayagua. This stop is a must for the view even if you are not hungry.

At the Casa del Valle de Yumurí, a Horizontes hotel, we found the restaurant overpriced and unappealing. For less money, good fried chicken, salads, and other fare were served by the pool in the evening.

Lodging

There are too many options in the Playas del Este for us to describe. Many hotels are listed in the general guidebooks for Santa María del Mar, Guanabo, and a few smaller towns on the *playas*.

In Guanabo we highly recommend Casa Alberto y Neisa. One guest room has a private entrance, bath, and small foyer with its own refrigerator. The other is in a self-contained cottage in the back yard. There is a sunny patio, and good meals are served by the friendly young couple that are your hosts. Casa Alberto y Neisa is a short walk from the beach at Calle 500 No. 5. The telephone number is 96-4503.

In Playa Jibacoa, the first likely stop for cycle tourists is Villa Loma Jibacoa, an Islazul hotel on a bluff overlooking the sea. Rooms are in scattered, two-story stone buildings. There is an upstairs suite in the building closest to the water, often rented to foreigners, with absolutely gorgeous views from a spacious private terrace. The food and service in the restaurant could be much better, but at $36 for a virtual apartment, the setting compensates for other failings. (There have been rumors that a new, expensive hotel complex will eventually replace this budget accommodation, but it may not happen quickly.)

Down the road, El Abra is a Cubamar *campismo* that aspires to be an eco-resort for an international clientele. There is tremendous potential here, but it is hampered by a poor restaurant and an uncertain water supply. Still, El Abra is adequate if you do not expect too much, and the beach is fantastic. Not far past El Abra is a brand-new, five star Superclub hotel. If you want to really splurge, this is a place to do it—the newest, most luxurious beach resort west of Varadero. Only 7 km from Matanzas City, the Casa del Valle de Yumurí is in a quiet valley with a lush, green setting. Though the rooms are just ordinary, the older reception building has great charm, and there is a nice pool.

In the center of Matanzas City, the Hotel Louvre is in a wonderful old building. There is a small atrium courtyard inside. We inspected a room that was rather dark, with a saggy mattress, but adequate. The Louvre could use a thorough renovation, but it is a possible option.

Route Directions

0.0 This route begins at Muelle La Luz, the small terminal from which the *lanchita* crosses Havana Harbor. If you spend any time in Havana, you will no doubt visit Plaza de Armas in Old Havana. To find Muelle La Luz from this plaza, just go one block to the waterfront and turn right. The harbor will be to your left. Follow signs to Iglesia de Paula and Muralla. You will pass the huge Sierra Maestra shipping terminal. Muelle La Luz is on the left immediately after the row of big terminals and warehouses. It is a tiny gabled structure on the waterfront with a sign that says LUZ. Boats depart from here to Regla and to Casablanca every 20 minutes or so, and you want Casablanca. Passengers wait in four lanes separated by railings, and the two lanes on the left are for Casablanca, one for pedestrians and one for cyclists. When you get off the ferry in Casablanca, cross the railroad tracks and ride up the small hill.

0.2 Follow the main road as it curves sharply to the right. This will take you through the old village of Casablanca. (The left around a tiny park climbs to El Cristo de Casablanca.)

1.0 Bear right at a fork and proceed straight through the crossroad that immediately follows; do not go uphill to the left. You are on the Carretera Casablanca, though there are no signs. A couple of kilometers from Havana, you will be in rural countryside. Casablanca has the look and feel of a small, rather dilapidated country town, even though it is directly across the harbor from a city of over 2 million people.

3.8 The road widens to four lanes.

4.7 Turn right on a busy, four-lane road with a divider. This is Avenida 15 (Avenida Vía Tunel) in the suburb of Antonio Guiteras. There are big apartment blocks across to the left; and on the right, shortly after the turn, there is a thatched snack bar and a CADECA.

5.3 Negotiate a traffic circle, the Rotonda de Cojímar. There is a thatched cafeteria on the right. Continue around the circle, **pass the exit for Havana del Este, and take the next fork to the right**, which is the Vía Blanca.

7.5 There is a sign on the right for Guanabo, Matanzas, and Varadero.

18.8 Pass the exit for Santa María del Mar, a major beach resort.

25.8 Pass the exit for Guanabo, where there are decent beaches and many *casas particulares*.

30.3 On the left is a Rumbos snack bar. Here you can sit at tables by the edge of the sea. Soon oil wells line the Vía Blanca most of the way to Santa Cruz del Norte.

35.9 There is another snack bar and a restaurant on the left.

45.0 A huge electrical generation plant on the right provides power for Havana.

47.3 Pass an exit for Santa Cruz del Norte on the right. In the town, which you can see from the Vía Blanca, there are apartment blocks first, then some modest residential areas.

48.5 Cross a small bridge and continue straight, passing a right turn to the Central Camilo Cienfuegos. The Habana Club distillery is ahead on the right. In another 2 or 3 km, riding through rather flat, open countryside, you can see distant cliffs above Playa Jibacoa.

55.1 Cross the bridge over Río Jibacoa, a landmark. There is a sign here for Villa Loma Jibacoa. You can now take a pleasant break from the Vía Blanca. Note: If you intend to stay at Villa Loma Jibacoa, take the following shortcut. Just 20 meters after the bridge, carefully make a left turn onto a dirt lane. It comes immediately before a bus shelter. This lane will pass through a gate in a chain-link fence, and the paving will resume. Proceed directly to the entrance to Villa Loma Jibacoa.

56.1 Take the exit ramp to the right, shortly after the bridge over Río Jibacoa, and bear right at the top of the ramp.

56.4 Turn right, following signs for Playa Jibacoa and El Abra. You will soon ride through a lovely row of trees that creates an arch over the road and provides the coolest shade on the entire ride so far—reason enough for taking this little detour along Playa Jibacoa.

57.2 The first paved road on the left, unmarked, goes to Villa Loma Jibacoa.

57.4 Another paved road, a sharp left, also goes to Villa Loma Jibacoa. There is a public beach near this intersection but no facilities. Continuing straight, you will pass a dollar store on the right in 100 meters. It had no sign when we were last there; you can recognize it by the green Cristal Beer awning over a second-floor patio. There is usually ice cream, cheese, crackers and cookies, beer, *refrescos,* and soap for washing clothes. Soon you will pass *campismo*-style resorts that are reserved for sugar workers. During winter harvest they are deserted, but in late summer and early fall vacationing families fill them.

59.6 Pass Campismo Popular Las Caletas on the left. Yellow bungalows with red roofs are scattered amid palm trees. This is an attractive holiday camp for Cubans with a nice pool, but it is closed except on weekends and in midsummer. We believe foreigners might talk their way in when the *campismo* is open and there are vacancies, but they might be asked to continue down the road to Campismo El Abra.

59.9 Campismo El Abra is on the left.

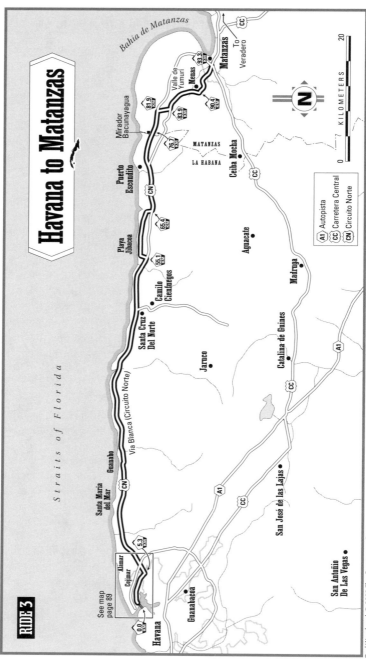

RIDE 3

Havana to Matanzas

Straits of Florida

Bahia de Matanzas

To Veradero

Matanzas

Valle de Yumurí

Menas 93.3 KM

81.9 KM

90.4 KM

83.9 KM

Mirador Bacunayagua

76.7 KM

MATANZAS

LA HABANA

Ceiba Mocha

Puerto Escondito

CN

65.6 KM

Playa Jibacoa

Aguacate

55.1 KM

Camilo Cienfuegos

Santa Cruz Del Norte

Madruga

Jaruco

Catalina de Guines

CC

A1

See map page 89

Mamar
Cojimar

5.3 KM

Santa Maria del Mar

Guanabo

Via Blanca (Circuito Norte)

CN

0.0 KM

San José de las Lajas

A1

CC

Havana

Guanabacoa

San Antonio De Las Vegas

A1 Autopista
CC Carretera Central
CN Circuito Norte

N

KILOMETERS

0   7   20

Paul Woodward, © 2002 The Countryman Press

60.4 Campismo Popular La Laguna is on the left. It does not look as nice as Las Caletas.

61.2 Bear right. (The sharp left here is the entrance to Villa Tropical, a resort only for patrons of an Italian travel agency.) As you ride uphill, you will pass the entrance to Superclub Breezes Jibacoa on the left.

65.4 Turn left onto the Vía Blanca.

75.6 Reach the top of a 3-km climb with panoramic views of sea.

76.7 Turn left into the driveway to the Mirador de Bacunayagua. This turn comes just a few meters after a small snack bar on the highway. The *mirador* is popular with tour groups and is well worth the visit. You can enjoy cold drinks, sandwiches, a crafts shop, live music, clean rest rooms, and a truly spectacular view. If you find yourself crossing the highest bridge in Cuba, you have missed the turn to the *mirador* by about 100 meters. After visiting the *mirador,* return to the Vía Blanca and continue across the bridge.

81.9 Turn right following signs to El Valle and Horizontes Casa del Valle de Yumurí. The signs indicate that it will be 2 km to the hotel, but don't believe it. In fact, you will have to turn again in 2 km and then ride another 5 km to get there. (If you continue straight along the Vía Blanca, you will reach the center of Matanzas in approximately 17 km. However, the ride via Casa del Valle de Yumurí is quieter and less monotonous, and the distance is almost the same.)

83.9 Turn left at a T-intersection, following the sign for Casa del Valle de Yumurí.

88.6 The clearly marked entry to the hotel is on the right. From here, you can backtrack to Playa Jibacoa and points west, or you can ride 7 km to the center of Matanzas by continuing to follow the route directions.

88.7 Turn right as you exit the hotel driveway.

89.1 Cross railroad tracks carefully. This is the Mena stop on the Hershey train. (Unfortunately, bikes are not allowed on this train.)

90.4 Cross an iron bridge and turn left at the T-intersection, following the sign to Matanzas. (Right goes to Corral Nuevo.)

92.1 Begin a fairly difficult, 1-km climb.

93.3 Bear left at a yield sign. The right here goes to Madruga. On the right at this intersection, we found pork sandwiches , with meat sliced right off the freshly roasted pig, for five *pesos*.

94.0 Bear right at the Y-intersection. Parque Rene Fraga is directly ahead. Continue downhill with the park on your left; do not take the right turn. You will be riding down Calle 83 into the center of town.

95.5 Reach Plaza de la Libertad. There is an Infotur office on the corner, and the Hotel Louvre is just ahead on the right.

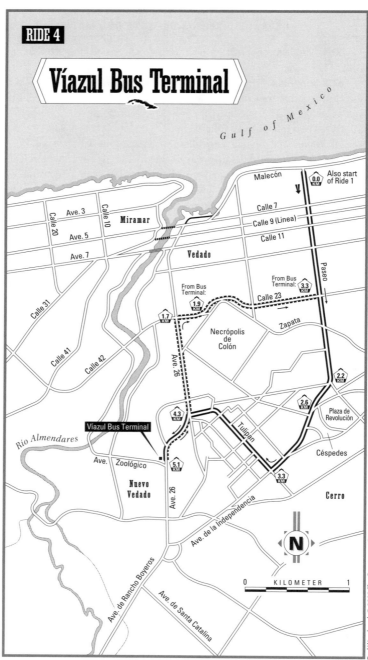

RIDE 4

Víazul Bus Terminal

Gulf of Mexico

Malecón

Also start of Ride 1

0.0 KM

Calle 7

Calle 9 (Linea)

Calle 11

Ave. 3

Calle 10

Calle 20

Miramar

Ave. 5

Ave. 7

Vedado

Paseo

From Bus Terminal: 1.9 KM

From Bus Terminal: 3.3 KM

Calle 23

Calle 31

1.7 KM

Necrópolis de Colón

Zapata

Calle 41

Calle 42

Ave. 26

2.2 KM

4.3 KM

2.6 KM

Plaza de Revolución

Víazul Bus Terminal

Río Almendares

Tulipan

Ave.   Zoológico

5.1 KM

Céspedes

3.3 KM

Nuevo Vedado

Ave. 26

Cerro

Ave. de la Independencia

N

Ave. de Rancho Boyeros

Ave. de Santa Catalina

0   KILOMETER   1

❹ Getting To and From Víazul Bus Terminal, Havana

Riding to the Víazul Bus Terminal

0.0 Follow the directions for Ride 1, Havana to Las Terrazas and Soroa, until km 3.3.

3.3 Turn right on Tulipán. Be careful! To make the turn safely, pull over to the left, against the grassy median, until the light turns red. Then walk your bike to the right, across two lanes of traffic that have stopped for the light, and proceed on Tulipán.

4.3 Turn left at a T-intersection with traffic lights. This is Avenida 26, a four-lane road. Be sure to cross all the way to the right lane on the far side. Follow Avenida 26 as it curves to the right, then to the left.

5.1 The Víazul bus station will be on your right, on the corner of Avenida 26 and Zoológico. This comes shortly after you pass a big CADE-CA on the right and begin climbing a gentle hill.

Riding from the Víazul Bus Terminal to Vedado and the Malecón

0.0 Starting out: The bus depot is on the corner of a two-lane road and a six-lane road. Cross the six-lane road carefully and ride to the left, downhill. You are on Avenida 26, which you will stay on as it bears to the right, then to the left.

1.3 Continue straight through a major intersection preceded by a sign indicating that Calle 23 and Miramar are ahead and Necrópolis de Colón is to the right.

1.7 Turn right onto Calle 23. There are traffic lights at this intersection. Avenida 26 continues ahead, but it becomes a narrower one-way street. On the right is a cafeteria called "23 y 26."

1.9 Make the gentle left turn. This is just 100 meters after a sign indicating that La Rampa is to the left and Plaza de la Revolución is straight ahead. Wait for a red light to stop traffic before attempting to walk your bike across this busy intersection. Follow Avenida 23 as it curves to the right, then to the left.

3.3 Reach the intersection with Paseo. This is a boulevard with shade trees and benches. There are traffic lights, a police kiosk, and corner-stones for identification. If you turn left on Paseo here, you will reach the Malecón in about 1.5 km. If you continue straight on Calle 23, it will become La Rampa, and you will reach the Malecón in 2 km, passing the Hotel Habana Libre on the right. This is the principal Vedado hotel neighborhood. If you are heading to Habana Centro or Habana Vieja, turn right on the Malecón.

Part II:
Pinar del Río

Near the border of Pinar del Río, billboards announce THE GARDEN PROVINCE OF CUBA. Though Cuba's westernmost province is known chiefly for fine tobacco, it is a rich and diverse agricultural region. The lowlands of Pinar del Río are a bright green sea of sugar cane, and cattle are raised on lush pastures in the south and on rough ranch land in the west. Farmers, many of whom who still plow their small fields with oxen, raise an abundance of fruit and vegetables.

Much of Pinar del Río is dominated by a chain of low mountains. Low, that is, until you are cycling through them. The Cordillera Guaniguanico mountain range is divided into the Sierra del Rosario in the east and the Sierra de los Organos in the west. These mountains are covered with forests, but productive farmland punctuated by Royal Palms is tucked into countless small valleys. To the north, the mountains descend almost to the sea. South of the mountains, and west of Guane as well, Pinar del Río is nearly flat. Though cycling is easiest in these lowlands, the best rides are in or near the mountains, where the work of climbing is repaid with stunning views of blue-green peaks, misty valleys, and lowlands stretching to the sea.

Our routes in Pinar del Río originate from Soroa or Las Terrazas, and from Viñales. With quiet roads, unpretentious tourist centers, and gorgeous, unspoiled scenery, this is one of the best cycle touring areas in Cuba.

Returning to Havana. You can return to Havana from the west by

RIDES 5·6·7·8

Pinar del Río Region

Havana

Mariel

Alquízar

Guanimar

A4

Guanajay

Cabañas

Artemisa

LA HABANA
PINAR DEL RÍO

Las
Terrazas

Soroa

Candelaría

Bahía Honda

San
Cristóbal

Ride 5

Los
Palácios

San Diego
de los Baños

A4

La Palma

Ride 6

Cayo Levisa

Gulf of Mexico

Consolácion
Del Sur

Viñales

CC

Pinar Del Río

Puerto
Esperanza

Santa
Lucía

Ride 7

Puente
De Cabezas

Ride 8

CC

Boca de Galafre

Playa Bailén

Dimas

Guane

Isabel
Rubio

Sandino

Miguel Lazo

Cayo Jutías

Mantua

Laguna Grande

La Fé

La Bajada

María la Gorda

Golfo de Guanahacabibes

Bahía de
Corrientes

Cabo
San Antonio

N

KILOMETERS

0   50

A4 Autopista
CC Carretera Central

Paul Woodward, © 2002 The Countryman Press

Bohio where tobacco leaves are cured

backtracking the route on the North Road to Viñales, or by backtracking the route to Las Terrazas and Soroa on the Carretera Central and the Autopista. Of the two routes, the North Road is better. The route back to Havana on the Autopista or Carretera Central is more difficult to follow, and riding through the suburbs of Playa and Miramar is more pleasant than riding through the industrial areas south of the city.

From the Las Terrazas-Soroa area, you can take the North Road Connection (see the sidebar on this route on page 72). If you get an early start, you may choose to head east. It is a little over 100 km from Soroa to Villa Cocomar by this route. It is 135 km all the way back to the city. You could also take the North Road and then stop in Bahía Honda for the night before heading east.

There are other ways to pick up the North Road. One that we have used cuts north from Bauta; you can pick it up from either the Carretera Central or at the Bauta exit from the Autopista. Another possibility is to ride on the Carretera Central all the way to Punta Brava. A road goes north to Santa Fe via Cangrejeras. It is narrow and unpleasantly littered in places, but it is a short, practical alternative. Note: You can also get back to Havana from Pinar del Río City or Viñales on the Víazul bus—in less than three hours for about $12.

❺ Soroa–San Diego de los Baños Loop

130 km, 2 days

This is one of our favorite rides in Pinar del Río, and it takes you right off the map! That is, part of the route follows a spectacular mountain road that does not appear in the *Guía de Carreteras,* the best collection of highway maps in Cuba, or on any other map but one. We found the road on an out-of-date provincial map, and even then it was drawn inaccurately.

On the morning of the first day, you will ride through remote mountains and valleys that are virtually untouched by tourism. The hills are challenging but the rewards are tremendous. Then you will leave the Sierra del Rosario on a long, long downhill to the Carretera Central. You will ride for a while in rolling countryside south of the mountains and arrive for the evening in the small resort town of San Diego de los Baños.

The second day takes you back to Soroa along the Carretera Central, which in this part of Cuba is just a scenic country road, and on a short, easy section of the Autopista. The only difficult climb on the second day comes in the last couple of kilometers before Villa Soroa.

Food

You will need plenty of water and some good things to eat for the first morning. We recommend that you discreetly raid the breakfast buffet at Villa Soroa if you are staying there. Some fruit and sweet rolls will see you through, perhaps supplemented with peanuts and sweets from the hotel shop, where bottled water is also available. Once you reach Niceto Pérez on your way out of the mountains (km 39.4), you will be able to buy more food. There are many possibilities for buying drinks and food on the Carretera Central. These places are mentioned in the route directions.

Lodging

Our favorite place to stay along this route is Hotel El Mirador, in San Diego de los Baños. It is an old-fashioned resort hotel, clean and well maintained, now run by Islazul. Try to get room 26 if you can; it is special. Sunlight pours in through casement windows on three sides of the room. Hotel El Mirador has a small, shallow pool where you can cool off at the end of the ride, and a poolside bar. Many Cubans come here to relax in the evenings and on weekends, and it is a pleasant and friendly place. Breakfast was included in the 2001 rate of $36 for two. Dinners were adequate, and the dining room was handsome, with French doors along one wall, Tiffany-style lamps over every table, and an adjoining gallery of arts and crafts.

Next to the hotel are the mineral baths that put this little town on the map, but one of our correspondents sent the following note: "I was really disappointed by the baths in San Diego de los Baños. They are in a bleak building and are not hot. We took a swim in the river that was much prettier, free, and full of healing sulfur. There are spots downriver from the bath-

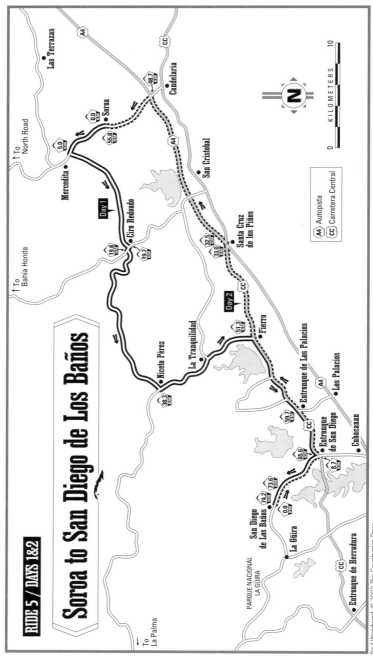

RIDE 5 / DAYS 1&2

Soroa to San Diego de Los Baños

To Las Terrazas

To North Road

To Bahia Honda

To La Palma

Las Terrazas

Candelaria

Soroa

Mercedita

Ciro Redondo

Day1

San Cristóbal

Santa Cruz de los Pinos

Niceto Pérez

La Tranquilidad

Day2

Fierro

Entronque de Los Palacios

Los Palacios

PARQUE NACIONAL LA GÜIRA

San Diego de Los Baños

La Güira

Entronque de San Diego

Cabacanan

Entronque de Herradura

0.0 KM
55.0 KM
5.0 KM
48.7 KM
19.8 KM
19.7 KM
32.5 KM
33.0 KM
38.3 KM
51.3 KM
59.7 KM
65.6 KM
73.6 KM
74.2 KM
0.0 KM
8.7 KM

A4 Autopista
CC Carretera Central

N

KILOMETERS

0   10

Paul Woodward, © 2002 The Countryman Press

The high road we call "Cuba's Skyline Drive."

house just past the bridges that are perfect." Another correspondent was disappointed by the massage that was offered at the baths.

Note: There are one or two licensed *casas particulares* in town.

Day 1: Soroa to San Diego de los Baños (74 km)

0.0 Turn left as you leave Villa Soroa.

3.7 Begin climbing a challenging hill, reaching the top at km 4.8. It gets harder toward the top.

5.0 Turn left onto an unmarked, paved road. This road appears almost immediately after you crest the hill; do not continue downhill, or you will have a long ride back up.

10.4 Note multiple signs on the right warning, in Spanish, VEHICLES, CHECK EQUIPMENT! There are pictures of cars crashing—no kidding! It will be a great downhill, but you must ride under control!

13.0 Pass through a small village at the bottom of the downhill run. After the village, you will resume intermittent climbing.

17.2 Start up a long section of switchbacks that is quite difficult but also rewarding because of the fabulous views. This is one of the high points of the ride, figuratively and literally.

19.7 Turn right at a T-intersection. (Note: Turning left will take you toward San Cristóbal. If you find the mountains too difficult, you can bail out and head for the lowlands. On this option you will cross the Autopista in 11 km and continue approximately 1.5 km to the Carretera Central. After riding west for about 15 km on the Carretera Central, you will reach the tiny

Alphabet Soup: Agricultural Reform in Cuba

When cycling through rural Pinar del Río and elsewhere in Cuba, you can't help noticing repeated abbreviations on thousands of signs by the side of the road. Some of the most important are INRA, CCS, CPA, ANAP, and UBPC. These abbreviations tell part of the story of remarkable transformations in Cuban agriculture and rural life.

Before the revolution, a wealthy 8 percent of farmers controlled 70 percent of the land. Many of the largest landholders were foreigners. The overwhelming majority of rural Cubans were agricultural laborers. They subsisted on low seasonal wages, and most lived in shacks without electricity or running water. They went without education and medical care.

In 1959 and again in 1963, radical redistribution of Cuba's agricultural land was carried out by INRA, the National Institute for Agrarian Reform, and 12,000 huge farms were expropriated. Small farmers kept their property, and more than 100,000 rural laborers were given free title to land. The number of small farms increased from 45,000 to 160,000. Housing, schools, clinics, stores, and community centers were built all over rural Cuba.

At the time of the reforms, Fidel Castro promised that small-scale farmers would never be forced to give up their farms, and the promise has been kept. To prevent reconsolidation of land into large, private holdings, farmers are forbidden to sell their land except to the government, but they can deed it to relatives and leave it to descendants in their wills.

In keeping with the revolution's socialist convictions, small farmers are encouraged to join cooperatives. CCS and CPA are two types of cooperative. CCS stands for Cooperative for Credit and Services. In these organizations, farmers retain individual ownership of land and earnings but negotiate collectively for loans and services, as the name implies. CPAs are Cooperatives for Agricultural Production. These are true cooperatives in which farmers pool their land, own and work it collectively, and share

earnings. A small minority of farmers chooses not to join any cooperative at all.

ANAP is the National Association of Small Producers, the umbrella organization to which all CCS and CPA farms belong. ANAP negotiates with government on behalf of its members concerning farm prices and policies.

At the time of the land reforms, the biggest proper-

Watering vegetables at an *organopónico*

ties—44 percent of all agricultural and ranch land—were retained by government and converted to state farms. In subsequent years the percentage of land in state farms increased. Former seasonal laborers became salaried employees. Highly mechanized, capital-intensive production methods were adopted by the state farms and by many CPAs as well. Cuba used as many tractors per acre as the U.S., and even more fertilizer.

Collapse In the 1990s These production methods made Cuba dependent on steady supplies of fuel, chemicals, and machinery parts. When Soviet aid and trade ended in 1990, supplies were cut off, and Cuba's farm production began to tumble. Tractors rusted in the fields, pumps stopped for lack of electricity and parts, crops died, and animals starved or were slaughtered. The average Cuban began to go hungry. It was the Special Period.

A UBPC–Basic Unit of Cooperative Production

Under these desperate circumstances, with practically no help from overseas, Cuban agriculture has been transformed once again, and food production has rebounded. The international aid organization OXFAM says this recent transformation should be studied as an example for the developing world.

UBPCs are part of the story. Government broke huge state farms into smaller units and turned over the land, rent free, to cooperatives of former employees. These are the Basic Units of Cooperative Production (UBPCs). The intent is to encourage more flexibility and diversity; and because members share the earnings of the cooperatives, there should be an incentive for higher production. Additional production incentives are now provided by markets in which farmers can sell a portion of their crops directly to consumers. Recently, government has experimented with incentive payments in U.S. dollars for extra production in some crops.

Farming methods also changed drastically in the 1990s. The few older farmers who still knew how to handle draft animals became the nucleus of nationwide training programs. Tractors were replaced by oxen on many farms. Research on organic production methods was quickly disseminated. Driven by necessity, Cuba managed a rapid transformation to ecological agriculture. And while inputs decreased, yields increased.

Organopónicos Perhaps the most visible change, one with a direct impact on the average Cuban diet, has been the establishment of *organopónicos*. You will see these big gardens when you cycle through the outskirts of nearly every city and town. Vegetables are raised by cooperatives and clubs for their members and for local distribution. Intensive gardening methods are used, including raised beds of soil mixed with organic compost. *Organopónicos* have become an urban gardening movement in Cuba. Production of vegetables doubled or tripled every year from 1994 to 1999, and it is still climbing.

hamlet of Fierro. Here you will rejoin the regular route at km 51.3, saving about 4 km of riding but missing more spectacular highland scenery. We have not ridden this alternative. A correspondent writes that the downhill out of the mountains is steep enough to be either thrilling or terrifying, depending on your taste in these matters.)

19.8 Turn left. This is the first paved road on the left, about 100 meters after the T-intersection where you just turned right. When you make this left turn, you will immediately do some more climbing.

21.1 The road drops like a stone. This is a terrific downhill, lasting nearly 1 km, and the road surface is in good condition so you can enjoy it. This downhill is followed by approximately 15 km of tough climbs and exhilarating downhills. You will reach high, windswept country and pass places where you can see all the way north to the Atlantic coast and south over the lowlands to the Caribbean. This wonderful ride reminds you why you love bicycle touring!

36.9 Pass a radio transmission tower on the left as you are beginning a downhill that gets quite fast and steep. Ride under control and be prepared to stop at a T-intersection that appears rather suddenly.

38.3 Turn left at the T-intersection. This is the road to Niceto Pérez.

39.4 Coast downhill into the center of Niceto Pérez village. There are vendors selling snacks, and a café set back from the road on the right.

44.6 Look out over rolling plains and a large reservoir, Embalse Bacunagua, far ahead and still downhill.

51.3 Turn right at a T-intersection onto the Carretera Central. The settlement here is Fierro. There is a Tiendas Panamericanas kiosk on the right shortly after the turn. (The kiosk is set back from the road and easy to miss.) You will now ride west on the Carretera Central through gently rolling country for about 14 km.

54.9 The Yuri Gargarin Farm is on the right, a feedlot for thousands and thousands of geese. The Carretera Central is quiet here, passing through expanses of grazing land and fields of sugar cane, with some corn and tobacco. Royal Palms and the Sierra del Rosario create a scenic backdrop.

59.7 Bear right at a fork in the hamlet of Entronque de Los Palacios. The left goes south to the Autopista and Los Palacios.

65.6 Turn right at a small crossroad following a sign on the right for Hotel El Mirador.

66.9 Villa Amistad is on the left. This is a modest but attractive resort for vacationing soldiers and their families. It is not open to the general public.

73.6 Bear right at the fork immediately after a Cupet gas station.

Landscaped grounds at Hotel El Mirador in San Diego de Los Baños.

Follow this road through several intersections in the small town of San Diego de los Baños.

74.2 Turn right immediately after a small cinema on the left.

74.3 Arrive at the Hotel El Mirador. The entrance gate is on your right after a steep climb of only 20 or 30 meters.

Day 2: San Diego de los Baños to Soroa (56 km)

0.0 Turn left as you exit the hotel gate, and then take the immediate left at the bottom of the short, steep hill. Backtrack from San Diego de los Baños to the Carretera Central.

0.7 Proceed straight, passing the Cupet gas station on your right. (There is a small convenience store attached to the gas station, a good place to buy bottled water.) Continue all the way to the Carretera Central.

8.7 Turn left at the crossroad onto the Carretera Central following the sign for Havana. The second time we did this ride, we had an early start, and the morning sun illuminated the brilliant green of sugar cane along the carretera, a striking contrast to the darker mountains in the background.

19.3 Pass the Yuri Gagarin Farm, now on your left.

22.9 Ride through Fierro, passing the Tiendas Panamericanas kiosk and the road on which you traveled down from the mountains on Day 1.

30.3 Enter Santa Cruz de los Pinos. Continue through town, staying on the Carretera Central as it bears right at a small triangular park. There is a Tiendas Panamericanas dollar store on the right just before the park. Also, we bought some street pizzas near this park that were among the best we've had—or perhaps we were hungrier than usual.

Following are directions for entering the Autopista by the safest, most direct route.

32.5 Cross a bridge over the Autopista. You will take the Autopista for the next 15 km. As you cross the bridge, notice that there is a dirt track below to the right that provides access to the Autopista. You will not be using this track because there is a better entrance for eastbound travelers, but the track is a useful landmark for identifying the next turn.

33.0 Turn left. You can identify this turn because there is access on the right to the dirt track. The left, which you will make, enters a residential area.

33.2 Turn left at a T-intersection. Then, in only a few meters, turn right. There may be small snack stands here.

33.3 Turn right onto the Autopista. At this point the Autopista has just two lanes and a gravel shoulder in each direction. You can ride on the right-hand paved lane. Bikes, pedestrians, and even horse carts customarily use this lane.

48.0 Pass the first of two signs for Soroa. Ahead in the distance is a bridge where the road to Soroa passes over the Autopista. This is the road you want, but it is easier to pass the exit ramp at km 48.6 and ride under the bridge.

48.7 Walk your bikes to the left across the Autopista through one of the gaps in the fence and bushes along the median, less than 100 meters past the bridge.

You are now at km 78.9 of the One-Day Autopista Option (see page 73). Simply follow the directions from the Cupet gas station back to Villa Soroa arriving at 55.8.

❻ Viñales–San Diego de los Baños Loop

125 km, 2 or 3 days

This is an exciting and challenging overnight ride. The first half of Day 1 is easy and delightfully scenic, but then some tough climbing begins. The route takes you to Cueva de los Portales, a hideaway that was Che Guevara's command post during the missile crisis. Hidden deep in the Sierra del Rosario, this is no ordinary cave. A river flows right through the wall of mountains. It is a beautiful spot as well as a historic landmark of interest to revolution buffs. Then there is more difficult climbing into the Parque Nacional La Güira, followed (at last) by some long, rough, downhill runs toward the pleasant village of San Diego de los Baños.

On Day 2, you can ride all the way back to Viñales on a route that is considerably easier than Day 1, completing the loop in two days. Alternatively, you could make Day 2 shorter by stopping for the night at Aguas Claras, a sort of eco-resort about 7 km north of Pinar del Río City. From there you could ride back to Viñales the next morning, or you might choose to explore Pinar del Río City.

Food

On Day 1 you should pack enough food for the ride. The first restaurant is at Campismo Popular Cueva de los Portales, if it is open when you get there and if there is food. You will want to eat long before then. There is also a restaurant in Parque Nacional la Güira, but we have never seen anyone eating there. Near the park entrance, a *peso* cafeteria sells *bocaditos,* but at this point you are only a few kilometers from San Diego de los Baños.

Meals at Hotel El Mirador in San Diego de los Baños were reasonably good and inexpensive when we were there in 2001. On the return ride, there will be several options for lunch or snacks along the Carretera Central.

Lodging

For overnight accommodations, we like the Hotel El Mirador. The *campismo* by the entrance to Cueva de los Portales, at km 43.2, is mentioned in guidebooks; but when we stopped there in 2000, it looked dismal, and we would not have recommended it. However, in 2001 this *campismo* was undergoing a major renovation. A few new cabins had been built, old ones were being repainted, new signs and sidewalks had been installed, an outdoor bar had opened, and a new restaurant was almost finished. Correspondents who were there in early 2002 said that there was no food in the restaurant yet, and the bathrooms still operated with buckets, so the upgrading was apparently incomplete. In any case, this might be an alternative for cyclists on a tight budget.

Aguas Claras offers adequate cabins, some with air-conditioning and hot water, a small swimming pool with bar, a pleasant setting, a poor restaurant, and usually, a congenial bunch of low-budget travelers from many countries. The eco-resort description is mainly justified by the labels on some of the trees and by the fact that loud music does not blare around the swimming pool. In 2001, cabins were $24 with a fan and cold water and $28 with air-conditioning and hot water—including a disappointing breakfast.

Day 1: Viñales to San Diego de los Baños (59 km)

0.0 Start from the plaza in the center of Viñales. With your back to the Casa de la Cultura, ride to the left on Salvador Cisneros.

0.5 Bear left at the Cupet gas station following signs to Las Cuevas (the Caves) and to San Vicente.

3.3 Turn right shortly after a faded sign to Laguna de Piedra. When you make the turn, tobacco fields will be on your left backed by a *mogote*.

7.7 Continue straight, following the sign to the Carretera Circuito del Norte (the North Road). Do not turn right to República de Chile. (This agricultural cooperative and housing complex was built around the time of Salvador Allende's assassination, and it was given this name in his honor.)

11.0 A pleasant downhill begins, but keep your speed under control because you will be making a sharp right turn.

11.2 Make the sharp right on an unmarked, paved road near the bottom of the hill. You will cross a few whitewashed bridges. La Resbalosa, a wonderful swimming hole, is at the third bridge.

15.0 La Resbalosa is below to the right. The easiest way to get there is on a path that descends from the left side of the bridge and crosses under it.

23.7 Ride through a small settlement. This is CPA Abel Santamaría.

27.5 There is a large sawmill, Complejo Agro-Industrial Forestal La Baria, on the left. You will be turning right in 200 meters.

27.7 Make a sharp right at an unmarked intersection. There is a bus shelter here. This is the first paved road after the sawmill.

30.1 Continue past a sign on the left for Centro Para el Desarollo de la Montaña Universidad de Pinar del Río (a center for economic development of the mountain region). On the right is a military zone. The next 3 km are hilly.

33.8 Turn left at an unmarked intersection. There is a bus shelter and a bench here, and there will probably be people waiting for rides. Immediately after this turn begin a short downhill. Watch out for bad potholes.

35.4 Notice a tiny schoolhouse on the right; the bust of José Martí is almost as big as the building! You will be riding in a pleasant, level valley for a while, passing some larger-scale farms growing rice, tobacco, and more coffee.

39.2 Follow the paved road as it bears right.

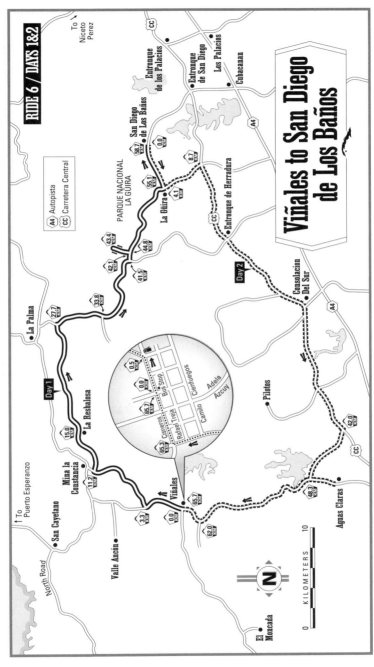

RIDE 6 / DAYS 1&2

To Niceto Perez

Viñales to San Diego de Los Baños

A4 Autopista
CC Carretera Central

PARQUE NACIONAL LA GUIRA

To Puerto Esperanzo

North Road

San Cayetano

Valle Ancón

El Moncada

0 KILOMETERS 10

Paul Woodward, © 2002 The Countryman Press

41.2 Pass an inconspicuous PNR control point on the right. Immediately afterwards, climb a short hill and begin watching for the next turn.

41.5 Turn left following the sign for Campismo Cueva de los Portales, which is immediately before the cave.

42.1 Turn left following a sign for Cueva de los Portales. (A sign also indicates that it is straight ahead to Cabañas. This refers to Cabañas de los Pinos, not the town of Cabañas. You will be going this way after visiting Cueva de Portales.)

43.2 Ride through the *campismo*.

43.4 Arrive at the cave. There is a shelter here for shade, and you can chain your bike to it. This is also a good spot for a picnic lunch. You will probably be approached and offered a tour. The tour is free, but a tip will be

Cabañas de los Pinos

Once upon a time, there was an extraordinary *campismo* in the hills of Parque Nacional La Güira known as Cabañas de los Pinos. Some guidebooks still mention it.

Small cabins were built, not on the ground, but high on stilts in the fragrant pines that grow at this altitude. The cabins were connected by a network of suspended walkways. Cabañas de los Pinos recalled the magical elfin wood of Lothlorien in Tolkien's *Lord of the Rings*. Celia Sánchez, a hero of the revolution and Fidel Castro's closest companion until her death, was responsible for creating this wonderful *campismo*.

Cabañas de los Pinos in 2000; now they are gone.

When we first visited in 2000, many of the cabins still existed, but they were uninhabitable, all facilities were gone, and the walkways were treacherous. Sadly, the place had been closed for several years. In late 2001, there was nothing left—nothing except piles of broken boards at the base of the trees that had once sheltered the cabins in their branches. In the drifts of pine needles along the side of the lane, we spotted a few paper receipts left behind by guests from years ago. At the entrance to Parque Nacional La Güira, there is still a painted billboard showing Cabañas de los Pinos in its prime, but the billboard gives no more than a hint of what this place must once have been.

Billboard still advertises Cabañas de los Pinos.

appreciated. Remember to show respect for this place; Che Guevara is still a great national hero, especially to the older people who act as guides here. Continue the ride by first backtracking through the *campismo*.

44.8 Bear left, passing a sign for the Carretera La Palma, which is 1 km to the right, the way you came. You are now heading toward Cabañas de los Pinos. (When we passed this spot in 2001, a smiling young man offered us a horse to ride. He said it would be easier than biking in the hills ahead. He was right, but the difficulty of the hills is mitigated by the quiet, in which bird calls are the loudest sounds, and by the fact that the last third of the climb is shady.)

48.0 Notice an unpaved road from the left with signs that are almost indecipherable. The route continues straight ahead. The left goes to Cabañas de los Pinos. Shortly after passing the turn to the cabins, ride a steep, twisting downhill. There are potholes and very rough pavement, so keep your speed down.

53.0 Gas pumps are soon followed by motel units on the right, and then a swimming pool and restaurant. The rooms and pool are reserved for vacationing soldiers and their families, but the huge, empty restaurant is open to the public. In two visits, we have never seen anyone eating, and there may not be any food, but cold drinks are available.

54.8 Continue straight, passing a paved lane on the right that leads to a basic *peso* cafeteria. Also, there are national park accommodations here. They are quite basic, however, and you are now close to San Diego de los Baños.

55.1 Turn left after passing through the fortresslike entrance to the national park. Notice ahead and to your right a billboard for Cabañas de los Pinos, giving a hint of what this place once was.

55.3 Continue straight, passing a paved road to the right. (You will use this road on the way back to Viñales.) There is a school here on the left.

58.7 Bear right at a fork. In less than 100 meters, pass a sign for San Diego de los Baños.

59.0 Cross a small bridge and enter town. If you can take the first paved road on the left after the bridge, it will bring you directly to the hotel. However, the road is often closed to traffic because a local school uses it as a play area. If this is the case, take the second left, ride two blocks, turn left again, then right, and continue to the hotel.

Day 2: San Diego de los Baños to Viñales (66 km)

0.0 Ride down the steep driveway of Hotel El Mirador. **Continue until you reach a T-intersection and turn right**. If the last block before the T-intersection is closed so that school children can play in the street, you will have to turn left at the barricade, then right, and then right again. (For the first 4 km of this ride, you are backtracking the route that you followed from Parque Nacional La Güira.)

4.1 Turn left on an unmarked, paved road. You passed this turn yesterday at km 55.3. There is a school on the right. If you reach the entrance to the national park, you have missed the turn; go back and take the first right.

8.7 Turn right at a major intersection. This is the Carretera Central. Traffic is light except when the road passes through towns. Often there are views to the right across rolling farmland to the mountains.

17.6 Continue straight through an intersection in Entronque de Herradura. There is a TRD Caribe dollar store on the right, and two dollar kiosks on the left. Also, roadside vendors sell *peso* snacks.

25.0 Be careful as you ride through the outskirts of Consolación del Sur. Traffic picks up—bicycles, cars, trucks, and horse carts.

26.7 Continue straight at the fork—do not bear left. This fork comes just after a large white building on the left, local headquarters of the Partido Comunista de Cuba (PCC).

27.4 Continue straight at the roundabout. There is a monument on the left to José Martí. At a gas station on the left, just after the monument, there is a ServiSoda—a convenience store with sandwiches, cheese, pastries, and cold drinks. As you continue through town, you will spot a dollar store on the right and a *peso* cafeteria on the left just after the town's main square.

29.1 There is a Tiendas Panamericanas kiosk on the left.

37.1 Continue straight through a crossroad. There is a Tiendas Panamericanas kiosk on the right. You will be turning right in less than 5 km.

42.0 Turn right following a sign to Campismo Aguas Claras.

48.3 Stop at a T-intersection. If you wish to go to Aguas Claras, turn left. In 3 km you will see Cubamar Disco Atlantis on the left. The entrance to Aguas Claras is just ahead on the left.

If you are continuing to Viñales, turn right and continue with the following directions.

51.2 Follow the main road as it curves sharply to the left. There is a billboard here with a portrait of Che Guevara and, in Spanish, the words HE LIVES IN THE HEARTS OF THE PEOPLE.

53.9 Climb through a set of switchbacks. For the next few kilometers there will be more climbs and some sweeping downhill runs.

61.7 Pass a sign indicating that Hotel Los Jazmines is 2 km; there is also a billboard listing other Horizontes hotels.

Scene along the Carretera Central in Pinar del Río

62.0 Bear right at a fork toward Viñales. (Turning left here will take you to Hotel Los Jazmines.)

62.9 The Viñales valley opens up below to the left. You will be riding a wonderful, curving downhill. The descent demands attention, so enjoy the view safely by pulling off the road.

64.6 Pass beneath overhead signs for Viñales, Cuevas del Indio, and La Ermita. Watch on the left for a billboard picturing Julio Antonio Mella, Camilo Cienfuegos, and Che Guevara. As we move inexorably closer to age 60, the slogan here has become one of our favorites: REBELS—FOREVER YOUNG! You are now entering Viñales, with more traffic, small houses, and many *casas particulares*. Continue straight through a confusing intersection with many signs until, very shortly, you reach a crossroad.

65.3 Turn right at the crossroad onto Salvador Cisneros, the main street of Viñales. There are signs indicating a left to El Moncada and a right to Cuevas de Viñales.

65.7 The route ends at the town plaza on your left.

❼ Viñales–Cayo Jutías Loop

134 km, 2 or 3 days

This multi-day loop offers wonderful variety. You'll encounter challenging hills and easy lowland riding, a pretty beach where you can spend the night in a tent, and a laid-back fishing port. There is even an opportunity to don a miner's helmet and explore the Western Hemisphere's largest system of caverns.

After 25 km of relatively easy riding, the route rises and falls through the Sierra de los Órganos, and there are a few hilltops between Pons and Santa Lucía from which you can see all the way to the north coast. Cayo Jutías has a pleasant if not spectacular beach, and Puerto Esperanza is a great spot for hanging out, popular with pleasure sailors who can't afford or do not want to spend the money for glitzy Marina Hemingway. There are *casas particulares* and a seafood restaurant. The return ride to Viñales winds past *mogotes* with picturesque farmsteads huddled at their base.

For simplicity we describe this as a two-day ride, and indeed it is quite possible to ride to Cayo Jutías in one day and return to Viñales by way of Puerto Esperanza the next. However, you will probably want to stay an extra night at Cayo Jutías or stop for a night in Puerto Esperanza, or both.

Distances in the route directions assume that you will skip the detour to the Mural Prehistórico but take time to visit the Gran Caverna de Santo Tomás. Yes, this does reflect our judgment as to the relative merits of these attractions.

Food

You can't count on finding food or bottled water on the first 48 km of this ride, so it is important to be prepared. Leave Viñales with plenty of water and snacks. On several occasions we were able to buy fresh bread at the Empresa Cuba del Pan, shortly after km 0.4. It doesn't hurt to ask.

Once you reach Villa Mary at km 48.5, food may no longer be a problem, but read the lodging section for more information. Mary operates both as a *casa particular* and a *paladar,* so you can get a good meal here, even if you

The beach at Cayo Jutías

are not spending the night. There is a snack stand and a *guarapo* stand just before Santa Lucía and a small dollar store in the center of town.

On the beach at Playa Jutías, there is a Rumbos restaurant; and in Puerto Esperanza, there is a seafood restaurant. Additional opportunities to buy snacks are noted in the directions.

Lodging

There are at least three places to spend your first night on the tour. The first and best is Villa Mary, on the outskirts of Santa Lucía. When we were there in 2001, Mary had one air-conditioned guest bedroom with a private bath— perhaps the tiniest bathroom we have ever seen, but it was immaculate. She was preparing a second bedroom for rent. Bad news came from two correspondents. They said that Mary had closed her *casa particular* in early 2002 because tourist business dropped so dramatically after September 11, 2001. By the time you arrive, we hope she will once again be open. If not, other correspondents report that another legal *casa particular* has opened in Santa Lucia. Just ask around.

The next accommodations are on the sands of Playa Jutías, next to the Rumbos restaurant. Here, it is possible to rent large tents ($20 per night for two) that the staff will pitch for you on the beach. The tents are equipped with a double air mattress, lounge chairs, and a beach umbrella. It could be fun to spend the night on the beach, but it can get chilly after dark so you must have your own sleeping bag or blanket, or at least some warm clothes.

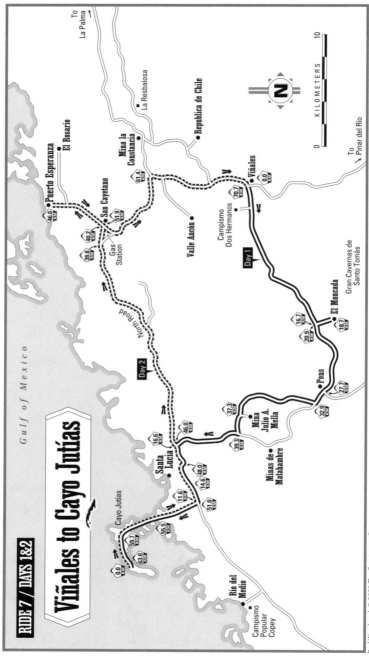

RIDE 7 / DAYS 1&2

Viñales to Cayo Jutías

Gulf of Mexico

To La Palma

La Resbalosa

El Rosario

Puerto Esperanza

Mina la Constancia

República de Chile

San Cayetano

Gas Station

Valle Ancón

North Road

Campismo Dos Hermanos

Viñales

Day 1

Gran Cavernas de Santo Tomás

El Moncada

Pons

Day 2

Mina Julio A. Mella

Minas de Matahambre

Santa Lucía

Cayo Jutías

Río del Medio

Campismo Popular Copey

To Pinar del Río

KILOMETERS

0   10

Paul Woodward, © 2002 The Countryman Press

Meals are available at the Rumbos restaurant. Be sure to check the restaurant hours. When we were there, it closed early, between 5 and 6 PM, so be prepared for an early dinner or bring food of your own.

A backup choice for the first night is Campismo Popular El Copey. This *campismo* is basic. When we visited on a weekend, it was occupied by a student group; but it is a friendly enough place, open year-round, and foreigners are welcome. Do not count on buying food. There is a cafeteria but it may not be open.

In Puerto Esperanza there are several *casas particulares.* For the best, seek out Villa Dora at km 46.1. This is a jolly place with four guest rooms, a pleasant patio restaurant in the back, and good seafood. Villa Dora is inexpensive—double rooms were $15 in 2001 and the priciest dinners were $8 per person. Dora and her friendly family have been operating this place for over a decade, and they know how to make you feel at home. Colorful graffiti scrawled on the walls by visitors from all over the world pay enthusiastic tribute to their hospitality.

Day 1: Viñales to Cayo Jutías (63 km)

0.0 From the main plaza in Viñales, with your back to the Casa de la Cultura, ride to the right on Salvador Cisneros. You will be heading south.

0.4 Continue straight toward El Moncada; do not follow signs to Los Jazmines and Pinar del Río. Empresa Cuba del Pan, the state bakery store, is on the left shortly after the intersection.

2.9 There are signs and a right turn for Campismo Dos Hermanos and the Mural Prehistórico. If you turn right here, you will ride toward a wall of *mogotes,* then through a shady gap between them. In just over 1 km, you will reach a gated entry on the right to the *campismo.* To the left, the Mural Prehistórico is clearly visible. This gigantic, gaudy painting on the face of a *mogote* depicts multicolored dinosaurs, among other things. It is promoted as a tourist attraction, but we find it to be certainly no improvement over the sheer limestone cliff upon which it is painted. Close to the mural, there is a restaurant. To continue the ride, backtrack to the main road and turn right at the T-intersection. This detour, if you take it, adds about 2.5 km to subsequent route distances.

5.2 On the road from Viñales to Pons, you will start up the first moderately steep hill of the day. There is a stunning view behind you of the lush Viñales valley, with *mogotes* towering over it.

14.2 Notice coffee bushes along the road and a sign UBPC El Moncada on the left.

16.7 Turn left, following a sign to El Moncada. This is the beginning of the side trip to Gran Caverna de San Tomás, a genuinely worthwhile attraction. These directions assume you will make a visit. However, you should allow at least two hours; so if you got a late start, you could skip this side trip, jumping to km 20.9 and subtracting 4 km from subsequent distances.

17.5 Cross a small bridge and immediately turn right. The facades of many small homes in El Moncada are decorated with elaborate patterns of colored brick and tiles.

18.1 Continue straight through a small roundabout.

18.4 Turn right at the fork. Soon you will see a sign on the right for the caverns.

18.7 Turn left into the small parking lot at the cavern headquarters. This is where you will meet a guide and begin your tour. There are clean rest rooms but no food service.

18.9 Turn right as you leave the cavern parking lot.

19.5 Continue straight through the roundabout,

20.2 Turn left and cross the bridge.

20.9 Turn left at the T-intersection. You are now on the main road from Viñales to Pons. (On the day trip from Viñales to the caverns, you now turn right and backtrack to town.)

Gran Caverna de San Tomás

Gran Caverna de San Tomás is one of the largest underground cave systems in the Americas. There are 46 km of passages on eight levels, with underground lakes and rivers as well. Fortunately the caves have not been improved with lights, walkways, or railings.

When you visit, you will be given a helmet with miner's lamp and battery pack to wear, and a guide must accompany you. The guide will point out innumerable details, and not incidentally, keep you from getting lost or falling down a dark hole. You will see stalactites that look like elephant ears. Tiny bats, hard to spot, sleep in crevices in the ceiling; and plants sprout from seeds in the bat droppings and then die in the dark. Crabs and crickets have adapted to life underground. Some mineral deposits at your feet look just like coral, or appear to be tiny pine forests seen from the air.

We were amazed to learn that a major storm once caused such terrible flooding in this region

In Gran Caverna de San Tomás

that furniture from nearby homes was carried by the underground river into the depths of the cave.

27.7 Turn right at a T-intersection in the small town of Pons, following the sign with distances to Minas de Matahambre and Santa Lucía. Watch for a *guarapo* stand on the left in about 0.5 km. Juice freshly squeezed from sugar cane will give you an energy boost for the next 4 hilly km.

31.7 Just after the crest of a hill, a 1-km downhill begins. The last 200 meters drop like a stone, so ride under control!

32.7 The downhill ends at small bridge.

32.9 Turn right after riding steeply uphill from the bridge. There is no road sign. (In fact, this well-paved road does not appear on any tourist maps that we have seen, but it is a less difficult route to Santa Lucía than continuing straight through Minas de Matahambre. *Less difficult* does not imply it is *easy.)*

37.3 Turn right at a T-intersection, following a sign to Santa Lucía and Minas de Matahambre. (The left goes to Julio Antonio Mella.) Watch out for potholes in a couple of hundred meters.

39.3 Turn right again at another T-intersection. Signs were down in 2001, but the right goes to Santa Lucía, while the left goes to Minas de Matahambre.

42.3 Approach a small bridge carefully. It is paved with loose metal plates and it is slightly hazardous.

46.0 Bear left, following a sign saying STA. LUCÍA, 2 KM. This is the intersection with the North Road. Villa Mary is on the left at this turn.

46.6 Bear left following the main road.

47.7 Follow the main road around a 90-degree curve to the right. Do not go straight on the unmarked, less traveled road.

48.0 Turn left, following signs to Campismo El Copey and Cayo Jutías. At this corner, there is a small, thatched snack stand with pizzas on the left, and a small *guarapo* stand on the right. Traveling west toward Cayo Jutías, the road is now almost perfectly flat. (If you were to continue straight here instead of turning left, you would arrive in downtown Santa Lucía after 0.2 km. In town, after a movie theater on the left and a basic, *peso* restaurant on the right, there is a TRD Caribe dollar store on the left. When we were there, this store had very little in stock.)

51.0 Turn right, following a sign for Cayo Jutías. (For Campismo Popular El Copey, do *not* turn here. Continue west on the North Road for over 9 km, and then turn right following a sign to the *campismo*. After a couple of kilometers (lots of potholes), you will reach the tiny village of Río del Medio, where you make a left to the *campismo*. The turn is unmarked, so you may have to ask.)

55.5 Stop at the toll gate at the beginning of the causeway. Admission

122 PINAR DEL RÍO

is $5 (U.S.) for foreigners. (Cubans pay only five *pesos*, so this is not one of those resorts whose policy is to keep Cubans off their own beaches.)

59.7 Turn left at a T-intersection, following the paved lane toward the beach and restaurant. There is a lighthouse to the right down a rough dirt track at this intersection, and the ocean is straight ahead. As you ride the next few kilometers, you will spot widely spaced trails to the right that lead to the beach.

63.0 Arrive at the Cayo Jutías parking lot just past the small restaurant on the right.

Day 2: Cayo Jutías to Puerto Esperanza (70.8 km)

0.0 You must first backtrack to the intersection where Villa Mary is located. From the Cayo Jutías parking lot, ride back toward Santa Lucía. The ocean will be to your left.

11.6 Turn left at the T-intersection onto the North Road.

14.6 Turn right at the T-intersection. This is still the North Road. The thatched snack bar is on the right here.

14.9 Follow the main road around a 90-degree curve to the left.

16.0 Follow the main road as it curves to the right, passing a turn to the left.

16.6 Bear left, immediately after Villa Mary. Pass the road back toward Minas de Matahambre on the right.

17.6 The road turns to dirt for a few hundred meters. This happens frequently for the next 7 or 8 km. Also, much of the road has potholes, gravel, or bumps nearly all the way to Puerto Esperanza. It is an enjoyable ride nevertheless, but you can't make fast time. Notice rice planted here and there, and fields of tobacco. Even if you despise smoking, you will have to admit that tobacco is a pretty plant, especially when its bright green leaves contrast with the deep red-brown soil in this part of Pinar del Río.

27.9 Cross a bridge where the greenery is so lush that you can barely see the small stream below. There is shade on the bridge, and it is a good place to stop and rest. During the next few kilometers, watch for a *guarapo* stand on the left. Only 50 *centavos*, hold the ice. The ride will become more scenic, with easy climbs and gentle downhills, as you approach the turn ahead for Puerto Esperanza.

39.8 Turn left at an unmarked fork. The road will quickly narrow, then just as suddenly curve to the right and become a boulevard. You have entered the small village of San Cayetano. (If you reach a gas station on the left, you have gone about 100 meters past the turn.)

40.2 Turn left at the crossroad. There is a Círculo Social Obreros on your left—a small recreation center for workers. This road will take you directly to Puerto Esperanza. It is a nicely paved, quiet country lane. The traffic count when we rode it: horse carts, 2; motorcycles, 0; and cars and trucks, 0.

44.1 Continue straight, passing the turn on the right to El Rosario. (A small hotel in El Rosario closed to the general public in 2001.)

45.1 Enter Puerto Esperanza, a pretty little town, much nicer than Santa Lucía.

45.3 Pass a TRD Caribe dollar store on the right.

46.0 The road ends at a waterfront park. There is a small monument here to José Martí. There are benches to the left scattered under trees, good for enjoying shade and a cool breeze off the water. (If you are going to Villa Dora for lunch or for the night, turn right at this monument. Then, in approximately 100 meters, turn left on a narrow paved lane. Immediately on your right, look for house number 5 with a small sign reading VILLA DORA. After visiting Puerto Esperanza, return to Viñales.

47.9 Continue straight, passing the turn on the left to El Rosario. There are beautiful views of mountains ahead.

51.9 Continue straight at the crossroad in San Cayetano, passing the road to the right on which you arrived from Santa Lucía.

52.6 Bear left onto the North Road. (There is a Cupet gas station with snacks and cold drinks about 100 meters to the right at this intersection.) You will pass a PNR control point to the left. For the next several kilometers, the terrain will be rolling and the views increasingly dramatic. As you approach a wall of *mogotes* ahead and to the left, you may wonder how you will ever get through them—or worse, over them. The road will swing to the left, however, and you will ride beside the sheer walls of the *mogotes,* so close that it seems you can almost reach out and touch them.

61.4 Bear right at an intersection following a sign for Pinar del Río and Viñales. Immediately pass a basic cafeteria, Cafetería Entronque La Palma, on the left.

62.7 Pass a turn on the right to Valle Ancón. Now continue straight all the way into Viñales.

70.2 Bear right onto Salvador Cisneros as you pass a Cupet gas station on the left.

70.7 Arrive at the Viñales town square.

❽ The Far West Tour

339 km, 5 or 6 days plus

You can begin this route from Viñales, Aguas Claras, or Pinar del Río City. The route winds through the western Sierra de los Órganos and across the flatlands beyond, all the way to Playa María la Gorda.

The scenery in the western mountains is similar to the beautiful valley of Viñales, but there are no signs of tourism at all. We counted far more horses and ox carts than cars or trucks on the quiet roads. Riding through the mountains is surprisingly easy—far easier, for example, than the loops to San Diego de los Baños in the Sierra del Rosario. We enthusiastically recommend that you cycle as far as Guane if you have a yen to explore a beautiful part of Cuba that is virtually untouched by tourism—and if you are flexible enough to do without the conveniences and the quality of accommodations that tourism development provides.

West of Guane the ride becomes—well—hot and boring is the only way to put it. This part of the route is made worthwhile by your eventual arrival at Playa María la Gorda. While the beach is pleasant, what lies beneath the sparkling surface of the Bahía de Corrientes is spectacular: Magnificent coral formations and abundant, colorful sea creatures make this one of Cuba's premier sites for diving and snorkeling. However, we recommend that you ride beyond Guane only if you have the desire, time, and money to stay for a few days at Playa María la Gorda.

Whether you turn back at Guane or continue farther west, the return to Pinar del Río City leads through small towns and gently rolling countryside, past some basic beach resorts that we have not visited, and into the rich tobacco country around San Juan y Martínez.

Food

Finding enough bottled water and food to keep you going is surprisingly easy along this route. There are small dollar stores, roadside vendors, or both in Cabezas, Sumidero, Guane, Sandino, and Manuel Lazo. All are noted in the route directions. Meals are available in the hotels and *casas* mentioned in the section on lodging.

Lodging

There is relatively little in the way of accommodations, so your ride must be planned to take advantage of what is available. If you start from Viñales, we recommend that you spend the first night at Finca La Guabina—a horse ranch where breeding stock is raised. There are four spacious bedrooms in

In the Valle de San Carlos

the former owner's luxurious home. It is surrounded by a reservoir on three sides. We enjoyed cool breezes off the water, and the large, airy living room had the most comfortable wicker rocking chairs we have ever sat on.

Food at Finca La Guabina was reasonably good. Rates in 2001 were $56 per couple for dinner, bed, and breakfast. With a large fruit plate for lunch plus beers and soft drinks, our bill was considerably higher, but it was still a good value. Because small groups occasionally stay at Finca La Guabina and there are so few rooms, it is important to make a reservation in advance. You can do this by stopping at the Rumbos office on Calle Martí in Pinar del Río City.

One of the advantages of staying at Finca La Guabina is that you can then ride all the way to Sandino or Laguna Grande the next day. However, if you start from Aguas Claras or Pinar del Río City and skip Finca La Guabina, you should plan on spending a night in or near Guane, which is a small, attractive town.

The guest house at Finca La Guabina

Just before Guane you could stop at Campismo El Salto. We did not spend a night there, but we saw that the *campismo* had basic cabañas in a pretty setting, with a cafeteria that is supposed to be open in the evening. Foreigners are welcome. In 2001 there were no licensed *casas particulares* in Guane, but we were twice offered private rooms within the first few minutes of our arrival at the plaza.

When you approach Sandino, the town appears uninviting at best. Drab, run-down apartment blocks rise from a flat landscape. However, we received an exceedingly friendly welcome and delicious meals at Motel Alexis, which is on a quiet residential street. Despite the name, this is a *casa particular;* the motel designation probably refers to the fact that each of the two guest rooms has its own private entrance along the side of the house. Highly recommended!

Another accommodation on the way to Playa María la Gorda is located along an alternative, slightly longer route. Villa Turística Laguna Grande is a quiet, out-of-the-way Islazul property on the shore of an artificial lake. Though billed as a fishing resort, we saw nothing of the sort going on. The simple cabins were roomy and clean, however, and the beds were comfortable. A couple of staff members spoke good English, and they were friendly and eager to please. The inexpensive restaurant was adequate, and it was the only place we stayed in Cuba with *caballo* (horse meat) on the menu. We passed on that treat and went for fish and chicken, which were also available, though fish was not on the menu. For variety, you could stay at

Hotel rooms are right on the beach at Playa María la Gorda.

Villa Turística Laguna Grande on the way west or on the return ride instead of spending both nights in Sandino.

Near the western end of the ride, there is relatively cheap accommodation at the Radar, a meteorological station just before La Bajada. Though the four guest rooms are clean and quiet, they are drab; and in 2001 there was no food available. Unless you are on a very tight budget, we recommend that you enjoy a couple of nights at Villa María la Gorda, on the beach of the same name and next door to the international dive center.

Villa María la Gorda offers two types of units. There are a few run-down rooms with unappetizing bathrooms in older wooden cottages, and much better, attractive rooms in modern two-story buildings. Fortunately the newer units are more numerous; beachfront rooms are most desirable. Rates in 2001 were $25 (single) and $40 to $56 (double). Tents for $10 per person were sometimes available, but only if all the rooms were full.

Unfortunately, *á la carte* meals were no longer offered in 2001. Instead, you could choose half-board (mediocre buffet breakfast and dinner) for $20 per person, or add lunch as well for an additional $10. We found the half-board adequate, and Villa María la Gorda was a pleasant place with an informal, friendly, international crowd. If you like snorkeling or diving and can spend a few days here, it is well worth the ride.

On the return route, accommodations are available at two basic beach resorts, which we have not visited, Playa Bailén and Boca de Galafre. Back in Pinar del Río City, there are hotels, which are described in the general

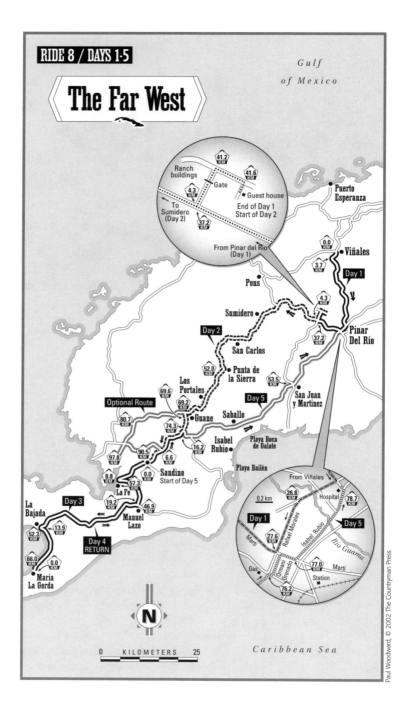

RIDE 8 / DAYS 1-5

The Far West

Gulf
of Mexico

41.2 KM

41.6 KM

Ranch buildings

Gate

4.3 KM

Guest house

To Sumidero (Day 2)

End of Day 1
Start of Day 2

37.2 KM

From Pinar del Río (Day 1)

Puerto Esperanza

0.0 KM

Viñales

3.7 KM

Day 1

Pons

4.3 KM

Sumidero

37.2 KM

Pinar Del Río

Day 2

San Carlos

52.0 KM

Punta de la Sierra

53.5 KM

San Juan y Martínez

Los Portales

69.6 KM

69.2 KM

Optional Route

80.7 KM

74.3 KM

Guane

Saballo

Day 5

16.2 KM

Isabel Rubio

Playa Boca de Galate

97.8 KM

90.5 KM

6.6 KM

8.8 KM

0.0 KM

Sandino
Start of Day 5

Playa Bailén

57.3 KM

La Fe

19.2 KM

46.9 KM

La Bajada

Day 3

Manuel Lazo

52.3 KM

13.9 KM

Day 4 RETURN

66.0 KM

0.0 KM

María La Gorda

From Viñales

0.2 km

26.8 KM

Hospital

78.7 KM

Day 1

Rafael Morales

Isabel Rubio

Day 5

Martí

27.6 KM

Ormani Arenado

Río Guama

Gas

77.0 KM

Martí

Station

76.2 KM

N

0 KILOMETERS 25

Caribbean Sea

Paul Woodward, © 2002 The Countryman Press

guidebooks, and many *casas particulares*. We were comfortable in the home of María Julia and Roberto Lee Ofrece at Calle Antonio Rubio No. 70, between Morales and Arenado.

Day 1: Viñales to Finca La Guabina (42 km)

0.0 Start from the town plaza in Viñales. With your back to the Casa de la Cultura, ride to the right on Salvador Cisneros.

0.5 Turn left following signs to Hotel Los Jazmines and Pinar del Río City.

3.7 Bear left soon after a sign that indicates Pinar del Río is to the left and Hotel Los Jazmines is to the right. In a few kilometers, the terrain will become rolling, with intermittent climbs and downhills.

14.6 Follow the main road as it curves sharply to right; the billboard with a picture of Che Guevara says HE LIVES IN THE HEARTS OF THE PEOPLE.

20.7 Pass the entrance to Aguas Claras.

25.8 Turn right at a busy intersection following signs to Ciudad, the city. This turn comes just after the entrance to Rumayor, a large nightclub on the right.

26.2 Cross a bridge over a small river. A large stadium will be visible far ahead to the left.

26.8 Bear left on Rafael Morales, following the sign to Guane. In a couple hundred meters, continue straight through an intersection with a traffic blinker.

27.6 Get off your bike at the traffic light on Calle Martí and walk to the right. The Hotel Vueltabajo is just across the street on the corner. Calle Martí is one-way to the left. Walking your bike 100 meters is better than riding around the block in these narrow, congested streets. (There are two *parqueos* on the right along this block. For a *peso* or two, you can safely leave your bike if you wish to explore downtown Pinar del Río on foot. Within easy walking distance, there are several dollar stores, an ARTex gift shop, a cigar factory, a post office where you can send e-mail, a Rumbos travel agency where you can make a reservation for Finca La Guabina, and a booking office for Campismos Populares. There is a selection of government restaurants and *peso* snack stands nearby as well.) Then get your bike and continue walking against the traffic on Martí. At the end of the block, Martí curves to the right. On the left is Plaza de la Independencia, a modest park with a small bandstand. Just to the left of the park, there are remarkable wall murals. See if you can make sense of them. As soon as you have passed the park, Martí becomes Calle Alameda, now with two-way traffic, and you can get back on your bike.

28.3 Continue straight, following a sign to the provincial prison and the Carretera Louis Lazo.

30.5 Follow the main road as it curves to the left.

31.2 A 24-hour gas station on left has a tiny convenience store.

31.5 The road narrows to two nicely paved lanes.

33.1 Pass the provincial prison on the right. Soon you will be riding gently downhill with views of the mountains ahead and to the right.

36.0 Continue past an unmarked, paved road on the left. It goes to San Juan y Martínez.

36.2 There is a large military installation on the right. Watch for the entrance to Finca La Guabina in 1 km.

37.2 Turn right just after a faded sign that indicates Sumidero is straight ahead and Plan Equino is to the right. A second sign says PLAN GENÉTICO EQUINOS LA GUABINA, the breeding stock farm where Finca La Guabina is located.

39.7 Pass through a brick gateway; be careful because there are metal grates on the ground that could catch a tire.

41.2 Turn right at a T-intersection. Corrals and ranch buildings are to the left. There is a dirt track continuing straight, which makes a pleasant route for a walk at dusk.

41.6 Turn right through a large wooden gate. This is the entrance to the guest house.

Day 2: Finca La Guabina to Sandino (90 km)

0.0 Ride down the Finca La Guabina driveway, through the gate, and continue straight.

0.5 Turn left, the way you came in.

4.3 Turn right at the T-intersection; you are now back on the road from Pinar del Río to Sumidero and Guane. In less than 1 km, intermittent climbing begins, but the grades are moderate.

6.5 Stop at a small memorial on the right honoring three men killed by the *shameful dictatorship* in 1958. There is a lovely view here. At this point you are climbing moderate switchbacks.

13.0 Pass a small lookout tower on the left, then a large medical building—there are no signs—and begin a downhill with great views into the valley ahead and to the left. You will coast for nearly 5 km! It seems certain, as you enjoy this long, downhill glide into a quiet valley, that there will be a terrible payback in the form of climbing ahead. In fact, there will be only a few modest hills, no difficult challenges.

22.0 Arrive in the small village of Cabezas. There is a TRD Caribe dollar store with cold drinks just before an iron bridge. Cross the bridge and continue straight, passing a turn on the right to Minas de Matahambre. There are many small bridges along the route. Be careful crossing them because they often have metal plates less than two feet wide on rough boards.

27.5 Stop at a little park on the right in the center of Sumidero, a pleasant small town. There will probably be vendors selling fruit and snacks; and just past the park, there is a TRD Caribe dollar store on the left. After a break, you will climb a short hill as you leave town.

30.0 The road gradually draws nearer to a wall of *mogotes*. It is extremely quiet here. Ox carts and horses should easily outnumber cars. For the most part the road continues to be level or gently downhill as it descends from one level of the valley to the next.

38.0 Ride through the tiny hamlet of San Carlos.

41.0 You are approaching a wall of *mogotes*. It seems that a tough climb is inevitable, but in fact the road winds slightly downhill through a cleft in the wall.

41.4 Stop as you approach a white bridge. Several meters before the bridge, there is a dirt track on the right. If you follow it for a few meters and then bear left, the track will take you through a small underpass, then under the bridge, where it now becomes a sandy trail and parallels the river. There are places down the bank for wading in the water, cooling off, and picnicking.

52.0 Turn right in front of a white-columned building in the village of Punta de la Sierra.

57.0 Pass a small school on the right. When we rode through here, there was so little traffic that people were spreading grain and beans to dry on the warm asphalt near the side of the road.

60.6 Enter the village of Los Portales and pass the bottling plant on the left.

65.0 Note a sign on the right indicating that Guane is 4 km ahead. In the distance you will see another sign on the left for Campismo El Salto. Should you decide to stop at this *campismo*, turn left at the sign onto a gravel lane. In another 20 meters or so, turn right at a T-intersection onto a narrow, paved road. In less than 0.5 km, turn left on an unmarked lane. You will see modern, whitewashed buildings up the hill—this is a water treatment facility, not the *campismo*. Ride up the hill, continuing past the treatment plant, and then go downhill to the *campismo* entrance. It is a climb to get in here, and a climb to get back out, so don't bother unless you intend to stop for the night.

68.9 Enter the town of Guane.

69.2 Turn left at a T-intersection onto the main street of Guane. (For an alternate route to Laguna Grande, turn right here. The information for this option is at the end of Ride 20, The Far East Tour.)

69.4 Continue straight, passing a small sign for a right to Isabel Rubio. You will be riding to Isabel Rubio, but *do not* turn right onto the narrow paved street after the sign. Instead, continue straight until you reach the small town park. Across from the park are dollar stores and snack stands. There is also a basic cafeteria in the park.

69.6 Turn right immediately after the park in Guane.

74.3 Turn right in Isabel Rubio, following the sign to La Fe. As you make this turn, there will be a small park on the left.

76.3 On the left a colorful billboard says SANDINO, ADVANCING WITH THE REVOLUTION. This is ranching country, sunbaked and hot.

84.0 Continue straight, passing a sign and a turn on the right for Villa Turística Laguna Grande.

89.7 As you enter town there is another Sandino billboard almost identical to the one at km 76.3.

89.9 Continue past signs saying MOTEL RENT ROOM on both the right and left. This advertisement is not for the Motel Alexis, and we can't recommend the property, though it could be a reasonable option. Ride ahead for another 500 meters.

90.4 Turn left just after a sign saying MOTEL RENT ROOM ALEXIS. There is another small RENT ROOM sign on the left. The *casa* is down the road on the left in about 100 meters, clearly marked with a sign saying MOTEL ALEXIS.

Day 3: Sandino to Playa María la Gorda (65 km)

0.0 With your back to the Alexis house, turn right, backtracking to the main road.

0.1 Turn left at the T-intersection. The road ahead is flat and straight as an arrow. This is ranching country with rough pastures, cattle, some corn, and very little tobacco.

8.8 Turn left at a T-intersection in the small village of La Fe. Most of the village is to the right.

17.3 As you ride through a small settlement, trees provide the first shade in several kilometers. The countryside becomes a little greener with more tobacco fields. You are approaching Manuel Lazo.

19.2 Turn right in the center of Manuel Lazo, following the sign to La Bajada. (Pinar del Río is straight ahead.) There is a Tiendas Panamericanas dollar store at this turn, which was well stocked when we were there. If you intend to stay at the meteorological station, you should pick up supplies here.

Simple church in Sabalo

19.5 Follow the main road as it bears to the right. After leaving town, the countryside is fairly well settled for a while, with houses and tobacco farms; but in another 5 or 6 km, you will be riding in scrubby, rather desolate land—and it continues for many kilometers.

51.6 The meteorological station (the Radar) is on the left, and there are rooms for rent. Then, on the right, is the Centro Ecológico. It is sometimes possible to hire a guide here for a trip to Cabo San Antonio, the westernmost point in Cuba. When we were there in 2001, the cape was closed for research on the environmental impact of possible tourism development. It was still possible to hire a guide for birding and nature walks.

51.8 Follow the paved road as it curves to the left.

52.3 **Turn left** at the T-intersection. This is shortly after a sign indicating that Cabo San Antonio is 54 km to the right and Playa María la Gorda is to the left.

60.0 Pass some nearly abandoned buildings on the left. The road here is lined with mangroves and palmettos, but you will soon see access points to several small beaches.

66.0 Arrive at Playa María la Gorda, about 700 meters after the entrance sign.

Day 4: Backtracking to Sandino (66 km)

0.0 From the hotel at Playa María la Gorda, backtrack along the shore. (Note: Be sure to top off your water bottles before you start this ride. Overpriced snacks are available at the hotel dollar store, but you might prefer to raid the breakfast buffet. We were able to buy a loaf of bread directly from the kitchen. It is almost 50 km to the first store in Manuel Lazo.) The terrain between Playa María la Gorda and Manuel Lazo will be flat or rising almost imperceptibly, so the cycling is easy.

13.9 Turn right. At the corner there is a small army post recognizable by a Cuban flag and a lookout platform on the roof. If the road turns to dirt, you have missed the turn.

46.3 Bear right at the fork following the main road into Manuel Lazo.

46.9 Turn left at the T-intersection in the center of Manuel Lazo.

47.2 Continue straight past the Islazul kiosk on the left. From here the road continues to be flat, without shade except from passing clouds, all the way to La Fe.

57.3 Turn right as you enter La Fe. There is a small bus shelter at this turn. If you ride through town and reach the water, you have gone 1 km too far.

62.0 Catch the first glimpse of mountains in the distance. This is striking after you have cycled 60 km along roads that have been nearly flat the entire way.

65.0 There is an army post on the right. You are arriving in Sandino.

65.9 Turn right at the sign for Motel Alexis. Welcome back.

Day 5: Sandino to Pinar Del Río (76 km)

0.0 Turn right as you leave Motel Alexis.

0.1 Turn right at the T-intersection. You will now backtrack 16 km to Isabel Rubio.

6.6 Continue straight, passing a paved road on the left. This road goes to the village of Bolívar and to Villa Turística Saguna Grande.

16.2 Turn right at a crossroad in Isabel Rubio, riding toward Pinar del Río City. There is a small park on the right at this turn. To the left is the road to Guane. In 100 meters you will reach a gas station and convenience store on the right; cold drinks and ice cream are available here.

20.6 Cross a bridge over a small river with a view of mountains to the north. You have left the flatlands behind and will be riding on rolling terrain with some moderate hills. There is little traffic, but beware of speeding tourists.

33.1 Enter the small town of Sabalo.

33.8 On the left is a tiny park with bright bougainvillea and an old church.

34.9 A road to the right goes to Playa Bailén, a basic beach resort with possible accommodations.

Downtown Pinar del Río

39.4 Another right goes to Boca de Galafre. There are possible accommodations here as well. Refer to any of the general guidebooks.

52.7 After crossing a small bridge you will enter San Juan y Martínez. On the right there is an El Rápido cafeteria. Here we enjoyed possibly the coldest beer and soda in Cuba, and also fresh popcorn, along with the usual sandwiches. As you continue through San Juan y Martínez, there will be a TRD Caribe dollar store on the left.

53.5 Turn right at a T-intersection on the Carretera Central.

53.9 Immediately after a whitewashed bridge, there will be a baseball diamond on the right.

55.4 At the top of a hill, there is a cafeteria on the right that is cleaner and more inviting than most *peso* establishments. If you look back, you will see a large billboard that says LAND OF THE BEST TOBACCO IN THE BEST HANDS.

You may have noticed that much of the tobacco around San Juan y Martínez is grown under the partial shade of guazelike netting. This tobacco is used for the wrappers of high quality cigars.

72.9 Continue straight at the overhead signs indicating that Industrial Zone, Centro la Caloma, and Ciudad are all to the right. Ciudad refers to the city of Pinar del Río, but this turn is meant to divert traffic away from some of the narrow streets in the city's center. On a bicycle it is easier and more direct to continue straight for more than 3 km, ignoring one or two more signs indicating that Ciudad is to the right.

76.1 Pass a Cupet gas station on the left. You are in the city now and will be turning in less than 100 meters.

76.2 Turn right after the gas station, and **then take the immediate left** on Avenida Ormani Arenado. Continue along this narrow, one-way street.

76.7 Arrive at Calle Martí, the main downtown street of Pinar del Río. From here, you can find your way to many choices of accommodation in Pinar del Río.

Follow these directions if you wish to head out of town and stay at Aguas Claras.

76.7 Turn right on Calle Martí.

77.0 Turn left on Isabel Rubio. You can recognize this turn because the Hotel Globo is on the right, and there is a post office on the left. (You can send e-mail from this post office.) Continue out Isabel Rubio for approximately 1.7 km. Watch for the provincial hospital on the left.

78.7 Turn left after the hospital. This is the road to Viñales, and Aguas Claras will be on the right in a little more than 5 km.

Alternate Route to Laguna Grande

This option begins in Guane on Day 2 of Ride 8: The Far West Tour, at km 69.2.

0.0 Turn right at the T-intersection in Guane instead of left. There is a service station on the right.

69.8 Both sides of the road are lined with apartment blocks. The rolling countryside ahead is largely devoted to cattle ranching, with some mixed farming and very little tobacco. Road conditions range from reasonable to fairly poor.

71.4 Stay on the paved road as it curves to the left.

79.8 Pass the paved entry to a large lumber mill on the left.

80.7 Bear left at a fork. There is a small, white bust of José Martí here, and also a bus shelter.

84.4 Watch for a sign saying WELCOME TO MANTUA. An important turn is coming up in 2 km.

86.0 Ride into a small settlement. There is a beat-up warning sign that indicates children in the road. You will turn in 0.2 km.

86.2 Turn left. You will be on a gentle, curving downhill as you approach this turn. There is a small cluster of buildings at the intersection.

88.7 This part of road has some very bad potholes. ¡*Cuidado!*

93.0 Continue straight through a crossroad. The small community of Bolívar is to the right.

97.6 Cross a small bridge over a spillway and then bear right. Laguna Grande, a man-made lake, is on the right.

97.8 Enter Villa Turística Laguna Grande. The *carpeta* (booking office) is on the left. If you hang out at Villa Turística Laguna Grande for a day, there is a nearby beach to visit. Just ride back to the crossroad at km 93 and turn left. From there it is an easy 13-km ride to Playa Colorada, though there are some rough patches in the road and the pavement briefly disappears. The water at Playa Colorada is shallow, but the sand is warm and the place is peacefully deserted except in summer, when the nearby youth camp may be in operation.

Villa Turística Laguna Grande to Playa María la Gorda or Pinar del Río

0.0 Leave Villa Turística Laguna Grande and cross the small bridge over the spillway. The lake is to the left.

4.8 Turn right at the crossroad. The village of Bolívar is to the left.

17.3 Arrive at the intersection with the main road between Guane and Sandino. If you are heading toward Sandino and Playa María la Gorda, turn right. You will be at km 84 of Day 2. **If you are heading back toward Guane and Pinar del Río, turn left.** You will be at km 6.6 of Day 5.

❾ Four Short Rides from Viñales

Viñales makes a wonderful base for cycle touring. If you do not wish to do the longer loop rides that start from here, you can still enjoy short outings on your bike. Each of these four outings uses parts of longer loops that we have already described.

If you are pressed for time, it is possible to have a wonderful Pinar del Río cycling vacation in a week or less. Simply take the Víazul bus from Havana and stay in Viñales for several nights to do these rides at a leisurely pace. Then use the bus once again for the return to Havana.

Viñales to Puerto Esperanza (50 km, 1 day)

A ride to Puerto Esperanza and back makes a splendid outing from Viñales, and it is especially worthwhile if you do not have time to do the Viñales–Cayo Jutías Loop. It is just under 50 km round trip. You can leave Viñales in the morning, explore the small fishing village of Puerto Esperanza, have a good lunch, and ride back to Viñales at your leisure.

From Viñales to Puerto Esperanza, you will be riding the last 25 km of Ride 7, the Viñales–Cayo Jutías Loop, but in reverse. Then you will use those same same directions for the return to Viñales. The information on food and accommodations in Puerto Esperanza appears on page 119. The following directions will help you get started from Viñales.

Route Directions

0.0 From the main plaza in Viñales, with your back to the Casa de la Cultura, ride to the left (north) on Salvador Cisneros.

0.5 Bear left immediately after a Cupet gas station on the right.

1.7 Notice a small fruit stand on the right. In early 2001, there were pineapples, green tomatoes, bananas, papayas, oranges, coconuts, and bars of *guayaba*. Prices were in *pesos*. There are similar stands ahead.

4.7 Pass the entrance to Cueva de Viñales on the left. Though it is possible to tour this cave, it is a tourist contrivance, with a bar in the cave entrance and disco dancing at night.

6.6 Pass the entrance to Cueva del Indio on the right. On the left, across from the cave, is a guarded parking lot that charges 25 cents for bicycles. Tourists line up at Cueva del Indio for short motorboat rides along an underground river. It is enjoyable, but we recommend skipping this cave in favor of Gran Caverna de Santo Tomás.

7.0 Pass the entrance to the Hotel Rancho San Vicente on the right.

8.0 Continue straight, passing a left at the bottom of a hill. (The left goes to Valle Ancón.)

9.3 Bear left onto the North Road. This intersection comes immediately after a basic cafeteria on the right, Cafetería Entronque La Palma. Soon you will be riding beside sheer walls of *mogotes* on your left.

12.2 Begin climbing. There will be some difficult hills during the next several kilometers; stop to rest and enjoy the views!

18.0 Continue straight, passing a PNR control point. Do not take the road here that goes to the right.

18.1 Pass a Cupet gas station on the right. Cold drinks and snacks are available here. You will be turning in a few hundred meters.

18.5 Make a sharp right. This turn is at the top of an easy hill after the Cupet gas station. You are now at kilometer 39.8 of the Ride 7, the Viñales–Cayo Jutías Loop (page 113). This is the road that suddenly narrows, then quickly widens to become the main street of the small village of San Cayetano. Simply follow the directions from here to Puerto Esperanza, and then back to Viñales.

Viñales to Valle Ancón (29 km, 1/2 day)

This short ride takes you to a quiet, scenic valley, not unlike the Viñales valley, but smaller and untouched by tourism. There is a coffee plantation in the valley, with workers' housing and a collection of schools that serve the local populace and also take boarding students from the surrounding countryside.

There are no tourist services in Valle Ancón. However, when we stopped to rest in the shade at the end of the paved road, a man soon greeted us and offered to take us on a walk around the area. He showed us the lookout described in the route directions below and invited us to his modest house to meet his brother and sister. They served us coffee and fresh coconut. If you spend an hour walking around Valle Ancón, you may enjoy a similar experience.

The road to Valle Ancón is quite hilly. Much of the time, you will be either climbing difficult grades or rocketing downhill. Watch for pigs wandering in the road. It is a good idea to do this ride in the morning when it is still cool, bring along a snack, and ride back to Viñales for lunch.

Route Directions

0.0 Follow the directions from the preceding ride to Puerto Esperanza, as far as 8.0.

8.0 Turn left to Valle Ancón instead of continuing straight. This turn is near the bottom of a hill, not long after a small white bridge, so ride under control and be watching for it. There will be some climbing on this road, and in some places it is very steep and narrow. Be sure to stay to the right—do not swerve or weave back and forth to ease the pitch of the climb.

11.3 Begin a long descent that is gentle at first, but with two steeper and faster sections preceded by warning signs. The road is rough with occasional potholes, so ride under control.

13.4 Ride past a coffee plantation on the left. On the right there will be a complex of schools and workers' housing.

14.0 Follow the road as it turns sharply to the right. The road becomes narrower and rougher, with sections that are washed out, but it is still passable with care. Soon there is a small primary school on the right.

14.3 The pavement ends and so does the cycling part of this route. On the left is the entrance to offices of the coffee plantation, and on the right is a thatched building with vines and flowers growing on the walls that is used for social events and music.

If you wish, you can continue a little farther on foot. The road turns into a dirt and gravel lane, soon becoming a deeply rutted path. You can walk your bikes when the ruts begin for another 100 meters or less, until you see a fence. It is there to control pigs, which roam all over the place in this area. You can open a gate in the fence—please close it as well—and proceed up the well-traveled path. After about 90 meters, watch on the right for another rough path, almost a gully, that goes steeply uphill. If you follow it for just 20 meters or so, you will reach an overlook on the right from which you can enjoy a scenic view of the coffee plantation and the valley.

Now you can return to your bikes and backtrack the 14.3 kilometers to Viñales.

Viñales to Gran Caverna de San Tomás (40 km, 1 day)

On this pleasant, moderately easy ride, you can visit the Mural Prehistórico, a bizarre work of art on the face of a *mogote* outside Viñales. It is promoted as a tourist attraction, but we find it faintly ridiculous.

The ride continues to Gran Caverna de San Tomás, an attraction that is genuinely worthwhile. Unfortunately there is no place serving food near the Gran Caverna de San Tomás. We recommend packing a lunch from Viñales. The grounds outside the cavern are a pleasant setting for a picnic.

To make this trip, simply follow the first 20 km of Ride 7, Viñales–Cayo Jutías Loop, and then backtrack.

Viñales to La Resbalosa (30 km, 1/2 day)

This is an easy, 30-km out-and-back ride on quiet country roads. It leads to a lovely swimming hole that is known to local residents as La Resbalosa (the Slippery Place). They refer to it as a natural swimming pool. La Resbalosa is not mentioned in any of the guidebooks. Indeed, the road to La Resbalosa does not appear on some maps.

This ride is simply the first 15 km of Ride 6, Viñales–San Diego de los Baños Loop. The terrain is level to gently rolling, with no extreme hills. The scenery is stunning, and it gets better the farther you go. This is a fine route

La Resbalosa

to do in mid-morning, bringing picnic supplies and a bathing suit for a lunchtime swim. Enjoy!

If you choose to ride past La Resbalosa for a few kilometers, the pavement becomes rougher but the scenery is even more beautiful—if that is possible.

From La Resbalosa, simply retrace the route back to Viñales.

Part III:
Central Cuba

Central Cuba has everything that lures visitors to the island: antique towns and vibrant cities, museums and sites of dramatic historical events, gently rolling countryside, a lofty mountain range, and sugary white beaches. Five of the routes in this section, taken together, comprise a great loop around the Sierra del Escambray, Cuba's second highest chain of mountains. The loop takes in the most important cities and towns in the region: Cienfuegos, Santa Clara, Remedios, Sancti Spiritus, and Trinidad.

If you are riding the Central Cuba Tour, it doesn't matter where you start. There is an international airport in Cienfuegos, so you may be able to fly directly to that city. An international airport is planned for Trinidad as well. Most visitors arrive in Havana, and it is easy to reach Santa Clara, Cienfuegos, Sancti Spiritus, or Trinidad by Víazul bus.

The entire loop is relatively easy. Any reasonably fit cyclist can do it. However, if you want to enjoy mountains by climbing them rather than merely viewing them from a distance, and if you are content to skip Sancti Spiritus, we describe a more difficult route between Santa Clara and Trinidad *over* the Sierra del Escambray. This is one of the most challenging paved routes in Cuba, comparable to La Farola in Guantánamo Province. Even if you are a strong cyclist, it will give you a good workout. The rewards are commensurate with the difficulty.

We also describe shorter loops that take a day or two, starting from

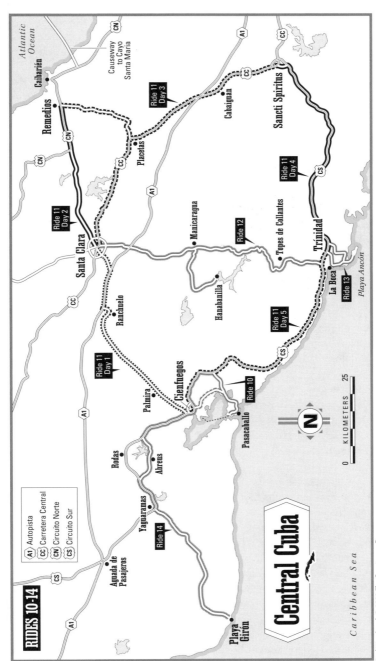

RIDES 10-14

A1 Autopista
CC Carretera Central
CN Circuito Norte
CS Circuito Sur

Atlantic Ocean

Caibarién

Causeway to Cayo Santa María

CN

A1

CC

Remedios

CN

CN

CC

Placetas

A1

Ride 11 Day 2

Santa Clara

CC

Ranchuelo

Ride 11 Day 1

Palmira

Cienfuegos

Rodas

Abreus

Yaguaramas

Ride 14

CS

Aguada de Pasajeros

A1

Ride 11 Day 3

Cabaiguán

Sancti Spíritus

CC

CC

Manicaragua

Ride 12

Topes de Collantes

Ride 11 Day 4

CS

Trinidad

Hanabanilla

Ride 11 Day 5

CS

La Boca

Ride 13

Playa Ancón

Ride 10

Pasacaballo

N

KILOMETERS

0   25

Caribbean Sea

Central Cuba

Playa Girón

Paul Woodward, © 2002 The Countryman Press

On the way to the Casa de Trova in Trinidad.

Cienfuegos, Santa Clara, and Trinidad. Finally, we give directions for cycling from Cienfuegos to Playa Girón on the Bahía de Cochinos, the infamous Bay of Pigs.

Cienfuegos

Cienfuegos, sometimes called the Pearl of the South, is a great place to start the Central Cuba Tour. It is a port and a major industrial center, but the refineries and factories are far from the commercial and residential areas you are likely to visit. The city is on a huge bay, and much of it is relatively clean and prosperous.

Cienfuegos is a great city for outdoor recreation. In the mornings you will see rowing teams in their racing shells on the bay. There seem to be more recreational cyclists in Cienfuegos than in any other Cuban city we have visited. Joggers and in-line skaters zip up and down the attractive Malecón all day long, and there is even a skating park on the waterfront.

The two areas of town with greatest appeal are the historic center around Parque Martí and the relatively upscale neighborhood of Punta Gorda, a peninsula that juts into the bay. These two areas are connected by the Prado, a handsome boulevard that becomes the Malecón along the bay.

In Cienfuegos, three hotels provide good accommodations. The high-rise Hotel Jagua in Punta Gorda has long been considered the best, but in 2001 the Hotel Unión, in the historic downtown near Parque Martí, was

With flags flying, Barbara rides east from Havana on the Vía Blanca, heading for the Playas del Este.

The world's finest cigar tobacco grows in the rich fields of Pinar del Río.

Cycling along the Carretera Circuito del Norte, the North Road, toward Bahía Honda and Viñales.

On a side street in Santiago de Cuba, a young girl lounges on her father's Russian-made motorcycle.

Tiny farmsteads huddle at the base of *mogotes* on the lovely route from Viñales to La Resbalosa.

This small girl on Cayo Granma, near Santiago de Cuba, will not be cooked for supper; she is getting a bath.

Santiago Alvares makes stringed instruments by hand at his workshop near Bahía Honda. He and his children are skilled musicians.

Bougainvillea blazes in Parque Céspedes, in front of Iglesia de Paula in the "new" part of Trinidad.

Many Cuban children, like this youngster in Trinidad, will ask tourists for *chicles* (chewing gum) or other treats.

Grupo Los Pinos Campesinos, a traditional music group, is a fixture in Trinidad. They can frequently be heard playing for tourists near Plaza Mayor.

View of the Valle de Viñales from a homestead high in the hills—accessible only to hikers or mountain bikers.

Gentlemen at ease on the central square of Remedios, a colonial town northeast of Santa Clara.

This elderly couple lives in a mountain community above Viñales. They are members of Los Aquáticos, a group who believe in the healing power of water. Their age and good health bear witness to its effectiveness—or to the benefits of hard work and simple living in an unpolluted environment.

Late afternoon sun lights up the laundry hanging from apartments along Havana's Malecón.

Greenery and wrought iron grillwork adorn buildings along this street near the Palacio Presidencial. The *palacio,* whose dome is visible in the background, now houses the Museo de la Revolución, an essential stop for anyone interested in modern Cuban history.

In Santa Clara, a schoolgirl contemplates a statue of Che Guevara.
Cuban children are taught "Seremos como el Che!" ("We will be like Che!")

Stunning scenery is the reward for cycling a difficult route through the Sierra del Escambray, from Santa Clara to Trinidad.

handsomely renovated. There is also an Islazul hotel, Hotel Puerta la Cueva, east of town on the way to the beaches at Rancho Luna.

We have always stayed in *casas particulares* in Cienfuegos, and we can recommend two. For excellent rooms and food, try the home of Jorge A. Piñeiro Vázquez at Calle 41 No. 1402, between Avenidas 14 and 16 in Punta Gorda. His e-mail is joma@tinocfg.jccc.org.cu.

The room and the meals may not be quite as good at the modest casa of María Antonia and her husband Napoles, but the welcome is just as warm and the setting is extraordinary. María's casa (at Calle 35 No. 22) is on a narrow neck of land overlooking the bay both in front and in back. There are always cool breezes. In the evening you can sit in back and watch the sun set over the water; then in the morning you can move to the front porch and see graceful racing shells skimming by.

⑩ Cienfuegos–Pasacaballo Loop

39 km, 1 or 2 days

This 39-km loop ride from Cienfuegos makes a great warm-up before starting on the Central Cuba Tour. It can easily be done in a single day, but you may wish to stop for a night or two at the beach. The route features a botanical garden, good swimming beaches, a Spanish fort, and two boat rides. You start in the heart of the city, but in just 7 km, you will be in quiet countryside, with views of the Sierra del Escambray in the distance. There are some challenging hills, but grand scenery and a swim in the Caribbean more than repay your efforts.

The route leads first to El Jardín de los Botánicos, once run by Harvard University and still loosely associated with it. This garden features over 1,400 species of trees, and for $2.50 per person, you can take a guided tour, which is well worth it.

The ride continues over a roller-coaster road to the best beaches in this part of Cuba. You can spend time swimming and then ride a few kilometers to Pasacaballo, where for $1 a small boat will take you across the narrow entrance of Bahía de Cienfuegos to Castillo de Jagua, a 17th-century fort. Another small, *peso* ferry runs regularly from the *castillo* back to the city. If you wish to spend a night or two by the sea, there is a good selection of *casas particulares* in the area of Faro Luna, a lighthouse on the coast.

Food

One good possibility for food along this ride is a picnic on the beach. It is easy to stock up in Cienfuegos—possibly a *bocadito* from the *agromercado*

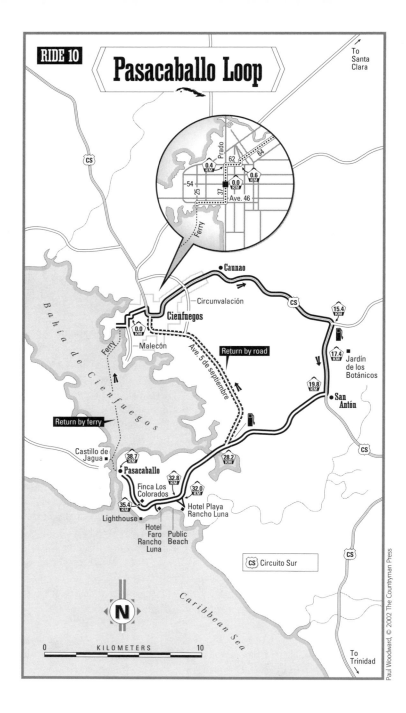

RIDE 10

Pasacaballo Loop

To
Santa
Clara

Prado

62   64

0.4
KM

54

25   37   0.0
KM   0.6
KM

Ferry   Ave. 46

● Caunao

Circunvalación

CS   15.4
KM

● Cienfuegos

Bahía   0.0
KM

Ferry   — Malecón   17.4
KM   Jardín
de los
Botánicos

de   Ave. 5 de septiembre   Return by road

19.8
KM

Cienfuegos   ● San
Antón

Return by ferry   CS

Castillo de
Jagua ■   38.7
KM

● Pasacaballo   28.2
KM

Finca Los
Colorados   32.8
KM

35.4
KM   32.0
KM

Lighthouse ■   Hotel Playa
Rancho Luna

Hotel   Public
Faro   Beach
Rancho
Luna

CS   Circuito Sur

N   CS

Caribbean   Sea

0   KILOMETERS   10

To
Trinidad

Paul Woodward, © 2002 The Countryman Press

Finca Los Colorados—like a small country inn

north of Parque Martí. Cold drinks to go with a picnic are available at Villa Rancho Luna, a bar on the public beach. Alternatively, you could buy lunch at either of the hotels along the beach—Hotel Playa Rancho Luna and Hotel Faro Luna. Near the end of the ride, lunch is available at Hotel Pasacaballo, or better, at Casa del Pescador, a seafood restaurant on the bay. However, the finest meals around are at Finca Los Colorados—see information under the section on lodging.

Lodging

If you are not pressed for time, consider stopping for a night or two at Finca Los Colorados, just 100 meters past the Faro Luna lighthouse. English-speaking José Pinero is both a kindly host and an excellent chef. His establishment is something between a *casa particular* and a small, comfortable inn, directly overlooking the sea. The exact location is in the route directions. If Finca Los Colorados is full, accommodations are also available at several *casas particulares* in the area, and at Hotel Playa Rancho Luna, Hotel Faro Luna, and Hotel Pasacaballo.

Route Directions

0.0 Start at the Prado and Avenida 54. Ride north on the Prado, away from Punta Gorda.

0.2 Pass a sign indicating that Havana is straight ahead.

Horse carts and cyclists on the Malecón in Cienfuegos

0.4 Turn right on Avenida 62, following a sign to Trinidad. There is a Baptist temple on the left just before this turn.

0.6 Turn left immediately after passing a small park. Then in one block bear right onto Avenida 64. Its name will change to Calzada Real de Dolores, a busy four-lane road.

3.5 Continue straight across another busy, four-lane road. There is a traffic blinker here, and signs indicate that Rancho Luna and Trinidad are to the right, that Havana is to the left, and that Cumanayagua is straight ahead. (The crossroad here is the Circunvalación.)

4.8 Continue straight, passing a right turn to the airport.

6.0 Pass a sign for Caonao. As you ride through this small town, the road will curve sharply to the right, then to the left, and will narrow considerably.

7.0 There is a large fruit and vegetable farm on the left. You will soon have a glimpse of the Sierra del Escambray ahead. From here, the ride will become increasingly hilly, though not difficult until after El Jardín de los Botánicos.

15.3 Continue straight through a crossroad; to the left you can see the Karl Marx Cement Factory.

15.4 Bear right at a fork; there is a Cupet gas station and a small convenience store, which has cold drinks. This road will climb, with increasingly scenic views of the mountains to the left.

17.4 Reach the clearly marked entrance on the left to the El Jardín

de Los Botánicos de Cienfuegos. A guided tour of the garden typically takes an hour, two at the most. As you leave the garden, turn left, continuing along the road on which you arrived. You will ride through high, scenic country, with cane on the left and rolling fields and cattle to the right.

19.8 Turn right onto an unmarked paved road. On the left is one of the most scenic bus shelters imaginable. The road you will now be on is like a roller coaster, with some difficult climbs, but also grand views and exhilarating downhills toward the Bahía de Cienfuegos far below.

27.5 Continue straight, passing a right to Cienfuegos.

27.7 Pass a service station on the right where cold drinks are available.

28.2 Bear left onto a major road. (Back in Cienfuegos, this same road is Avenida 5 de Septiembre.)

28.6 Cross a bridge, immediately followed on the left by a small restaurant serving *criollo* meals and seafood.

32.0 Note a signed road to the left that goes to Playa Rancho Luna. (There is an all-inclusive hotel at the end of this road catering to German and Canadian package tourists. We do not find it appealing, but it was being renovated, and you can use the *good* beach even if you aren't staying there.)

32.8 Turn right at the bottom of a marvelous hill with views of the sea below. (The left follows the shore to Playa Rancho Luna.)

33.0 Pass the entrance to Villa Rancho Luna, a bar on the pleasant public beach, on the left. Sun chairs and umbrellas are available for rent. The entrance to Faro Rancho Luna is just 60 meters past Villa Rancho Luna (also on the left). This small Cubanacán resort is named for a lighthouse that is a little farther down the coast. The all-inclusive hotel is reputed to be better than the one at Playa Rancho Luna. Along the lane to Hotel Faro Rancho Luna, there are at least four small *casas particulares* renting rooms and serving meals.

35.3 Pass the lighthouse from which the hotel gets its name, Faro Luna, on the left. There are two *casas particulares* on the right immediately after the lighthouse. The second, Finca Los Colorados, is more like a tiny inn, and we recommend it highly.

38.7 Turn left down a dirt lane toward the shore for a boat to Castillo de Jagua. This turn is directly opposite a driveway on the right leading up to the Hotel Pasacaballo. If you continue straight past the boat landing and the Hotel Pasacaballo, you will reach the end of the road in another 1.5 km. The seafood restaurant, Casa del Pescador, sits at the very end of the point. To return to Cienfuegos, first take the boat from Pasacaballo to Castillo de Jagua. This should cost a dollar or two. Don't try for a boat all the way back

Looking across to Castillo de Jagua from Pasacaballo

to Cienfuegos; it would be expensive if you could find one. Once you get to Castillo de Jagua, just across the narrow entrance to the bay, you can wait for another small, public ferry that will take you 10 km back to Cienfuegos for a *peso* or two.

Backtracking along the Coast

A hurricane swept across central Cuba in late 2001 just after we rode this loop. In early 2002 a correspondent told us that the restaurant, Casa del Pescador, was closed. More importantly for completing this ride, he said it was impossible to get a boat at Pasacaballo. It is likely that when you ride this loop, everything will be back to normal. However, if there is still no boat available, it is not difficult to ride back to Cienfuegos. We have done it, and it takes just over an hour because you do not have to return via the botanical gardens.

Backtrack along the coast, and just after Villa Rancho Luna, **bear left up the hill**. In less than 5 km you will see the road to the right where you rode from El Jardín de los Botánicos. Do not take it, however. **Continue straight**, and you will soon pass a service station on the right. You will be on Avenida 5 de Septiembre.

In another 10 km, in the busy outskirts of Cienfuegos, notice a huge Grecian-style building on the left, the entrance to the Cemetery Tomás Acea. About 2 km past the cemetery, you will come to a T-intersection at Calle 45. **For the Punta Gorda area, turn left at the T-intersection, and then take the next right**. In four blocks you will reach a T-intersection on the Malecón. Punta Gorda is to the left. For the Parque Martí area, turn right at the T-intersection (at Calle 45) and take the next left; it is four blocks to the Prado.

⑪ Central Cuba Tour

350 km, 5 days or more

This 350-km tour is divided into five days of riding, and it can certainly be done in that amount of time. However, you will surely want to spend at least a couple of days in Cienfuegos and Santa Clara, and probably longer than that in Trinidad. The Central Cuba Tour would be perfect for a two-week vacation.

The second day of the tour, from Santa Clara to Remedios, can be turned into an enjoyable two-day loop by returning from Remedios to Santa Clara instead of continuing on to Sancti Spiritus.

Day 1: Cienfuegos to Santa Clara (67 km)

Santa Clara, where Day 1 ends, is an important university town. It is not often visited by tourists, but it deserves to be. We particularly admired the awesome memorial to Che Guevara, and we have enjoyed concerts at Teatro La Caridad, a beautiful 19th-century theater that offers musical performances two or three evenings each week. We also like stopping at the provincial office of the National Union of Writers and Artists of Cuba (UNEAC) on Máximo Gómez between Parque Vidal and Plaza del Carmen. UNEAC is a friendly place, with an art gallery and occasional recitals in the afternoon.

Parque Vidal is a handsome square in the center of town, one of the most impressive in Cuba, full of families and children on warm evenings, busy all the time. There is a pedestrian mall along several blocks of Independencia with sidewalk cafes and restaurants. Santa Clara is a lively, congenial city.

The terrain on this 67-km ride is mostly flat or rising slightly, never steep enough to present real difficulty. There are a few rolling hills before Santa Clara. The only real challenge on this ride is headwind—it can be strong, especially on the Autopista.

Food

You can pick up enough sandwiches and fruit or other provisions in Cienfuegos, but there are also two towns along the way that offer all you need. Palmira, just 11 km from the start, has the biggest selection; and you can find basic fuel for your body and a dollar store in Cruces, 29 km from Cienfuegos. Just 10 km before the end of the ride, there is a clean, air-conditioned rest stop on the Autopista with ice cream and plenty of other Rápido-style foods.

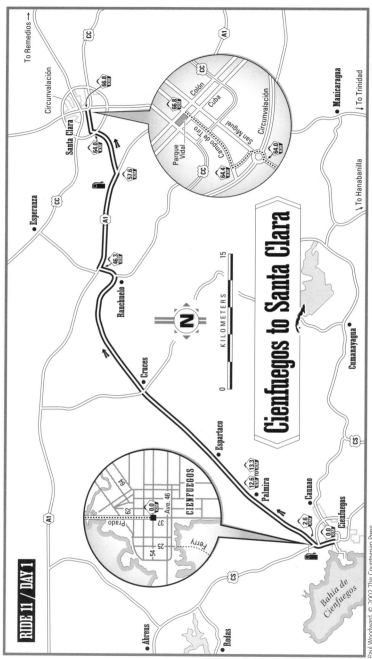

RIDE 11 / DAY 1

Cienfuegos to Santa Clara

To Remedios →

Circunvalación

66.8 KLM

Santa Clara

64.0 KLM

57.6 KLM

Esperanza

A1

46.3 KLM

Ranchuelo

Cruces

Colón

CC

66.8 KLM

Cuba

San Miguel

Campo de Tiro

Circunvalación

Parque Vidal

64.4 KLM

CC

64.0 KLM

Manicaragua

→ To Trinidad

↓ To Hanabanilla

N

KILOMETERS

0   15

Espartaco

12.6 KLM TO KLM   13.3 KLM

Palmira

Prado

CIENFUEGOS

Ave. 46

0.0 KLM

37

-54   -25

Ferry

Caunao

2.6 KLM

Cienfuegos

0.0 KLM

Cumanayagua

CS

Bahía de Cienfuegos

Abreus

Rodas

Paul Woodward, © 2002 The Countryman Press

Lodging

Santa Clara's principal tourist hotel, Los Caneyes, is an attractive place, far nicer than the dreary Hotel Santa Clara Libre in the center of the city. Our room at Hotel Los Caneyes was nicely furnished, and the buffet dinner was adequate. We enjoyed surprisingly cool water in the small but very clean swimming pool. However, this hotel is pricey for what you get. In late 2001, a single night with breakfast and dinner for two came to nearly $80. When we stayed there, the buffet breakfast was poor, and Hotel Los Caneyes was the only hotel in Cuba that charged for a cup of plain hot water for Barbara's tea—$1 per cup! You can check descriptions of other hotel options in the general guidebooks, but on our next visit to Santa Clara, we chose a *casa particular.*

We liked Casa María on Calle San Pablo #19. This *casa particular* faces Iglesia del Carmen, a national monument on its own small, photogenic square. It is a short walk along Máximo Gómez to the center of town at Parque Vidal. Alina and Eliar, the young couple who are the hosts at this casa, will store your bicycles indoors. There are many other *casas particulares* in Santa Clara as well.

Route Directions

0.0 The route begins in Cienfuegos at Calle 37 (the Prado) and Avenida 54. Ride north on the Prado, away from Punta Gorda. On the Prado, a four-lane boulevard, cyclists ride in the left lanes next to the center divider. (Just one block from the start, a sign indicates that Santa Clara is 74 km ahead. This distance agrees neither with our measurements nor with the best maps. The correct distance is closer to 67 km, depending on your exact destination in Santa Clara.)

0.2 Continue straight through the intersection with Avenida 62. (This is where you turn on the ride to El Jardín de Los Botánicos and Pasacaballo.)

0.9 Notice a sign indicating that the cycle lane *(ciclo vía)* has changed to the normal, right lane. You are still on a busy four-lane road, and the cycle lane is now separated from traffic by speed bumps.

1.9 Leave the cycle lane and continue straight on the main road. (The cycle lane turns right toward Pastoria, a neighborhood that is off the route.)

2.2 Continue straight through a major intersection with the Circunvalación.

2.6 Continue straight, passing a turn towards the Autopista and Havana. (This is the road to Rodas. It is part of the route to Playa Girón.)

3.2 There is a modern service center on the left—a good place to pick up cold water if you are low.

Children in goatcarts circle Parque Vidal in Santa Clara.

11.6 Enter the town of Palmira.

12.6 Turn right at a T-intersection and **then immediately turn left**. You will be riding alongside a small park in the center of town. On the right are stands selling fruit and vegetables, *bocaditos* with hot *chorizo, batidos,* and more. Just past the park, as you continue straight, there is a café with pizzas on the right and a well-stocked dollar store on the left. There is also a government bakery. If there is plenty of bread on hand, you can buy a fresh loaf for a few *pesos.*

13.3 Turn right (straight ahead, the road turns to dirt), and **then turn left** immediately after crossing the railroad tracks.

23.7 Take care riding over another railroad crossing because the tracks protrude above the surface of the pavement and cross at an extreme angle.

29.4 In the town of Cruces, there are street vendors, a dollar store, a pizza place, and a basic cafeteria.

30.2 Stay on the paved road as it curves to the left. In another 100 meters, note a sign indicating that Ranchuelo is 14 km.

44.0 Enter Ranchuelo. Snacks including ice cream are available on the Carretera Central. The central part of town is off to the right. If you look down the side streets, you can spot a TRD Caribe dollar store and other services.

45.9 As you are leaving Ranchuelo, there is a sign indicating a service station ahead and to the right. Watch for the next paved right, in about 400 meters.

46.3 Turn right on an unmarked, paved lane. This is the entrance to the Autopista toward Santa Clara. If you cross a bridge over the Autopista, you have missed this turn.

55.9 On the left, there is an attractive stone and thatched café followed immediately by a modern service center with an air-conditioned snack bar. There are clean rest rooms.

57.6 Bear left at the Y-intersection toward Santa Clara. A sign indicates that Santa Clara is 7 km. (You are leaving the Autopista, which continues right to Sancti Spiritus.) The next few kilometers will gradually become hillier.

64.0 Stop at a complex intersection with a small traffic circle. **Proceed straight**, following the sign toward Plaza de la Revolución. **In a few meters you will have to bear left** following a sign to Hotel Los Caneyes. **Then immediately turn right** onto an unmarked road. (Do not continue toward Hotel Los Caneyes—unless you plan to stay there, of course.) After just 50 meters, **turn left on the first paved road**. Very soon you will see towering lights ahead and to the right; these illuminate the Plaza de la Revolución. (Note: If you are staying at Hotel Los Caneyes, continue left at the traffic circle, onto the Circunvalación. Watch for a sign in a few hundred meters indicating a left to the hotel. Take care when you cross the Circunvalación. Shortly after you leave the Circunvalación, you will come to a T-intersection. Turn left, and the thatched roofs of the hotel will appear on your right in about 1 km.)

64.4 Turn right at a T-intersection onto Campo de Tiro, a major, six-lane road. The huge monument to Che Guevara is just ahead on your left. After the monument, the road narrows to an ordinary, two-lane city street named Rafael Trista. (If you wish to visit the monument now, turn left into the parking lot immediately *after* passing the monument; do not attempt to enter via the turn on the left *before* the monument.)

65.5 Watch for a warning sign on the left for a dangerous intersection ahead. It lists deaths, accidents, and injuries. It's no joke! At the upcoming intersection, a busy road with two-way traffic, it can be difficult to see cars approaching from the right.

66.8 Arrive at Parque Vidal. You must walk your bike here; the entire circumference of the park is a pedestrian zone. It is a fine place to get your bearings, and there are several *casas particulares* in the area, including Casa María.

Day 2: Santa Clara to Remedios (47 km)

Remedios, only 47 km from Santa Clara, is often compared to Trinidad. That is an overstatement, but Remedios is one of the oldest towns in Cuba, and it certainly has antique charm. While Remedios lacks Trinidad's rich selection of restaurants, galleries, and music, it also lacks crowds of tourists—which can be an attraction in itself. For cyclists intent on a serious beach vacation, it is only 13 km from Remedios to the beginning of a scenic 40-km causeway that leads to Cayo Santa María.

The ride from Santa Clara to Remedios passes through areas with small farms, diverse vegetation, and the hills of the Alturas de Santa Clara. The terrain is generally rolling, with moderate climbs in the Alturas. From Remedios, the Central Cuba Tour continues to Placetas and on to Sancti Spiritus. If you do not aim to do the whole tour, it is possible to return in one day from Remedios to Santa Clara, thereby completing an easy two-day loop. Directions for returning appear at the end of the Remedios–Sancti Spiritus segment.

Food

The ride from Santa Clara to Remedios is neither long nor difficult, so it is possible to do it between breakfast and a late lunch. There are, however, street vendors, a dollar store, and a Rápido-style cafeteria in Camajuani, about midway between Santa Clara and Remedios.

In Remedios, there are two basic restaurants—one for *pesos*, and a Rumbos restaurant for dollars, on Plaza Martí. The best food, however, will be either at the Hotel Mascotte, also on Plaza Martí, or in *casas particulares*.

Lodging

There are plenty of good places to stay in Remedios. The Hotel Mascotte on Plaza Martí is in an old building that has been tastefully restored. The rooms are nicely furnished, and the dining room is elegant in an understated way. This is a small, friendly hotel, with only a dozen guest rooms.

Tour groups fill it up two or three nights a week; on other nights, it may be nearly empty. The Mascotte is a bargain, considering its quality. Check it out.

Several *casas particulares* are also located near Plaza Martí. We stayed in the roomy, second-floor apartment of Gladys Aponte Rojas. Her address is Brigadier González No. 32, just a few doors off Independencia. This apartment is in a Colonial building and has a roof terrace with a view. If you stay there, you may notice a small shrine in the corner of the living room. Gladys is a *santera*, and if you would like to learn more about *Santería*, the fusion of Catholicism and African religion that is so important in Cuba, this might be a good place. We found it somewhat inconvenient to haul our bikes up

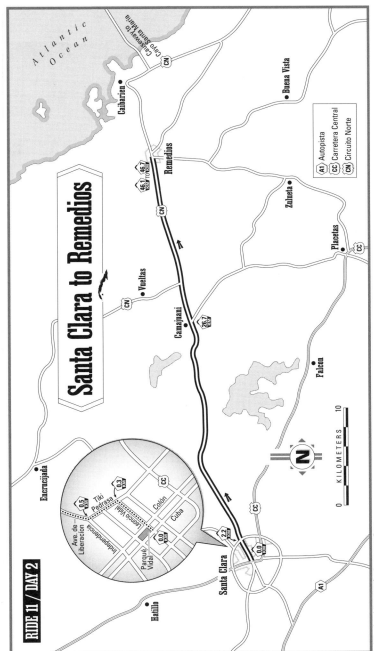

RIDE 11 / DAY 2

Santa Clara to Remedios

Atlantic Ocean

Caibarien

Causeway to Cayo Santa María

CN

46.7 KM TO Cayo Santa María

46.1 KM

Remedios

Buena Vista

Zulueta

CN

CN

Vueltas

Placetas

CC

Camajuani

26.7 KM

Encrucijada

0.5 KM

Tiki Pedraza

0.3 KM

Ave. de Liberación

Independencia

Leoncio Vidal

Colón

Cuba

Parque Vidal

0.0 KM

CC

Santa Clara

2.2 KM

0.0 KM

CC

Falcon

Hatillo

A1

Autopista CC Carretera Central CN Circuito Norte

N

0 KILOMETERS 10

Paul Woodward, © 2002 The Countryman Press

Che Guevara and the Billboards

When we first arrived at the memorial to Che Guevara in Santa Clara, we cycled into the wrong parking lot and were immediately confronted by members of the Policía Nacional Revolucionaria. They firmly directed us to the correct entrance. Security was tight. Entering the monument, we had to check bags and cameras.

After visiting the dimly lit mausoleum where Che's remains are interred, we toured the museum. We saw the photographs, mementos, and explanatory text about Che's youth in Argentina; his years in medical school; the journeys that taught him about the suffering of South America's peasants and workers; his years as a *guerrillero* with Fidel Castro in the Sierra Maestra; his roles in the revolutionary government; and his final, quixotic efforts to support freedom fighters in the Congo and then to ignite a revolution in Bolivia, where he was finally captured and murdered.

As we left the museum, we were suddenly approached by one of the police who had stopped us in the parking lot. We felt a moment of apprehension, but he was only curious about Americans who were visiting the memorial to Cuba's secular saint. He walked around the monument with us, talking about Che, translating inscriptions, and explaining the bas-relief sculptures on granite blocks beneath the huge, bronze statue. He pointed to the plaza below us and said that the pattern of tiles symbolizes one of Che's ideals—people of all races and nationalities joining hands around the world.

The pattern of the tiles symbolizes racial harmony.

The Billboards As you cycle around Cuba, you will see billboards near all the towns and cities. They display exhortations to revolutionary virtue from A TRUE REVOLUTIONARY NEVER LIES to the ever-popular SOCIALISM OR DEATH, and our personal favorite, REBELS, FOREVER YOUNG! These billboards are part of a decades-long campaign that began with Che in the early days of Cuba's revolutionary government.

In 1959, Cuba was taken over by a group of young revolutionaries who had almost no practical experience in government. They were former workers and peasants, professionals, intellectuals—idealists all, and Che Guevara was the most fervent idealist of all. He was convinced of the need to develop El Hombre Nuevo. This New Man would be motivated not by material gain, but by joy in serving others and by dedication to building a just society. Creating the New Man would require a transformation of consciousness that could be achieved only by education—that is, education if one supported the effort, indoctrination or propaganda if one did not. The effort initiated by Che to reshape attitudes has continued for more than two generations.

It has been at least partly responsible for some of the revolution's undeniable

Che—his example lives, his ideas endure.

achievements—read the sidebars entitled Education in Cuba (page 87) and Latin American School of Medical Sciences (page 80). It also led to mistakes when hard work and sacrifice alone were expected to overcome inexperience and lack of expertise. In any event, signs of the effort to create a New Man are still evident all over Cuba—on the billboards, in government-controlled radio, television, newspapers, and magazines, and even in the lessons and recitations of school children.

Has any of this has had a real effect? Are the values of Cubans in general significantly different from those of people in other countries? This is a difficult question, but we believe the correct answer is probably yes. Even though some Cubans are discontent and envious of North American material culture, most are still unusually willing to make sacrifices for their country.

The evidence? The simple fact that most doctors do not drive cabs to earn dollars—they continue to staff the hospitals and care for their patients while earning $30 a month. Most teachers do not quit to seek jobs as waiters and tour guides—they teach their classes for $20 per month. Buses and trains keep running, after a fashion, and so do stores and farms and factories. In the depths of the Special Period, with conditions that would have brought riots and rebellion to many nations, Cuba remained calm, and this was not because government cows the people into submission. If the history of Cuba shows anything at all, it shows that Cubans have never been afraid to rise against tyranny.

We think that Cuba held together through extraordinarily difficult times because, to at least some degree, Che's ideals of discipline and dedication have taken hold. That is not to say that the New Man is alive and well in Cuba, nor that the social achievements of the past can't be undone by continuing adversity. But Che's picture is on the billboards and hanging on the walls of many Cuban homes because people still hope to realize the ideals he believed in. Some of the billboards say HIS EXAMPLE LIVES; HIS IDEAS ENDURE and HE LIVES IN THE HEARTS OF THE PEOPLE.

to the second floor, but otherwise we liked this *casa* very much. There are several more *casas* renting rooms nearby.

Route Directions

0.0 This ride starts at Parque Vidal in Santa Clara on the corner of Leoncio Vidal. This is near the southeast corner of the park, directly opposite the tall and ugly Hotel Santa Clara Libre. Ride on Leoncio Vidal away from the park. Count the blocks; you will turn left at the third block.

0.3 Turn left on Pedraza, the third left after leaving Parque Vidal.

0.5 Turn right at a T-intersection on Independencia/Liberación, following signs to Camajuani and Universidad Central.

0.7 El Tren Blindado (the armored train) is on the right. You will ride across the very tracks on which the armored train carrying Batista soldiers was traveling when Che Guevara and his followers derailed it. The battle of Santa Clara was the final, decisive victory of the revolution.

1.1 Watch on the right for an extraordinary, life-sized statue of Che Guevara, striding forward with a child in his arms. It is in front of the headquarters of the Provincial Committee of the Communist Party.

1.5 A new Cupet gas station on the right houses a small dollar store.

2.2 Proceed straight through a rotary following signs to "Universidad."

7.7 Pass the entrance to the Universidad Central de Villas Claras on the right. The campus continues another kilometer or more. From here, the road will become increasingly rural, with easy rolling hills.

19.4 Large concrete signs indicate you are leaving the *municipio* of Santa Clara and entering Camajuani.

20.1 Note the welcome sign on the left to Luis Rosa, sugar *central,* complete with a handsome steam locomotive. *(Central* literally means "center" or "head office" in Spanish, but in Cuba is often used for the sugar refineries that are the industrial centers of huge sugar-producing farms.) The road becomes even more scenic, with hills, small farms and fields, and Royal Palms.

26.7 Enter the town of Camajuani. Watch on the left for a couple of interesting *organopónicos*. One of them produces flowers, and a decorative fence bears paintings of various blossoms and the romantic characteristics associated with each. A second *organopónico* raises vegetables, and its fence is painted with illustrations and lists of the nutritional benefits derived from each vegetable.

27.2 There is a small complex with a gas station, cafeteria, and dollar store on the right in Camajuani. Also in town you can find several street pizza vendors and many other snacks, including *batidos* and ice cream.

Busy pedestrian mall in Sancti Spiritus

28.4 Watch on the right for a remarkable sign that faces oncoming traffic from Remedios. It is capped on either side by statues, one of a toad prince, one of a goat. These are symbols of the neighborhood teams into which this town divides for the *parrandas,* competitions in December to see who can create the most elaborate floats and spectacular fireworks. Remedios and several other towns in the region are famous for these events.

39.3 Enter the *municipio* of Remedios.

46.1 Stop at a crossroad as you are entering the town proper. The bus depot is on the right. You will proceed straight ahead on Independencia, a street that narrows considerably. (Route directions for leaving Remedios on Day 3 begin at this intersection.)

46.7 Independencia comes to T-intersection beside the beautiful Iglesia de San Juan Bautista; and the central square, Parque Martí, is immediately to the left. The Hotel Mascotte is also to the left, one block farther.

Day 3: Remedios to Sancti Spiritus (71 km)

The next section of the Central Cuba Tour is a beautiful 71-km ride from Remedios to Sancti Spiritus. It is also possible to loop back to Santa Clara, and we give directions for this 61-km option as well. In either case, you will first ride through the hilly country between Remedios and Placetas—hilly enough to be scenic, that is, but still not difficult.

To Zulueta the grade will be rising more than falling, but none of it is memorably difficult. You will first pass rough pastures, rocky enough to rival the worst in New England. Then the ride becomes increasingly scenic, with hills, small fields, rows of handsome Royal Palms, and diverse agriculture.

From Placetas, you will ride on the Carretera Central. Whether you go west to Santa Clara or southeast to Sancti Spiritus, the Carretera Central will be surprisingly quiet, at least once you are away from the cities.

Sancti Spiritus seems to be a city in which visitors merely stop when they are on their way to somewhere else. This has been true for us as well, we must admit. It appears to be a pleasant town that would reward you for time spent there. In any case, Sancti Spiritus is the beginning of one of the loveliest rides in central Cuba. So often the most scenic routes owe their beauty to hills that the cyclist must climb, but this time less work is required. From Sancti Spiritus to Trinidad, you will ride beside the Sierra del Escambray much of the time, but you do not have to climb the mountains to enjoy the view.

Food

After Remedios, the first available food, as well as a dollar store, is in Zulueta. We prefer to stop for a break in Placetas. Placetas has a large, shady park, an exceptionally well-stocked dollar store, and a good selection of street food. If you are riding toward Sancti Spiritus, be sure to top off your water bottles and have lunch or a snack in Placetas; it will be at least 23 km before the next available bottled water.

Lodging

In Sancti Spiritus, we have stayed at Villa Los Laureles, a hotel in the western outskirts of town on the Carretera Central. Villa Los Laureles consists of small, clean, and modern bungalows on pleasantly landscaped grounds. There is an adequate restaurant beside the large swimming pool. While not an outstanding bargain, it is clear that Islazul is trying to build this place into a modest but attractive resort. Several handsome new villas were under construction when we were there in late 2001.

A reputedly better and more expensive hotel is Villa Rancho Hatuey. This is the Sancti Spiritus hotel that tour groups use. It is also on the Carretera Central, just 0.5 km past Villa Los Laureles, so it would be easy to compare them if you wish. There are a number of *casas particulares* around Parque Serafín Sánchez in Sancti Spiritus proper.

We have also stayed at Hotel Zaza, 10 km east of Sancti Spiritus. The best thing about this hotel is its location on Cuba's largest reservoir.

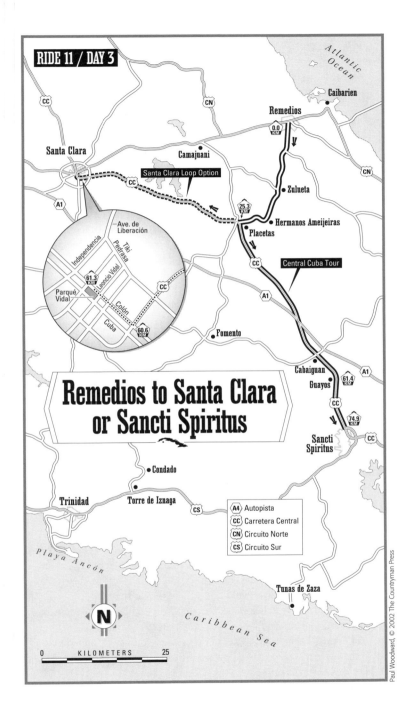

RIDE 11 / DAY 3

Atlantic Ocean

Caibarien

CC

CN

Remedios
0.0 KM

Santa Clara

Camajuani

CN

Santa Clara Loop Option

CC

Zulueta

A1

25.3 KM

Hermanos Ameijeiras

Ave. de Liberación

Placetas

Tiki Pedrosa

Independencia

Central Cuba Tour

61.3 KM

Leoncio Vidal

CC

Parqué Vidal

Colón

A1

Cuba

60.6 KM

Fomento

Cabaiguan

Guayos

61.4 KM

A1

CC

Remedios to Santa Clara
or Sancti Spiritus

74.9 KM

Sancti Spiritus

CC

Condado

Trinidad

Torre de Iznaga

CS

A4	Autopista
CC	Carretera Central
CN	Circuito Norte
CS	Circuito Sur

Playa Ancón

Tunas de Zaza

N

Caribbean Sea

0   KILOMETERS   25

Otherwise it is adequate, with a large swimming pool, but probably not worth the extra distance if you are riding on to Trinidad.

Route Directions

0.0 This ride begins in Remedios at the intersection by the bus station—see km 46.1 of Day 2, Santa Clara to Remedios. Follow the sign toward Zulueta.

13.3 Arrive in Zulueta. There are snack vendors and a dollar store in town. When we cycled through here, streets were torn up for installation of water or sewer lines, and banks of mud and gravel were piled along the pavement, which was full of potholes. Because some of the streets were impassable, we had to wander around and pick our way through town. Because it is unlikely that you will find your way through Zulueta in quite the same way we did, there may be some discrepancy between our subsequent distances and your cycle computer's readings. Less than 2 km past Zulueta, the road reaches the high point of this ride and a great downhill begins with expansive views to the right.

19.3 Ride through Hermanos Ameijeiras, a small village and sugar *central* of the same name. On the left, note a welcome display that features another antique steam engine.

25.3 Turn left at a tiny triangular park with benches and a small monument on the left. Do not take the sharp left that precedes the park. The main road curves to the right, merging with the Carretera Central, through the center of town. If you want food or drinks, you should continue into town and then ride back to this turn. **If you are returning to Santa Clara rather than continuing to Sancti Spiritus, do not take this left. See Loop Option on next page.**

26.7 A sign on the right says CONSEJO POPULAR BENITO JUÁREZ. The terrain now is gently rolling, and the road is straight for several kilometers. You can see the Sierra del Escambray in the distance, off to the right.

46.5 Cross a small bridge and enter Sancti Spiritus Province.

49.7 Continue straight, crossing a bridge over the Autopista. There are signs that indicate a right for Havana and Fomento and straight ahead for Sancti Spiritus and Cabaiguán. Before you cross the bridge, there is a rest area below to the right with cold drinks, toilets, and shade.

51.9 There is a dollar kiosk on the right in the small town of El Diamante.

55.7 Ride through the center of Cabaiguán. You will be on a boulevard with shade trees and benches. As you leave town, continue straight, passing a sign for a right to Santa Lucía.

Cabañas at Villa Los Laureles

61.4 In the town of Guayos, there is a small Tiendas Panamericanas dollar store on the right. Immediately after the store, roads angle off to the left and right; **take the center road across the bridge**.

66.8 Pass a tiny dollar store and a cafeteria on the right in the small town of La Aurora.

67.4 Cross a bridge and enter the *municipio* of Sancti Spiritus.

69.7 Enter the Sancti Spiritus city limits. 69.8 Pass a big, new service center on the left with a dollar store and an El Rápido cafeteria.

70.6 Continue straight, passing under a bridge. (There is a right for the Autopista and Yaguajay, a left for the airport.)

71.4 Villa Los Laureles is on the left, across the Carretera Central. Villa Rancho Hatuey is another 0.5 km ahead on the right. If you wish to go downtown for a *casa particular*, continue by following the first 5 km of Day 4, Sancti Spiritus to Trinidad or La Boca.

Santa Clara–Remedios Loop Option (108 km, 2 days)

From Placetas, it is easy to ride back to Santa Clara on the Carretera Central. There are rolling hills and little traffic until you enter the outskirts of Santa Clara. Along the way, there are several stops for food and drink noted in the directions.

At kilometer 25.3 of the preceding directions, follow the main road to the right instead of turning left at the tiny park. You will ride on the Carretera Central through the center of Placetas, a bigger and more prosperous-looking town than Zulueta. Then continue as follows.

Route Directions

26.2 Pass a large park with benches and shade trees on the right, a good spot for a break. There is a small dollar store just before the park on the left and an exceptionally well-stocked dollar store on the street to the left at the far end of the park. There is also plenty of street food on the Carretera Central after the park.

27.0 Cross a high bridge over railroad tracks. Stay on the Carretera Central all the way to Santa Clara. There are rolling hills as you approach the city, and of course, the traffic will increase near the end of the ride.

39.0 In the small town of Falcon, there is a TRD Caribe dollar store on the left.

44.6 Cross a bridge and enter the *municipio* of Santa Clara.

45.7 There is another small dollar store on the left in the tiny village of Manajanabo.

58.4 Go straight through a large rotary. (To accomplish this, take the *third* right as you ride around the rotary.)

59.8 Note large apartment blocks on the right.

60.1 Watch for Patio Bar El Bosque on the right. It has a bizarre statue out front, and it comes immediately before a bridge. Then watch for a 24-hour Cupet service station, also on the right. You will turn right in one block.

60.6 Turn right on Colón. There is a traffic light at this busy intersection. The name of the street is on a small plaque on the building just across the intersection on the right. Colón leads directly to Parque Vidal, in about seven blocks.

61.0 Arrive at Parque Vidal.

Day 4: Sancti Spiritus to Trinidad or La Boca (76 or 82 km)

This 82-km day is a special treat because it is surprisingly easy for a ride with such grand views. Once you leave Sancti Spiritus, you will cycle along a gently rolling road through farms and pastures and then through drier cattle country. A long downhill will bring you to the floor of the Valle de los Ingenios (sugar mills). A very short detour to the Torre (Tower) de Iznaga is included at km 60.7. There is a pleasant restaurant here, and the view from the top of the tower is absolutely not to be missed. The only challenging part of the ride is between the valley and Trinidad.

First settled by a few Spanish families in 1513, Trinidad is a hugely popular tourist destination. Trinidad surely has more museums, galleries, and restaurants than any other Cuban town of its size. Strolling through its maze of ancient streets and pastel buildings is a delight, especially early in the morning, in the glowing light of late afternoon, or during the cooler time near dusk.

Nevertheless, Trinidad is not a good town in which to cycle. The most attractive and historic part of town has been designated a World Heritage Site by the United Nations. This means the wonderful Colonial buildings are being preserved, and so are the cobblestone streets, which turn cycling into a shuddery ordeal. Fortunately there are plenty of places to park your bike, and the historic center can be thoroughly enjoyed on foot.

From Trinidad, it is easy to visit Playa Ancón, the only beach we know of on the south coast that compares with Cuba's superb northern beaches. We love Trinidad, but we love the beach as well, so we have twice chosen to stay in La Boca, a nearby fishing village on the coast that is only a short ride from either Trinidad or Ancón.

Food

There are many places to buy food and water in Sancti Spiritus, but once you leave the city, the first place for bottled water, cold drinks, and snacks is Banao, about 25 km along the route. Be sure to stop there, *topoff* your water bottles, and have an ice cream; the next opportunity for food and bottled water will be 35 km later, at the Torre de Iznaga.

Lodging

There are so many good *casas particulares* in Trinidad and La Boca that it seems crazy to pay for Motel Las Cuevas, a moderately expensive hotel that is favored by tour groups. The other hotel in town is La Ronda, an Islazul establishment near Parque Céspedes that is said to be a bargain. (At the end of 2001, site preparation was underway for a new hotel behind the facade of an old building on Martí, facing Parque Céspedes.)

There are scores of *casas* renting rooms, possibly the best selection in Cuba. We can recommend the immaculate little home of Martha Puig Jimínez. Her address is Francisco Cadahia No. 236, between Colón and Lino Pérez. *Casas* around Plaza Mayor may be more appealing to many tourists because of their picturesque location, but Martha is a charming woman who speaks excellent English, and her home is on a quieter block just a few minutes walk from all the town's principal attractions.

Though we enjoy Trinidad very much, we actually prefer to stay a few kilometers outside of town at La Boca, a small fishing village. Hostal Sol y Mar in La Boca is, we think, one of the cleanest and friendliest *casas particulares* in Cuba, with some of the best food too. Joaquín Pomés Figueredo and his wife Olga are delightful hosts. There are many other *casas* renting rooms in La Boca. We have also stayed at Casa del Capitán, about 0.5 km past Hostal Sol y Mar. Cuca Casanova, the host at Casa del Capitán, is a pleasantly eccentric widow who makes you feel at home. While her house is not quite as comfortable as Hostal Sol y Mar, the back terrace has one of the most beautiful views we have enjoyed at any *casa*, and meals are good too.

Our route directions continue through Trinidad and on to La Boca. La Boca is about 20 minutes by bike from the center of Trinidad, and also 20 minutes from the beach at Ancón. As you first enter La Boca, it is not terribly appealing, but then you reach the modest waterfront—unfortunately stripped by a hurricane in 2001—where the houses have lovely sunset views over the water. It is easy to get hooked on this place. A family of Norwegians meant to stop for a single night at Hostal Sol y Mar when we were there; they ended up abandoning most of their travel plans and staying for nearly a week!

It is also possible to stay at one of the tourist hotels on the beach at Playa Ancón. In 2001 there were three hotels open, and two more were planned. The best of the bunch by far was the brand new, expensive Hotel Brisas Trinidad del Mar.

Route Directions

0.0 Leaving Los Laureles, turn left onto the Carretera Central. (Note: These route directions start at Villa Los Laureles, a few kilometers north of the center of Sancti Spiritus on the Carretera Central. If you don't stay at this hotel, you can pick up the directions at the main plaza in the center of town, Parque Serafín Sánchez, at km 4.8.)

0.6 Pass Villa Rancho Hatuey on the right.

1.2 Pass the run-down Hotel Deportivo on the left. Continue straight.

1.6 Navigate a traffic circle, following the signs straight ahead to Ciudad.

1.8 Continue straight, passing a left turn to Ciego de Ávila and the Circunvalación.

3.4 Pass a large hospital complex on the left and the central ETECSA office and post office on the right.

4.0 Turn right on Avenida de los Mártires, following the sign to Trinidad. (Ciego de Ávila is straight ahead.) There are traffic lights at this busy corner, and an overhead pedestrian walkway crosses the Carretera Central.

4.5 Avenida de los Mártires narrows to a single lane.

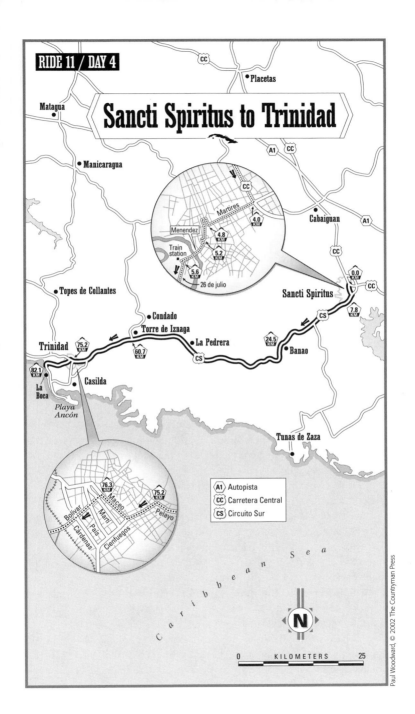

RIDE 11 / DAY 4

Sancti Spiritus to Trinidad

Placetas

Matagua

Manicaragua

Cabaiguan

Martires

Menendez

Train
station

26 de julio

Sancti Spiritus

Topes de Collantes

Condado

Torre de Iznaga

La Pedrera

Banao

Trinidad

La
Boca

Casilda

Playa
Ancón

Tunas de Zaza

Bolivar

Maceo

Marti

Pais

Cardenas

Cienfuegos

Pelayo

A1 Autopista

CC Carretera Central

CS Circuito Sur

C a r i b b e a n   S e a

N

0   KILOMETERS   25

Paul Woodward, © 2002 The Countryman Press

The ride from Sancti Spiritus is surprisingly easy.

4.8 You must turn right, following a sign to Trinidad. Parque Serafín Sánchez, the principal plaza in the center of town, is now on your left. You will ride around three sides of the park.

4.9 Turn left at the end of the park, following another sign to Trinidad.

4.95 Quickly turn left again, continuing around the park. You are now riding on Máximo Gómez. Stay on this street, leaving the park behind.

5.2 Turn right at a T-intersection at a large church, following the sign to Trinidad. **Then, immediately turn left** on Jesús Menéndez. (The signs for Trinidad, you may notice, disappear just when you need them most.)

5.3 Stay on Jesús Menéndez, following the sign to Reparto Colón. Do not turn onto Plácido.

5.5 After crossing a small bridge, Jesús Menéndez widens briefly to become a boulevard.

5.6 Bear left as the boulevard ends in front of the train station, and then quickly bear right. You are now on 26 de Julio.

6.0 Signs reappear for Trinidad straight ahead.

6.8 Again, you will see signs for Trinidad straight ahead; you are on the right track.

7.8 Merge onto the main road for Trinidad. The Circunvalación comes in from the left.

8.0 A sign says TRINIDAD 66 KM, LA GÜIRA 28 KM, AND BANAO 17 KM.

15.7 Continue straight through Entronque Guasimal. There is a left for Guasimal and Tuna de Zaza. The riding now is beautiful, through gently rolling cane and cattle country, with the foothills of the Sierra del Escambray

Trinidad's cobbled streets are better for horses than for cyclists.

on the right and higher peaks behind them and ahead in the distance.

18.1 Note a sign for Consejo Popular Banao. The town is 5 or 6 km farther. You are entering a rich horticultural district, noted especially for garlic. Medicinal plants are also grown here.

23.5 Enter the town limits of Banao.

24.5 There is a Rumbos cafeteria about 100 meters off the road on the right; it is inconspicuous and easy to miss. You can buy cold soft drinks and ice cream; and there are chairs and tables under simple pavilions, so you can rest in the shade. As you continue through the village, there is a dollar store on the left. This is your *last* opportunity for a long while to buy bottled water.

After Banao, the countryside gradually changes character. From relatively lush land supporting a mixture of sugar cane and horticultural crops, the rolling hills become drier and are used mainly for grazing cattle. You will often pass horsemen along the road, complete with spurs and lariats. The countryside has an austere beauty, and there are occasional glimpses of the Caribbean in the distance ahead and to the left.

39.1 Enjoy a downhill to a small bridge, and enter the *municipio* of Trinidad. Grades tend to become longer if not steeper, and at km 44, there is a particularly stunning view of the Valle de los Ingenios far ahead and below. You will gradually wend your way down to this broad valley, and the countryside changes once again. Soon you will be surrounded by seas of sugar cane, with the stacks of sugar mills here and there in the distance—all backed by mountains in the north and west. Beautiful! You will ride through several tiny villages in the valley including La Pedrera, Fidel Claro, and Caracusey, but there are no dollar stores or other services until Manaca Iznaga.

59.5 Pass a few high-rise apartment buildings on the left (worker housing) and a pulp mill on the right. Note a sign for Manaca Iznaga. You will be turning soon.

60.7 Turn right. There is a sign here for Condado and Limones Cantera. However, coming from Sancti Spiritus, there is nothing to indicate that this is also the turn to Torre de Iznaga.

61.1 Cross railroad tracks and turn right immediately, up the cobblestone lane to the restaurant and tower. You may want to walk your bike. In the parking lot, a security guard will look after it, but don't leave valuables in sight. **After visiting the tower, backtrack to the main road**.

61.6 Turn right toward Trinidad, back on the main road.

70.0 Climb a long hill with marvelous views to the right over the Valley de los Ingenios. This is an outstanding photo opportunity, especially in the lowering sunlight of late afternoon. Just 0.1 km past the crest of the hill, there is a lane on the right that climbs steeply to a *mirador* and restaurant. This *mirador* is included in Ride 13, Trinidad–Ancón Loop.

73.4 Continue straight toward Trinidad, passing a left to Casilda, Ancón, and Cienfuegos. Soon you will be riding through the outskirts of town.

75.2 Turn left in town, following another sign to Cienfuegos. (There is also a sign saying STRAIGHT AHEAD TO THE MOTEL LAS CUEVAS.) You will be riding on a street named Camilo Cienfuegos, and you will pass a historic church, Iglesia de Santa Ana, on the right.

75.7 Turn right on Maceo. There is a tiny park and a map of the historic center of Trinidad on the left at this intersection; on the right is Cafetería Punta Brava. This is the most direct route through town and on to La Boca, and it will give you a small taste of riding on Trinidad's cobblestones. Once on Maceo, you will want to turn left in a block or two if you are staying near Parque Céspedes. For Plaza Mayor, the center of the old city, continue on Maceo to Bolívar and turn right. This ride turns left on Bolívar and proceeds to La Boca.

76.3 Turn left on Bolívar. There is no street sign at Bolívar. The corner is one block after Casa Habanos, a fancy cigar store. At the corner of Bolívar, La Cremería is on the right and Restaurant Casa Mimbre is on the left.

76.8 Continue straight through the intersection with Cárdenas.

Iglesia de Santa Ana, one of Cuba's oldest churches

(Cárdenas is the most direct route out of town toward Cienfuegos.) In a few blocks you will cross railroad tracks, pass a few apartment buildings, and suddenly leave the town.

81.1 Pass a sign on the left with a large swordfish saying WELCOME TO LA BOCA.

81.3 Bear right. (The road uphill to the left is the one on which you travel when returning to Trinidad.) In a few hundred meters, the waterfront will be on your right.

82.1 Hostal Sol y Mar is on the left. You have already passed a few other *casas particulares* renting rooms, and Casa del Capitán is 0.5 km ahead on the right.

Day 5: Trinidad to Cienfuegos (83 km)

During the first half of this 83-km ride, the road parallels the coast, and the Sierra del Escambray is just to the north. There are views of the sea here and there, but the water is out of sight most of the time, and the higher mountain peaks are usually obscured by nearer, less impressive foothills.

After Guajimico, when the road turns inland, it gradually climbs into dry, rolling cattle country, and the high mountains are clearly in view. This part of the ride has a special beauty that faintly reminded us of the American West. Overall, this is not as spectacular as the similar coastal route west from Santiago de Cuba, but neither is it as difficult.

Food

There are no towns on this route, and although there are enough places to stop for a meal or a cold drink along the way, it is a good idea to carry fruit and snacks from Trinidad. About 26 km from the start there is a simple café and attractive thatched restaurant at Río Yaguanabo. This is a good place to stop for lunch if you are not too early. In the 55 km between here and Cienfuegos, there are places for cold drinks but nothing in the way of meals. Less than an hour past Río Yaguanabo, a roadside stand sells cold drinks; and on both occasions when we stopped, there was fresh-squeezed orange juice—delicious!

In another 25 km you can buy cold drinks and ice cream at a gas station with a convenience store. This will energize you for the last 15 km into Cienfuegos proper.

Lodging

Both times that we have cycled this route, we have ridden all the way to Cienfuegos without difficulty. However, if you should wish to stop for a night along the way, there are a couple of choices. The first good one is an inexpensive Islazul hotel, Villa Yaguanabo. The staff is friendly, and tourists who stayed there told us their rooms were large and clean. The drawback is that this place is only 26 km from Trinidad, so you will probably want to go farther.

About 40 km from Trinidad, you can turn off the route to Villa Guajimico. This is an upscale campismo on the sea that caters to tourists. We should mention that a couple of European cyclists told us their room was dirty and overpriced, but we have not visited the place. Its reputation is fairly good, and the folks we met may have been fussy and cheap. In any event, from Guajimico it is less than 45 km to Cienfuegos.

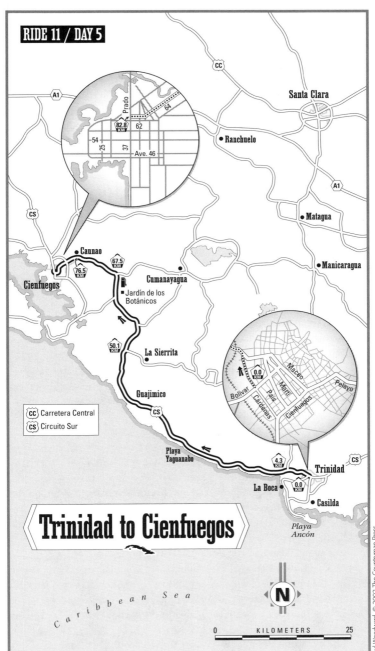

RIDE 11 / DAY 5

Santa Clara

A1

Prado

64

82.8 KM   62

54   37   Ave. 46
25

Ranchuelo

A1

CS

Matagua

Caunao

87.5 KM   Cumanayagua

76.5 KM

Cienfuegos

Jardín de los Botánicos

Manicaragua

50.1 KM   La Sierrita

Macco
Marti
País
Cárdenas   Cienfuegos   Pelayo
Bolívar

0.0 KM

Guajimico

CS

CC Carretera Central
CS Circuito Sur

Playa
Yaguanabo

4.3 KM   Trinidad

CS

0.0 KM

La Boca

Casilda

Trinidad to Cienfuegos

Playa
Ancón

Caribbean Sea

N

0   KILOMETERS   25

Paul Woodward, © 2002 The Countryman Press

Have you ever seen a statue of a shrimp?

Route Directions

0.0 This ride starts in Trinidad at the intersection of Bolívar and Cárdenas. Ride west on Cárdenas. If you have approached this intersection on Bolívar coming from La Boca, just follow the sign for Cienfuegos. Coming from the historic center of town on Bolívar, Cárdenas will be the fifth right after Maceo. Once you are out of town and on your way, stay on the main road all the way to Cienfuegos.

4.3 Continue straight past the sign and the right to Topes de Collantes. There is a 24-hour café on the left.

5.3 Start a lovely downhill to Playa Río Caña. There will be a small beach and a very basic motel on the left.

14.2 Leave Sancti Spiritus Province and enter Cienfuegos Province as you cross a bridge over Río Cabagan.

25.3 Pass an aquaculture facility and a shrimp research station on the left. How often have you seen a statue of a giant shrimp?

26.0 Cross Río Yaguanabo. After the bridge is Villa Yaguanabo. There is a cafeteria and a handsome dining room overlooking the sea.

39.4 A small bar and sandwich place is on the left.

40.5 The entrance to Villa Guajimico on the left is marked by a statue of an Indian. Grades will become more pronounced from here to Cienfuegos, but they are never really difficult. And from about km 45 to Cienfuegos, there are views of the higher peaks of the Sierra del Escambray to the right.

50.1 Continue straight past a right to La Sierrita. There is no sign, but

Horseman on a road to Cienfuegos

the junction is unmistakable because there is a small memorial here to Rafael Lay Apestequia, a distinguished orchestra conductor who died on this spot in the 1980s. You are now riding through cattle country—the mountains to the north are the backdrop for rolling grasslands where cattle graze, and you may see almost as many men on horseback as you do cars and trucks. (The road to La Sierrita looks excellent here. It appears on the map that this road could be used for a great loop back to Trinidad via Topes de Collantes. However, if you are thinking of trying it, please read the sidebar "The Road Not Taken" on page 192.

55.8 Continue straight to Cienfuegos through an unmarked intersection.

63.3 Continue straight at the top of a long hill, but first stop to enjoy the view. (The road to the left goes to Pasacaballo.)

65.7 Pass the entrance to Jardín de los Botánicos de Cienfuegos on the right.

67.5 Turn left at a T-intersection. There is a Cupet service center with cold drinks and ice cream. (The right goes to Cumanayagua.)

67.7 Stay left, then continue straight through an intersection. (To the right is the entrance to a cement factory.)

76.5 Bear left, and then ride straight through the town of Caunao. There is a small dollar kiosk on the left in town. The road will become increasingly busy as you ride into the outskirts of Cienfuegos.

Downtown Cienfuegos

79.6 Continue straight through a busy intersection with a traffic blinker. There are signs indicating a right to Havana and straight ahead to Ciudad—the city of Cienfuegos.

81.6 Continue straight, following the sign to Ciudad. There is another sign for a right to Havana.

82.5 Follow the main road as it bears right and becomes one-way. Pass a small park on the left.

82.8 **Reach the intersection with the Prado.** This intersection is preceded by signs indicating that Jagua is to the left and Havana is to the right. The Prado is a busy boulevard. If you are headed to Punta Gorda, turn left here, following the sign to Jagua. Notice that on the Prado, cyclists ride on the left, nearest the median.

⑫ Santa Clara to Trinidad Over the Sierra del Escambray

144 km, 2 or 3 days

This is a great ride if you enjoy the challenges of climbing. The Sierra del Escambray is the second highest and most rugged chain of mountains in

Cuba. The route we use is paved all the way so a mountain bike is not required, but don't try it without low gears!

It is 73 km from Santa Clara to Topes de Collantes, a small mountain resort with accommodations, and only 22 km farther to Trinidad. Many cyclists—including us, when we are in shape—think nothing of a 95-km ride. However, only the strongest cyclists should consider riding from Santa Clara to Trinidad in one day. For the rest of us, we give directions for a two-day route, including a detour and overnight stay at a scenic lake in the foothills of the mountains. A second overnight stop at Topes de Collantes would turn this into a three-day ride.

Day 1: Santa Clara to Hanabanilla (54 km)

Hanabanilla is a long lake, actually a reservoir *(embalse)* that snakes among the hills south of Santa Clara almost like a river. It is a popular spot for boating and fishing. You may be interested in riding to Hanabanilla as an overnight outing and then returning to Santa Clara, or you can take the challenge of cycling over the Sierra del Escambray to Trinidad.

Between Santa Clara and Manicaragua, you will ride through rolling, gradually rising cattle country toward the distant wall of mountains. This section of the ride has a few long, moderately difficult climbs. From Manicaragua the route turns west and becomes relatively flat and easy for about 12 km. When you turn south again, on the last leg of the ride to Hanabanilla, you will work hard. Some of the hills, especially near the end, are challenging.

We rode to Hanabanilla intending to take a boat from the north end of the lake to the landing near Jibacoa. We ended up not using a boat because it would have broken our budget. You may want to try it, however, especially if you are with friends who can share the expense. In late 2001 the public relations office at Hotel Hanabanilla would arrange a small speedboat and driver to carry two cyclists for $40, or a larger launch that would accommodate a small group for $60.

There was also a small, slow, early morning ferry that would have taken us to Jibacoa for *pesos,* but when the pilot saw our bulky bikes, he waved us off. On another morning, you might be allowed on board, but the ferry goes all the way to Jibacoa only a couple of days each week. The location of the ferry landing is noted in the directions.

In any event, if you do not take a boat down the lake, you can cycle back to Manicaragua as we did and then continue south over the mountains. This is a difficult ride, but it is one of the most spectacular in Cuba.

Food

As always, it is a good idea to carry snacks. It is possible to leave Santa Clara early and arrive at Hanabanilla in time for a late lunch, but you will probably want to eat something in Manicaragua, almost halfway to Hanabanilla. Bottled water, drinks, and snacks including street pizza are available in Manicaragua. *Guarapo* is also sold at a stand in front of a house as you ride into town. It should also be possible to buy snacks in La Moza and Ciro Redondo, but these places are such a short, easy ride past Manicaragua that we have not bothered.

Lodging

There is a *peso* hotel in Manicaragua, but it might not admit foreigners, and you might not enjoy staying there. As far as we know there are no licensed *casas particulares* along the route. The logical option, therefore, is the Hotel Hanabanilla, a big, slightly run-down Islazul property perched on a bluff above the lake. Although the rooms are Spartan, they are clean enough, and many have small balconies with lovely views. The hotel is lively and popular with Cubans who come for fishing holidays, and some Canadian and Italian groups stay there as well.

Route Directions

0.0 Start at Parque Vidal, on the corner in front of Hotel Santa Clara Libre. Ride south on Cuba.

0.7 Continue straight across the Carretera Central. There is a traffic light at this busy intersection. Soon Cuba changes its name to 7 de Diciembre.

2.2 Turn right just before a small, triangular park on the left. **Then, in another 50 meters, turn left**. You are now on the road to Manicaragua. (Note: If you miss this turn, 7 de Diciembre will end at a curb and a sidewalk. Simply walk your bike across the sidewalk to the busy road immediately ahead and turn left.)

2.4 Proceed straight across the Circunvalación. (Take care and wait for the traffic light; the Circunvalación is six lanes wide at this point.)

9.8 Enter the *municipio* of Manicaragua.

10.3 Stay to the right. A paved road veering off to the left is an unmarked exit from the Autopista. Don't ride up it! In about 200 meters you will cross a bridge over the Autopista.

14.1 Ride through the tiny town of Ceibaba.

18.6 Continue straight, passing a right to Cardoso, La YaYa, and Jorabada.

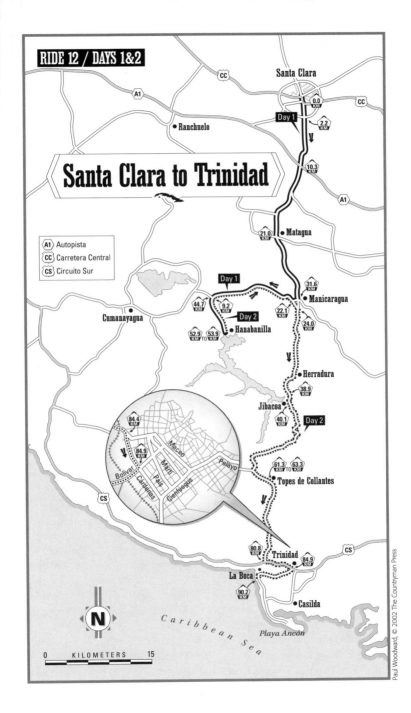

RIDE 12 / DAYS 1&2

Santa Clara

Day 1
0.0 KM
2.2 KM

• Ranchuelo

10.3 KM

A1

Santa Clara to Trinidad

21.0 KM • Matagua

A1 Autopista
CC Carretera Central
CS Circuito Sur

31.6 KM • Manicaragua

Day 1

44.7 KM 9.2 KM
Day 2 22.1 KM

Cumanayagua 52.9 KM TO 53.9 KM • Hanabanilla 24.0 KM

Herradura

38.9 KM

Jibacoa

40.1 KM Day 2

84.4 KM

84.9 KM Maceo Pelayo

Bolivar Marti Pais Cardenas Cienfuegos

61.3 KM TO 63.3 KM
• Topes de Collantes

CS

80.8 KM • Trinidad CS

84.9 KM

La Boca •

90.2 KM

• Casilda

N

C a r i b b e a n   S e a

Playa Ancón

0 KILOMETERS 15

Church in Manicaragua

21.0 Pass through Matagua. The Sierra del Escambray, a wall of mountains in the distance, looks more formidable as you approach. You will be riding into treeless foothills with several climbs, sometimes long but not terribly steep.

31.6 Turn right in Manicaragua, following a sign to Hotel Hanabanilla. There is a dollar store on the left just before this turn, and a white church on the right shortly after you have made the turn.

32.3 Continue straight just over the top of a hill, but notice a signed left to Jibacoa. If you cycle from Hanabanilla to Topes de Collantes and Trinidad tomorrow, you will make this turn at km 22.1. In the next 12 km, the road passes through a series of small towns. La Moza, at about km 38, is the biggest.

42.5 Enter the town of Ciro Redondo. There are tall apartment blocks to the left in an otherwise rural area, and also an explosives factory. To reach Hanabanilla, you must turn left in about 2 km; but when we toured in late 2001, there was no sign at the turn. Shortly beyond Ciro Redondo, there is a smaller village (Campaña) that is not on the *Guía de Carreteras,* and it is less than 2 km before the turn.

44.7 Turn left on a well-paved road; this road is at the top of a small hill. Immediately after turning left, you will climb another short, steep hill. From here to Hanabanilla there will be several longer climbs, the most difficult of which is near the end.

52.4 Continue straight, passing a turn on the right for Hidroeléctrica Hanabanilla. The dam is just above on the right. You have been climbing a fairly steep hill, and it will get even steeper.

52.9 The lake is now below you. **Bear right** and ride across the top of the dam. (If you bear left instead of crossing the dam, the ferry landing will be ahead on the right. There is only a set of rough steps down the steep bank to the lake; you will have to ask locals in the area if the ferry is running and when it will depart. When we were there, the ferry left at 7 AM sharp, but as noted, we were not allowed on board with our bikes.)

53.9 The road ends at Hotel Hanabanilla.

Day 2: Hanabanilla to Topes de Collantes or Trinidad (64 or 85 km)

This is a difficult but rewarding ride through the Sierra del Escambray to the south coast of Cuba. Beyond Jibacoa, the road climbs for many kilometers among precipitous, pine-covered slopes, eventually reaching the cool mountaintops. The end of the ride is even more spectacular as you rush down the south slope of the Sierra del Escambray toward the Caribbean far below.

There are a couple of variations that could shorten this challenging day. If you take a boat down the lake from Hanabanilla to Jibacoa, you will skip 19 km of cycling and avoid one long, difficult hill. Don't worry, you won't have missed all the fun; the killer climbs are after Jibacoa.

Also, you may opt to spend a night at Topes de Collantes, about 20 km short of Trinidad. This is a small resort high in the mountains, noted for hiking trails and waterfalls.

Food

If you do the whole route by bike, as we did, the first practical food stop is in Manicaragua, where we bought filling street pizzas (for breakfast!). *Guarapo*

Barely getting started up the hills to Topes de Collantes

was also on sale for *pesos* near the center of town. (Food may be available sooner in La Moza, but you will probably breeze right through.)

In Jibacoa there is a small dollar kiosk with little more than water and soft drinks. There are also a couple of cafeterias along the route, which are noted in the directions. La Cañada, a small cafeteria 35 km from Hanabanilla, looked nice, but it will probably be closed if you ride through before lunch as we did.

Meals are available at both hotels in Topes de Collantes. On the way out of the mountains, cold drinks are sold at the *mirador* snack bar, km 64, and again when you reach the coast road at km 80.

Lodging

We have not spent a night in Topes de Collantes; we like Trinidad and La Boca so much that we were eager to get there. However, there are two hotels that welcome tourists. The massive Kurhotel is so ugly that we would not want to stay there despite the fabulous setting. Hotel Los Helechos is smaller and more attractive. Refer to any general guidebook for details.

When you are deciding whether to stop for the night in Topes de Collantes or continue to Trinidad, keep in mind that there is still more climbing ahead. Yes, it is downhill for a while from Topes de Collantes, but the road climbs over a few more difficult hills before its final plunge to the coast.

Route Directions

0.0 Leave Hotel Hanabanilla, and backtrack to Manicaragua. The ride will be downhill almost all the way to the Manicaragua road.

9.2 Bear right at the Y-intersection and merge with the Manicaragua road. You will ride through Campaña, Ciro Redondo, and La Moza.

22.1 Turn right, following the sign to Jibacoa. (If you need to buy bottled water, visit a dollar store, or find a street pizza, you may wish to continue straight for about 0.7 km to the center of Manicaragua, then backtrack to this point and turn left, adding about 1.4 km to subsequent distances.)

24.0 Turn right at a T-intersection.

27.2 A sign warns of PENDIENTES Y CURVAS PELIGROSAS (steep grades and dangerous curves). There is a climb just ahead, but it is gentle for a kilometer or more. Then it gets much steeper and more difficult until km 32.

32.5 Start downhill.

33.1 In the tiny village of Herradura, there is a small restaurant on the right—not open when we passed through in the morning. From here, the road will wind and dip through small valleys with rugged hills all around. It is a lovely area, but the road surface is rough at times.

34.9 An attractive brick cafeteria, La Cañada, is on the left. It was closed when we passed through, but it looks like the sort of place that might be patronized by bus tours. In less than 2 km, you may notice coffee bushes along the sides of the road.

36.7 Stay left, following the main road.

38.8 Signs indicate a left up ahead to Ancón Naranjo and Pico Blanco. A coffee factory is on the left, where beans are dried in the sun, then soaked to remove the dried hulls before further drying and roasting.

38.9 Bear right at the Y-intersection immediately after the coffee factory.

40.1 Turn left following the sign to Topes de Collantes and Trinidad. Shortly after making the turn, you will pass beneath overhead signs for Topes de Collantes and Trinidad. Then you will ride through the center of Jibacoa, a small, attractive town. (Another sign at this intersection, shortly before the left, says straight to Presa Jibacoa, Manantiales, and Guanayara. If you took a boat from Hanabanilla down the lake, you would cycle up this road and turn right to go through Jibacoa and on to Topes de Collantes and Trinidad.)

40.5 In Jibacoa there is a dollar kiosk on the left with water and cold drinks. Past Jibacoa, the ride continues to be easy and pleasant as the road rises and dips through small valleys.

45.0 Cross a small bridge and enter Sancti Spiritus Province. A sign on the left warns of hills to come. Soon climbing will begin with few interruptions for about 7 km. Though this is certainly a long climb, it is neither steep nor terribly difficult.

54.1 Pass a steel *mirador* on the right. There is a good view, but some of the structure is badly rusted, so if you climb up, be careful where you step. Now there will be a little more climbing, a short, pleasant downhill, and some rolling terrain.

55.5 A sign warns of a dangerous downhill. While it is not terribly steep, the road is rough with occasional potholes, so use caution—and your brakes.

58.8 Cross a small bridge and begin climbing again. In a few hundred meters, the road surface changes from asphalt to concrete. This is not a good sign—concrete indicates a particularly difficult grade. In fact, for a few hundred meters, the climb will be horrifically steep, perhaps 14 percent or more. Then the surface changes back to asphalt, and the climb is merely very steep.

60.5 Continue straight, passing a right turn into Parque Nacional Guanayara. The climbing will be extremely steep again for a while. (The road on the right is dirt, and quite rough. It goes all the way to La Sierrita.)

61.4 Reach the top of an extremely steep section—hard to believe it was less than 1 km! You are now approaching Topes de Collantes, and the huge, ugly Kurhotel is occasionally visible ahead.

63.1 Near the bottom of a downhill, there is a sign indicating a right to Trinidad. We turned here, obediently following the sign, but you *should not!* The concrete pavement of this road is in reasonably good shape, but it involves a short hill that is even steeper and more difficult than the hardest ones on the route so far. Instead of turning, continue straight toward the Kurhotel.

63.3 Turn right before the steep entrance to the hotel. This is the road that is normally used by vehicles bound for Trinidad. Hotel Los Helechos is down this road on the left. After Topes de Collantes, you might expect that the rest of the ride to Trinidad would be easy, mostly downhill. Not so! There is a climb to km 69.1, some of it difficult, followed by a short, fabulous, fast downhill, and another difficult climb that continues for a few kilometers with only one brief respite.

69.3 Watch for a *mirador* and snack bar on the right. Many tourist buses stop here, and there is an extraordinary view over the distant Caribbean below. *Very* cold drinks are available. From the *mirador* there is a downhill of more than 7 km. It is like descending in an airplane, and you should stop along the way to enjoy the view.

Coffee dries in the sun

80.8 Turn left onto the coast road between Trinidad and Cienfuegos. There is a 24-hour café at the intersection.

82.2 Pass a monument on the right to Alberto Delgado—an undercover agent of the Castro regime who was a martyr in the struggle against counterrevolutionary bandits in the Sierra del Escambray.

83.0 The entrance to Finca Recreo María Dolores is on the right. We were told that a new hotel is planned for this recreation area. Soon, on the left just before a bridge, there is a dirt road entering Parque el Cubano. There is a waterfall here, and horseback rides are available at Finca Recreo María Dolores. Rides can be booked through all the tourist hotels in the area.

83.7 Pass a striking display on the left that welcomes you to Trinidad de Cuba, Patrimonio de la Humanidad.

84.4 Bear right. The Celia Sánchez Policlinic is on the left, and there is a long mural of the city just ahead. **Then, almost immediately bear right again at a Y-intersection**, passing a small park on the left. You are on Cárdenas. (If you bear left at either of these points instead of right, you will enter the historic part of Trinidad via a tangle of narrow, rough cobblestone streets that always seem to be one-way in the wrong direction. They are great for strolling, but they are dreadful on a bicycle, and you will almost certainly get lost to boot.)

Welcome to Trinidad, a World Heritage Site.

84.9 Stop at the intersection of Cárdenas and Bolívar. There are signs just before this intersection indicating a left to the Centro Histórico, a right to La Boca, and straight to Sancti Spiritus. **If you are going to the historic center of Trinidad, turn left on Bolívar**; it goes straight to Plaza Mayor. **To continue to La Boca or to the hotels at Ancón, turn right on Bolívar.** After a few blocks, you will cross railroad tracks, pass apartment buildings and a dollar kiosk on the right, and quite suddenly you will have left Trinidad.

89.2 Pass a sign on the left with a large swordfish saying BIENVENIDOS A LA BOCA.

89.4 Bear right. (The road uphill to the left is the one on which you will travel when returning to Trinidad.) For the next couple hundred kilometers, La Boca is not terribly inviting. Soon, however, the waterfront will be on your right.

90.2 Hostal Sol y Mar, one of our favorite *casas* in Cuba, is on the left. You have already passed several other good ones, and Casa del Capitán is less than 0.5 km past Hostal Sol y Mar, on the right.

⑬ Trinidad–Ancón Loop

37 or 57 km, 1 day

This day trip takes you first to a *mirador* with a panoramic view of the Valle de los Ingenios. If you have not ridden through the valley and visited Torre de Iznaga, it is worth doing so as part of this ride. (A detour is described at the end of the route directions that adds about 20 km to the basic loop.) Then the route continues to the beautiful, white beach at Ancón. It returns along the austere, rocky coast near La Boca, with views across the water of the Sierra del Escambray, truly spectacular in the warm light of late afternoon.

Food

There is no shortage of places to stop for food and drinks. There is a restaurant at the *mirador* and another at Torre de Iznaga. There are a couple of pleasant outdoor cafés serving lunch right on the beach at Ancón. In La Boca, there is a bar and restaurant on the waterfront and a dollar kiosk where you can buy bottled water or a cold drink.

Route Directions

0.0 Begin the ride on Calle Martí at Parque Céspedes. Ride on Martí (it is one-way) one long block past the park.

0.1 Turn left on Cienfuegos—a block after Parque Céspedes—following the sign for Sancti Spiritus.

0.7 Pass Iglesia Santa Ana on the left, near the top of a hill.

0.8 Turn right, after you pass the church, onto Fausto Pelayo. This will become the road to Sancti Spiritus.

2.5 Go straight, following the sign for Sancti Spiritus. In a few more meters you will pass the sign for leaving Trinidad. (There is a right for Playa Ancón and Casilda. You will be turning here on the return ride.)

3.2 Follow the main road as it curves to the left. (The right goes to an asphalt plant.)

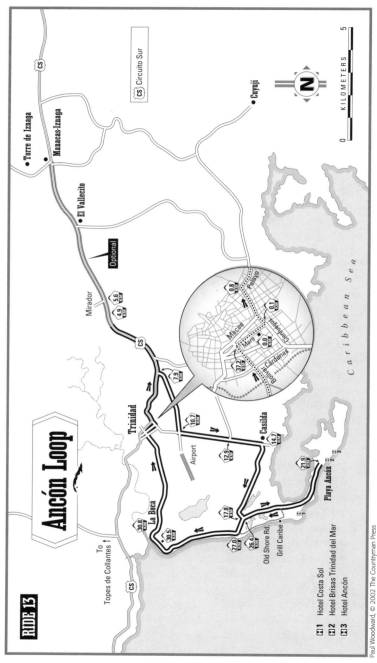

Ancón Loop

RIDE 13

To
Topes de Collantes ↑

Trinidad

Mirador

Torre de Iznaga
Manacas·Iznaga

El Vallecito

Optional

Cuyují

CS Circuito Sur

Caribbean Sea

Airport

La Boca

30.8
KM/H

30.5
KM/H

27.0
KM/H

26.4
KM/H

Old Shore Rd.

Grill Caribe

17.8
KM/H

12.9
KM/H

10.7
KM/H

7.9
KM/H

4.9
KM/H

5.6
KM/H

Casilda

14.7
KM/H

21.9
KM/H

Playa Ancón

Pelayo

0.8
KM/H

0.1
KM/H

0.0
KM/H

Macao

Martí

Cienfuegos

Cárdenas

Bolívar

37.2
KM/H

H1 Hotel Costa Sol
H2 Hotel Brisas Trinidad del Mar
H3 Hotel Ancón

N

0   KILOMETERS   5

Paul Woodward, © 2002 The Countryman Press

The sugary beach at Ancón

4.9 Turn left to visit the *mirador* and enjoy views of Valle de los Ingenios. This turn is near the top of a moderate hill. The roughly paved road up to the *mirador* is steep—for a few meters, *extremely* steep. If you want to climb the hardest part, bear left at the entrance to the parking area and try to make it all the way to the top! At the *mirador* there is a bar and restaurant. A few gifts and crafts are sold, and a potter and a painter are sometimes at work. After visiting the *mirador,* ride back down to the main road.

5.6 Turn right on the main road, back toward Trinidad. Or, if you have not ridden through the Valle de los Ingenios or visited Torre de Iznaga, this is the time to do it. Take the detour described at the end of the route directions.

7.2 Follow the main road as it curves to the right. (The left goes to the asphalt plant.)

7.9 Turn left, following the sign to Casilda and Playa Ancón. (This is the road you passed at km 3.3.)

10.7 Turn left at a major intersection, following the sign to Playa Ancón. There is a Cupet gas station on the right at this turn.

12.9 Bear right, following signs to Ancón and Hotel Costa Sur.

14.7 Bear right, passing a turn to the left. (You may be tempted to turn here because you can see the main Ancón hotels off to the left. However this turn goes only to the small port, which is closed to the public.) The road you stay on curves to the right, seeming to go in the wrong direction, away from the main beach and the hotels at Ancón. In fact, it is

New Hotel Brisas Trinidad del Mar at Ancón.

going in the wrong direction, but in 3 km you will be able to turn left along the shore.

17.8 Turn left, following the sign to Ancón. (The road straight ahead goes to La Boca; you will take it on the last part of the ride.)

18.8 The Grill Caribe is to the right on the old shore road, about 30 meters up a well-used dirt crossing.

19.1 A Cubanacán café is on the right on the old shore road, just like the Grill Caribe. (If you visit either of these places for lunch, return to the road on which you were traveling and turn right. Do not take the old shore

The Road Not Taken

We had planned to use the road through Parque Nacional Guanayara and La Sierrita as part of a great loop ride. Our idea was to ride west from Trinidad along the south shore, then east through La Sierrita to Topes de Collantes and back to Trinidad. We met Belgian cyclists who intended to do the very same thing. It looks great on a map!

However, when we arrived at this junction with the road from La Sierrita, two Dutch couples in a brand new Audi needed help pushing their car up onto the paved road. The car was covered with dirt and had overheated several times. They said the road to La Sierrita was unpaved, very rough, and steep for many kilometers. In fact, they insisted that the road should not be used by wheeled vehicles of any sort!

In fact, this road might be a good challenge for intrepid mountain bikers . If you want to try it, start from the end near Topes de Collantes so that the ride will be more downhill than up.

The waterfront at La Boca, hit hard by a hurricane in 2001

road; in late 2001, it ended in the midst of new hotel construction that was barely underway.)

21.9 Turn right for a convenient access point to the beach. Ride a couple of hundred meters to a small parking lot, then push your bike to one of the conveniently located palm trees just a few meters from the water. This turn comes about 200 meters before the entrance to the new Hotel Brisas Trinidad del Mar. The older, high-rise Hotel Ancón is a bit farther, and the road ends at a Puerto Sol marina, where visiting yachts tie up and big sailboats and motor yachts can be chartered.)

22.3 Return to the main road and turn left after enjoying your time at the beach.

26.4 Turn left toward La Boca. (This is where you were at km 18.6.)

27.0 Bear right at the small, thatched bar. From there, the road will follow the shore, which is rough pitted limestone. The view of the mountains ahead is especially wonderful just before sunset.

29.8 Pass Casa del Capitán on the left. In a few more meters, you will see the sign for La Boca.

30.3 Pass Ranchón Playa La Boca on the left. This is a waterfront bar and restaurant run by Islazul.

30.5 Hostal Sol y Mar is on the right. If you are going back to Trinidad, continue straight for a few hundred meters.

30.8 Bear right; then bear right again at the bottom of the hill. You will be on the main road from La Boca to Trinidad.

31.5 Pass the sign on your right with a large swordfish saying BIEN-VENIDOS A LA BOCA. Continue straight to Trinidad.

36.5 Pass a dollar kiosk and an apartment block on the left. Almost immediately you will cross railroad tracks and enter the city proper, riding along busy, narrow Bolívar.

36.8 Cross Cárdenas.

37.2 Turn right on Martí and return to Parque Céspedes at km 37.7.

Detour to Torre de Iznaga

5.6 Turn left at the T-intersection toward Sancti Spiritus instead of right toward Trinidad. In less than 100 meters, you will start a fast, 1-km downhill with more great views of the Valle de los Ingenios. Watch for a pullout on the left for a photo; in some ways, the view is more photogenic from this point than from the much higher *mirador.*

15.0 Turn left, following a sign to Torre de Iznaga. This road also goes to Condado and Limones Cantera.

15.4 Cross railroad tracks and turn right up the cobblestone lane to the tower. (This is km 61.1 on Day 4 of Ride 11, Sancti Spiritus to Trinidad or La Boca.) After visiting the tower, retrace your steps—back down the cobblestone lane, left over the railroad tracks, and right onto the Sancti Spiritus—Trinidad road.

25.4 Reach the top of the long hill out of the Valle de los Ingenios, and pass the entrance on the right to the *mirador.* You are back at km 5.6 of the loop.

⑭ Cienfuegos to Playa Girón

89 km, 1 day

Playa Girón is a long but easy 89-km ride from Cienfuegos. The quiet beach was the principal landing site in the 1961 Bay of Pigs invasion by U.S.-backed Cuban exiles. Over 160 loyal Cubans died repelling the invasion, most of them teenaged military cadets who arrived before the regular army troops. About 1,100 of the invaders were captured. Cubans take pride in their costly success and call it the Victory at Girón.

Today, Playa Girón is promoted as a resort, but the nice beach is enclosed by a long sea wall that obstructs the view. It was built for defense after the invasion, but we don't quite see the point because there are plen-

"The first great defeat of Imperialism in Latin America."

ty of landing places beyond the wall, if the Miami exiles were ever foolish enough to try again. At least the wall is good for walking at sunset or sitting and fishing.

Although the beach is rather disappointing, there is a fine museum at Playa Girón. It pays tribute to the young fighters who scored, as the billboards say, THE FIRST GREAT DEFEAT OF IMPERIALISM IN LATIN AMERICA.

We have speculated about riding from Playa Girón back to Cienfuegos via the coast road that is shown on some maps. We asked about it and rode the first dozen kilometers. Shortly after Caleta Buena, the road turns to dirt with drifts of sand. It should be passable by mountain bike—country buses crash some of the way along it—but locals advise against trying it. If you are returning to Cienfuegos, it is easy enough to backtrack.

Food

The best stop for food and water along the way is in the attractive little town of Abreus, about 24 km into the ride. You can also buy water and snacks at Yaguaramas and Horquitas.

In Playa Girón, there is a dollar store on the road to the hotel across from the museum, and a dollar kiosk in front of Casa Silvia. If you go straight at the crossroad in the village instead of turning right toward Playa Larga, you will find a Rumbos snack bar with sandwiches, chicken, fries, and cold drinks. There are meals at the hotel, of course, but they were overpriced when we were there. Your best bet for dinner is a *casa particular.*

Lodging

In Playa Girón we have stayed at the tourist hotel, Villa Horizontes Playa Girón, but we much prefer an excellent *casa particular* nearby, Casa Silvia. Silvia Acosta, her daughter, and other family members house you in comfort and provide good meals. If the guest room is occupied, you can count on Silvia to find you another good place in town. She often coordinates accommodations in Playa Girón for bicycle tours run by the International Bicycle Fund. Sylvia's house, distinctive because of the thousands of seashells inlaid on arches and walls, is a few hundred meters north of Girón center on the road from Yaguaramas and Cienfuegos. Her telephone number is 59-4249.

Route Directions

0.0 The first 2.6 km of this route are identical to Day 1 of Ride 11, Cienfuegos to Santa Clara. Start at the Prado (Calle 37) and Avenida 54, and ride north on the Prado, away from Punta Gorda. Remember to ride in the left lane.

0.9 The cycle lane switches to the right.

1.9 Leave the cycle path and continue straight on the main road. (There is a sign indicating that the cycle path turns right toward Pastoria; this is a neighborhood that is off the route.)

2.2 Continue straight through a major intersection with the Circunvalación.

2.6 Take the exit for the Autopista and Havana. You will be on the road to Rodas. In fact, the Autopista is many kilometers away, beyond Rodas, and you will turn onto quiet back roads long before you reach it.

10.3 Pass a prison on the right.

15.0 In the small town of Ariza, there is a Tiendas Panamericanas dollar store on the left.

17.7 Be on the lookout for a Methodist temple on the right, followed in a few hundred meters by a yellow Catholic church, Ave María, also on the right. You will be turning left 0.8 km after the Catholic church.

18.8 Turn left—this is the road to Abreus.

22.3 Turn right following the main road. There is a water treatment plant on the left before this turn.

24.4 Cross a bridge over a small, pretty river. You will soon be in Abreus. As you enter Abreus, the roadside is decorated with shrubs and flower beds lined with whitewashed stones. Abreus seems to show more civic pride than many other towns of similar size.

26.2 As you ride through town, the road turns into a pleasant boulevard with benches, flowers, and a small pavilion. On side streets to the right and

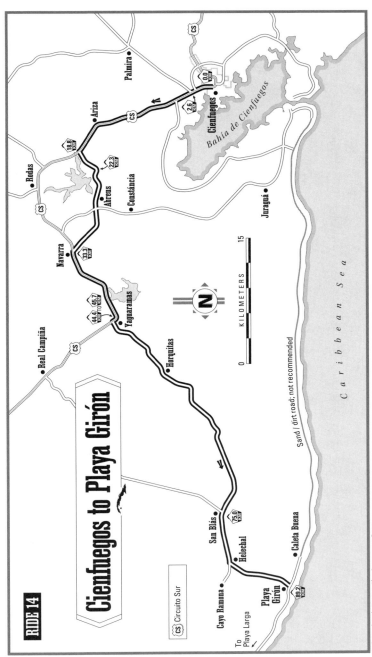

RIDE 14

Cienfuegos to Playa Girón

CS Circuito Sur

Paul Woodward, © 2002 The Countryman Press

Casa Silvia is decorated with tens of thousands of seashells.

left of the pavilion, there are dollar stores and vendors selling snacks—even peso ice cream, not Coppelia, but sweet and cold.

26.8 Continue straight, passing a left to Juragua.

33.3 Turn left at a T-intersection toward Yaguaramas. The right goes to Rodas.

41.2 Cross a small bridge over a reservoir. You may see herons and waterfowl in the wetlands on both sides of the road.

44.4 Turn left into the town of Yaguaramas. There are large, conspicuous electrical transformers just before this turn. From here, follow the route directions carefully; they will help you weave through the town and find your way onto the road to Horquitas and Playa Girón.

45. 2 Cross a set of railroad tracks and then turn left.

45.3 Turn right at a three-way intersection. You will immediately pass a large radio transmission tower on the right; this is the center of town, such as it is.

45.6 Follow the pavement to the left; the road straight ahead is dirt.

45.7 Bear right, passing a small monument on the left. You are now leaving Yaguaramas.

54.8 In the busy agricultural village of Horquitas, there is a dollar kiosk on the left, and street food as well. After Horquitas, you will ride through a highly productive farming area, with long, rolling irrigation booms at work in the dry season. At different times of year we have noticed beans, rice, corn, *malanga,* yuca, papaya, bananas, sugar cane, and other crops that we didn't recognize, as well as cattle and goats. In a few kilometers the irrigation ends and the land becomes, first, dry grazing land, and then gradually, scrub that is uninhabited by man or beast. The next 10 to 15 km are flat, one of the loneliest stretches of road that we have ridden in central Cuba.

75.0 Bear left at San Blas toward Playa Girón.

81.3 Continue straight, passing a right turn to Cayo Ramona.

89.2 Arrive at the crossroad in the center of Playa Girón. Casa Silvia is on the right a few hundred meters before this crossroad. There are more *casas particulares* on a side street to the right, as well as one on the main road just past Silvia's. For the hotel, turn right at the crossroad; this road leads to Playa Larga and on to Matanzas. In a few hundred meters, turn left onto paved road that goes past the museum and shops to the hotel. Backtrack to return to Cienfuegos.

Part IV:
The Oriente

Cuba's Oriente is a region of stunning diversity and stark contrasts. There are tropical beaches on the north shore of Holguín province, while due south in Granma and Santiago de Cuba provinces, Cuba's mightiest chain of mountains, the Sierra Maestra, looms over the coast. Far to the east is Baracoa, Cuba's oldest city, and some maintain, its most beautiful. Baracoa is also Cuba's rainiest city; but less than 60 km over La Farola, a precipitous mountain highway, cacti grow on the Caribbean shore in the hottest and driest part of the country. Santiago de Cuba, the second largest city in Cuba, is the heart of the region, a heart that throbs to the beat of Cuba's best traditional music.

The Oriente is also where the most dramatic episodes in Cuban history occurred. It was in Bayamo, the quiet capital of Granma Province, that Carlos Manuel de Céspedes first declared rebellion against Spain. Antonio Maceo and José Martí landed in Guantánamo Province to launch the second phase of Cuba's 19th-century independence struggle, which ended with the battle at San Juan Hill and the surrender of Spanish forces in Santiago de Cuba. It was also in Santiago de Cuba, in 1953, that Fidel Castro launched the first strike in the 20th-century revolution. Granma Province is named after a small, overloaded yacht that landed here three years later, with Castro and his comrades aboard to begin the two-year war that ended in defeat of General Fulgencio Batista's dictatorship. The Sierra Maestra was

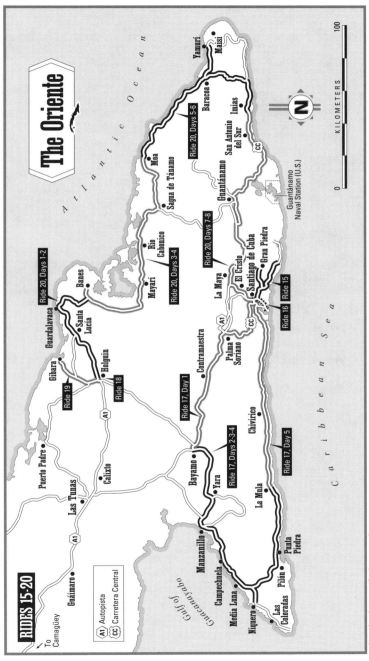

RIDES 15-20

The Oriente

To Camagüey

Autopista A1
Carretera Central CC

Guáimaro

Puerto Padre

Las Tunas

Calixto

Ride 20, Days 1-2

Santa Lucía

Banes

Guardalavaca

Gibara

Holguín

Ride 19

Ride 18

A1

Ride 17, Day 1

Atlantic Ocean

Mayarí

Río Cabonico

Ride 20, Days 3-4

Sagua de Tánamo

Moa

Ride 20, Days 5-6

Baracoa

Yamurí

Maisí

N

Imías

San Antonio del Sur

Guantánamo

CC

Ride 20, Days 7-8

La Maya

El Cristo

Santiago de Cuba

Gran Piedra

Ride 15

Ride 16

A1

Contramaestre

Palma Soriano

CC

Bayamo

Yara

Ride 17, Days 2-3-4

Chivirico

Ride 17, Day 5

La Mula

Manzanillo

Campechuela

Media Luna

Niquero

Las Coloradas

Pilón

Punta Piedra

Golfo de Guacanayabo

Caribbean Sea

Guantánamo Naval Station (U.S.)

KILOMETERS
0   100

Paul Woodward, © 2002 The Countryman Press

The second War of Independence. "They left us a beautiful flag of unity."

the first and most important stronghold of rebel forces, and Castro delivered his victory address in Santiago de Cuba.

The Oriente offers the longest and most challenging cycle tours in this book. This section in the Oriente is divided into two parts. The first describes a multi-day 500-km loop that begins and ends in Santiago de Cuba. The loop passes through Bayamo, continues to Niquero, a town near the site of the Granma's landing, and then returns along the south coast of Granma and Santiago de Cuba provinces over what is arguably the most beautiful road for cycling in all of Cuba. This route is not easy, but it is immensely rewarding, surely one of the best tours in the country. A superb one-day outing from Santiago de Cuba is also described in detail, and other short rides are suggested. You may want to try one or more of them before setting out on the loop, especially if you need to acclimatize.

The second part of this section covers a 500-km tour from Holguín city to the lovely beaches of the north coast, on to Banes, Moa, and Baracoa, then over La Farola to the austerely beautiful coast of Guantánamo province, and finally to Guantánamo City and Santiago de Cuba. By continuing to Bayamo and then north to Holguín, it is possible to turn this route into a 700-km loop. The first couple of days from Holguín are great for any cyclist, but the complete tour is only for the experienced and determined. Short, easy outings from Holguín and Baracoa are included as well.

Santiago de Cuba

Santiago de Cuba is called the Heroic City. This is not mere local puffery; Fidel Castro officially gave the city this designation in 1984, the only place in Cuba to be so honored. Santiago has been a center of resistance in all of Cuba's independence struggles. The city's motto is REBELLIOUS YESTERDAY, HOSPITABLE TODAY, HEROIC ALWAYS. You can gain a sense of the revolutionary heritage by riding from Santiago to Siboney.

In Santiago de Cuba, the cultures of Africa and Europe have created a darker, richer brew than anywhere else in Cuba. For example, most of the great musicians in the Buena Vista Social Club came from the Oriente, and Santiago's Casa de la Trova is Cuba's most famous venue for traditional music. There are many museums and art galleries, some magnificent architecture, and a picturesque, if tattered, Colonial core. The atmosphere is bustling but relaxed, and people are friendly. They are proud of their city and its heritage, and they do not, in general, care for Havana.

Santiago de Cuba lies on the shores of a huge bay nearly surrounded by mountains. While the natural setting is beautiful, it is a bowl that catches and holds exhaust and pollution from the city's motor vehicles and industry. The streets are often narrow and always busy. To thoroughly enjoy cycling in the city, you must develop a taste for danger and diesel fumes. Well, perhaps it's not that bad. We love Santiago de Cuba and recommend that you visit if you possibly can. If Santiago itself is not a great place for cycling, it is a wonderful hub from which to begin cycling adventures in eastern Cuba.

Food and Lodging in Santiago de Cuba

There are so many places to eat and stay in Santiago de Cuba that they fall far beyond the scope of a cycling guide. However, as a cyclist you may want to check out the Hotel San Juan, partly because of its location. It is inside the San Juan Hill historic site, perhaps the prettiest setting of any hotel in the city, and it is possible to pick up our cycling routes from this site without riding through the most congested areas. At the same time, it is not far from downtown by bike. Though we have not stayed at the hotel, we have visited and seen that it is recently refurbished and relatively inexpensive.

In Santiago de Cuba we have always stayed in *casas particulares*. There are scores, possibly hundreds. On our last trip, we stayed with the wonderful family of Luis Raúl Mercaderes Pérez. Señor Mercaderes is a very old gentleman, full of wit and fun. Most hosting duties are now handled by his son-in-law Gery and his wife and daughters. There is absolutely nothing fancy about

Great Names in Cuban History

As you cycle around Cuba, you will notice the constant repetition of a handful of names on streets, parks, statues, billboards, and signs of all sorts. If you are unfamiliar with Cuban history, you will eventually wonder who these people were. Here is a guide to some of the names you will most often see, beginning with 19th-century figures who are associated with Cuba's two wars of independence from Spain.

Carlos Manuel de Céspedes was a sugar planter in the Oriente. On October 10, 1868, he freed his slaves and proclaimed Cuba's independence (the *Grito de Yara*). He was a leader in the struggle that followed, and for a while, president of the revolutionary government. He was killed in a skirmish with Spanish troops in 1874. The goal of Céspedes and his fellow revolutionaries was first to win independence from Spain and then to join the U.S.. In fact, soon after the proclamation of independence, Céspedes led a delegation to the U.S. to petition for statehood.

José Martí is the intellectual father of Cuban independence. He was a brilliant journalist, poet, and orator. As a young man, Martí was exiled to Spain and then lived in the U.S., where he organized and raised funds for Cuba's independence struggle and headed the revolutionary government in exile. In 1895 Cuba's second War of Independence began, and Martí returned, but he quickly threw his life away in battle. Decades after his death, Martí's ideas assumed greater importance than ever before. In his prolific and eloquent writings, Martí argued not only for independence from Spain, but for also for anti-imperialism, racial and sexual equality, and social and economic justice.

Antonio Maceo was a leader in both of the independence wars against Spain, and he is generally considered to be Cuba's greatest military hero. He rose from private to general in the 1868–1878 war. Even as a general he always fought in the front lines, participating in over nine hundred battles and skirmishes. He was wounded 26 times. He was a brilliant military strategist as well as a courageous fighter. Maceo was a mulatto, sometimes referred to as the Bronze Titan, and he was determined to end slavery and achieve racial justice in Cuba. On one occasion, when he was criticized for favoring blacks over whites, he asserted, "The revolution has no color."

Calixto García also rose through the ranks during Cuba's first, 10-year War of Independence, and with Maceo, he was a commander of the rebel army in the final struggle from 1895 to 1898. García's troops played an important role in the ultimate victory but were barred by the Americans from marching into Santiago de Cuba when the Spanish surrendered. Cuban military leaders were excluded from the ceremony. García's eloquent letter of protest to the U.S. military commander is a key document in the history of Cuban nationalism.

Máximo Gómez served in the Dominican Army before emigrating to Cuba and settling in Bayamo, where he was an ally of Céspedes. In the first Cuban War of Independence, he was promoted to general and worked closely with Calixto García and Antonio Maceo. From 1895 to 1898 he was commander in chief of the rebel army. When the four-year American occupation ended and the Republic of Cuba was founded in 1902, Gómez turned down a suggestion that he run for president. He said, "Men of war for war, men of peace for peace."

In the early days of the independence struggle, Céspedes and Gómez were joined by several other planters and ranchers in the Oriente, and their names also appear on streets and parks all over Cuba. They include Ignacio Agramonte, Salvador Cisneros, Bartolomé Masó, Pedro Figueredo, and Francisco Vicente Aguilera.

Parks and streets are not as often named after 20th-century heroes, but their names constantly appear on patriotic billboards, hospitals, cooperatives, and other institutions.

Julio Antonio Mella was a popular and influential student leader who led demonstrations for university reform and in opposition to the dictator Machado. In 1925 he co-founded the Cuban Communist Party and was elected its first secretary-general. Mella was imprisoned by the Machado government and led a hunger strike that attracted international attention. He was deported to Mexico and was assassinated there in 1929, when he was only 24 years old.

Camilo Cienfuegos was a member of the Granma expedition who became an important *comandante* of the rebel forces. After the victory, he was appointed chief of staff of the new Revolutionary Armed Forces. Handsome and cheerful, Camilo was one of the most popular of the revolutionary leaders, but he apparently died in 1959 when his light plane was lost on a flight from Camagüey to Havana. His memory is still honored every year when school children cast flowers into the sea on October 28th, the day of his disappearance.

Camilo Cienfuegos smiles down on Avenida Garzón in Santiago de Cuba

Che Guevara is undoubtedly the most revered 20th-century figure in Cuba today. See the sidebar entitled Che Guevara and the Billboards. Che, Cienfuegos, and Mella are often depicted together on billboards, symbols of young men who gave their lives for the revolution. Our favorite of these billboards bears a slogan that appeals to us as we get older: REBELS, FOREVER YOUNG!

Ciro Redondo, one of Fidel Castro's closest comrades, was on the Granma and fought in the Sierra Maestra. He was appointed a lieutenant, then a captain. Before long, however, he was killed in a battle with Batista forces. Che was also a close friend; and when Ciro died, Che wore his cap until he lost it and replaced it with the trademark black beret. Che named his column in memory of Redondo, and it Finfrom the country.

Frank País was a student leader and resistance fighter. He led an uprising in Santiago de Cuba on November 30, 1956, that was planned to coincide with the landing of the Granma. Although País and his followers briefly took control of the city, the Granma was delayed by three days, so Batista forces had time to concentrate on defeating País before turning their attention to the rebel landing force.

Although País evaded capture, police in Santiago de Cuba shot him to death in the street one year later.

Abel Santamaría was Fidel Castro's close friend and his designated successor in the early days of the rebel movement. He participated in the attack on Moncada in 1953 and was captured and tortured to death by Batista forces. See the sidebar entitled Abel Santamaría.

Haydée Santamaria, Abel's sister, was one of two women who participated in the assault on Moncada. She was arrested and jailed but released six months later. Haydée became a director of the 26th of July Movement and helped organize resistance to the Batista dictatorship. She held important positions in the revolutionary government and founded a center for the study Latin American culture.

Celia Manduley Sánchez was a leader of the 26th of July Movement, a hero of the revolution, and a lifelong companion and confidante of Fidel Castro. She was in charge of smuggling men and weapons to the rebels in the Sierra Maestra under the noses of Batista troops. She participated in the Battle of Uvero, becoming the first woman combatant in the rebel army. After the victory she held several important government positions, but her most influential role was in her relationship with Castro; she was said to be the one person who could tell him things he did not want to hear.

this *casa*, but the family is one of the kindest we have met in Cuba, and that is saying something! The room they rent is by itself on the third floor, breezy, pleasant, and private, while bikes stay safely on the first floor. The food is excellent. This *casa* is in the old part of town, several blocks from Parque Céspedes at Hartmann #262, between Havana and Maceo. (Hartmann is also known as San Felix.)

We also like the *repartos* (zones) of Vista Alegre and adjoining Ampliación de Terrazas, both near the Hotel Las Américas. It is easy to cycle in and out of the city from here. Try the home of Edgardo Gutiérrez, just a few blocks from the Hotel Santiago de Cuba and Hotel Las Américas. Edgardo speaks excellent English and his wife Miriam is a gracious hostess. They will find you another place if their two guest rooms are occupied, which they often are. The address is Terraza No. 106, Reparto Ampliación de Terrazas. Edgardo's telephone number is 4-2536.

All our routes from Santiago de Cuba begin or end in the eastern part of the city at the busy traffic circle beside the Hotel Las Américas. The landmark Hotel Santiago de Cuba is only a block away. Despite the confusing tangle of six or seven streets that converge here, it is a good place to know because so many important or useful roads meet at this spot. Avenida Victoriana Garzón (or simply Garzón) goes west to the city's historic and commercial district. Moving counterclockwise around the circle, Avenida

Traditional music is sung all over the Oriente

Raúl Pujol heads southeast, passes San Juan Hill, and continues to Siboney and the Baconao Biosphere Reserve. Avenida Manduley is noteworthy because it is the main boulevard passing through Vista Alegre, once Santiago's poshest suburb and still a lovely area with many attractive homes and inviting rooms for rent. Avenida General Cebrero flows into the Autopista in a kilometer or two. It is the best route to and from Guantánamo. Avenida de las Américas leads to the Plaza de la Revolución, an essential stop on any visit to Santiago, and it continues to the Carretera Central, El Cobre, and on to the west.

⑮ Santiago de Cuba to Siboney and Baconao

31 km, 1 day

There are more sites of historic importance packed into this 40-km, out-and-back ride than into any other of similar length that we know. Near the start, it passes San Juan Hill, where Cuban and U.S. troops won the final land battle in Cuba's War of Independence against Spain. You can visit a historic park at the site and even see what remains of the very tree under which Spain's surrender was signed. The ride continues to Playa Siboney, about 15 km from the start. This is where the U.S. landed its interventionist forces in 1898.

Near Playa Siboney is Granjita Siboney, a modest country home that is one of the most hallowed sites in Cuba's 20th-century revolution. In 1953, over 120 men and two women converged on Santiago de Cuba for an attack on the Moncada garrison, the Batista government's most important military stronghold in eastern Cuba. On the night of July 25th, all the young rebels assembled here at Granjita Siboney, where cars and guns had been hidden in advance. As they waited through the night for the predawn attack, some of them made whispered speeches of encouragement, and the words of Fidel Castro and Abel Santamaría are recorded on enameled plaques in the house. Photographs, news clippings, diagrams of the action, and bloody memorabilia are also on display.

At about 5 AM on July 26 the rebels crowded into 16 cars and set out for the city. They were poorly armed for an attack against overwhelming numbers of regular troops; surprise was their only slim hope. As you cycle back to Santiago de Cuba and the Moncada garrison, you will be on the route that they followed. Along the way, notice modernistic monuments erected to the memory of those who died.

In fact, only eight of the rebels were killed outright in the defeat at Moncada. Many more were captured, however, and 61 of the prisoners were beaten and tortured to death. Smuggled photographs of these atrocities were published in Cuban newspapers and magazines, and widespread

Abel Santamaría

Abel Santamaría, a young accountant, was one of the people crowded into Granjita Siboney on the night of July 25th, preparing to attack Moncada the next morning. He had first met Fidel Castro in 1952. The two men quickly developed a close friendship, and Santamaría would have assumed leadership of the movement if Castro had been killed at Moncada.

These were Santamaría's words to the comrades that night: "It is necessary that we all go tomorrow with faith in our victory, but if destiny is against us, we must be valiant in defeat. What happens at Moncada will be known someday, history will record it, and our willingness to die for our country will be emulated by all the youth of Cuba. This example will make the sacrifice worthwhile and will mitigate the pain of our parents and loved ones. To die for the fatherland is to live! Liberty or Death!"

In the morning, Santamaría was captured by Batista soldiers. He was tortured, and one of his eyes was gouged out with a bayonet. It was shown to his sister Haydée, one of two women who participated in the assault, with the warning that his other eye would be taken if she did not give information about the leaders who escaped. Haydée said that if her brother would not talk when his eye was gouged out, how could she do so? Santamaría died under torture that afternoon. He is revered today as one of the greatest heroes of the revolution.

El Moncada, attacked on July 26, 1953

revulsion at the government's brutality helped make Castro's group—subsequently called the 26th of July Movement—the preeminent force in the struggle to overthrow the dictatorship.

After visiting the Moncada garrison, you can continue the ride to Parque Céspedes, in the heart of Santiago de Cuba's historic district. This is where Castro gave his victory speech on January 2, 1959.

If this sounds like a lot of serious history to absorb without a break, the beach at Siboney, despite its coarse gray sand, is a great place for lunch and a swim, and it is deservedly popular among Cubans and tourists alike.

The Baconao Biosphere Reserve is also on this route. This is a huge area extending east from Santiago de Cuba that has been recognized by UNESCO for its biodiversity. There are several hotels, historical sites, and tourist attractions within this protected area. It is easy to detour from the route to see more of the reserve. It is also possible—but emphatically not easy—to cycle up to Gran Piedra, a giant boulder atop a mountain, which is one of the great *miradores* of Cuba.

Route Directions

0.0 From the traffic circle at the Hotel Las Américas, ride out Avenida Raúl Pujol, following the sign for Carretera Baconao. You should immediately pass the international clinic and the offices of Havanatur, a national travel agency, on the right. Continue straight through the next intersection.

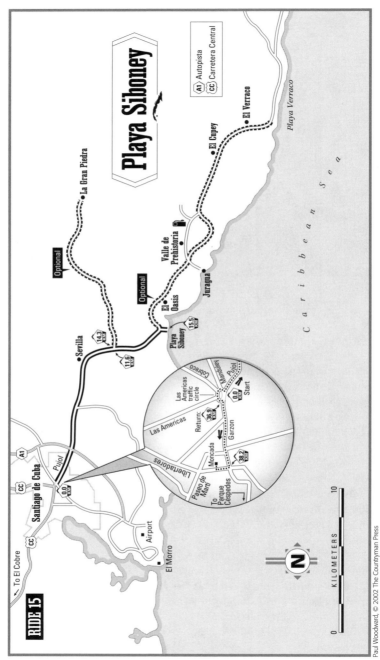

RIDE 15

To El Cobre

Santiago de Cuba

A1

CC

CC

Pujol

0.0 KM

Airport

El Morro

Sevilla

11.6 KM

14.3 KM

La Gran Piedra

Optional

Optional

El Oasis

Playa Siboney

15.5 KM

Valle de Prehistoria

Juragua

El Cupey

El Verraco

Playa Verraco

Caribbean Sea

Playa Siboney

A1 Autopista
CC Carretera Central

Las Americas traffic circle

Las Americas

Libertadores

Paseo de Martí

To Parque Céspedes

Moncada

Garzon

Return: 36.9 KM

38.2 KM

Cobreco

Heredia

Pujol

0.0 KM Start

Mandulev

N

KILOMETERS

0   10

Paul Woodward, © 2002 The Countryman Press

On top of Gran Piedra

0.8 Pass the entrance to the zoo on the right.

0.9 Two stone gate posts adorned with U.S. and Cuban seals mark the entrance to a historic site. Here, under a large tree, Spain surrendered to the U.S. in 1898, ending the "Spanish-American War." At this point, Cuba had been battling Spain for generations and had nearly won independence on its own. However, the Americans did not allow Cuban officers to participate in the surrender ceremony; they barred rebel soldiers from the city; and when Spain's flag was lowered, they replaced it not with the Cuban flag but with America's stars and stripes. You will reach the entrance to the San Juan Hill historic site in another hundred meters. It is on the right and marked by a sign for Villa San Juan. This is where Teddy Roosevelt's Rough Riders participated in the final land battle of the war. It is well worth a visit.

1.9 Cross a bridge over the Circunvalación. The Carretera Baconao narrows to two lanes. The ride becomes more scenic as you leave the city behind. You will draw nearer to towering mountains, their peaks often wreathed in clouds.

8.2 You are entering Sevilla, a tiny village at the top of a short, steep hill.

10.0 Bear left to stay on the main road. (The right to El Brujo quickly turns to dirt.)

10.3 A sign indicates that Playa Siboney is in 5 km, and a long downhill begins.

11.6 Continue straight, passing the left to Gran Piedra. (The ride up to Gran Piedra is nearly 14 km, much of it very steep. We did it in 2000, and it was probably the hardest hill we have ever climbed. If you have an unloaded bike with very low gears and lots of energy and patience, the hill is doable, but we recommend it only if you get an early start and if the mountains are not wreathed in clouds. Why do all that work and miss the view? By the time you reach the top, restore your strength with cold drinks or lunch at the restaurant, and ride back down the shatteringly rough, steep access road, you will be ready for a swim at Playa Siboney!)

13.5 Granjita Siboney is on the right. You are allowed to bring bicycles through the narrow gate and park them on the left. Shortly after Granjita Siboney you will pass a museum on the right devoted to the Spanish-Cuban-American War.

14.3 Continue straight ahead for the beach. The left continues farther into the Baconao Biosphere Reserve.

15.5 Arrive at Playa Siboney. Uphill to the right is a small Rumbos restaurant with cold drinks on a shady terrace but no food when we were there. Food vendors ply the beaches, and cold beer and soft drinks are also available. Many homes in Playa Siboney rent rooms, and seafood meals are offered in homes. To return to Santiago de Cuba, backtrack by continuing to follow the route directions. Ride away from the beach the way you came.

16.7 Bear left as you merge with the Carretera Baconao.

22.8 Pass through the village of Sevilla. There will be a very fast downhill, and the ride back to the city from here is easy.

29.3 Cross over the Circunvalación. You will pass San Juan Hill and the zoo on the left.

30.9 Continue straight, following the sign to Plaza de la Revolución.

31.2 Reach the end of Avenida Raúl Pujol, where you began the ride. There is a park on the right. **You must turn right and then ride around the traffic circle, bearing left**. *Do not* take the right on Avenida Manduley (where there is a sign to Zum-Zum Restaurant); and *do not* bear right on Avenidas General Cebrero or Las Américas (toward the huge Hotel Santiago de Cuba). Just continue around the rotary until you find yourself on a broad, busy, four-lane road. This is Avenida Garzón. **Ride carefully on Garzón toward the center of the city**.

32.5 Turn right on Avenida de los Libertadores. This turn comes immediately after the Coppelia ice cream park on the right. There are traffic lights here, and a sign to Parque Abel Santamaría.

32.6 The imposing Palace of Justice is on the right. Moncada is the next complex of mustard-colored buildings, also on the right. Though most of

El Oasis, an artist's cooperative in Baconao.

El Oasis and the Valle de la Prehistoria

If you have time to ride farther into the Baconao Biosphere Reserve from km 14.3, there are many things to see. Just 2.8 km past the turn to Playa Siboney, you will find El Oasis, a group of stone buildings on the right that house a small art cooperative. There are galleries in the homes of the painters, carvers, and sculptors who live and work here. The people of El Oasis are welcoming, and we never felt pressured to buy.

At El Oasis, a right turn leads to Bucanero, an all-inclusive hotel. Across the main road from El Oasis is a dollar restaurant, aquarium, and rodeo, a tourist contrivance that may not be in operation when you pass by.

If you continue still farther out the Carretera Baconao, you will reach the Valle de la Prehistoria on the left. Huge stone figures of dinosaurs are scattered among the hills. Seen against a mountainous backdrop, the effect is bizarre. There is an admission fee to the park, but we found the view from the road to be sufficient. A bit farther is a Cupet gas station with a small dollar store and El Rápido cafeteria. There is also a museum of old cars.

We have ridden as far as Playa Veracco, a brown sandy beach with accommodations (two-story cabins) meant for Cubans. We enjoyed our visit to this beach, and there was none of the hustling that goes on at popular Playa Siboney.

If you ride out this far, remember that it is nearly 20 km back to Siboney and another 15 km to the city. It is best not to ride through Santiago de Cuba in the dark. Alternatively, there are several hotels in the Baconao Biosphere Reserve if you want to stay overnight.

the garrison building has now been turned into a school, there is a museum here. It covers much the same information as the displays at Granjita Siboney. Across Libertadores from Moncada is a park honoring Abel Santamaría and José Martí.

If you wish to continue from Moncada to Parque Céspedes in the heart of the old city, be careful because you will be cycling on streets that are even more busy and congested than they have been so far. Ride back to Avenida Garzón and turn right. In 0.2 km you will reach Parque Martí. Turn left at the end of the park. Ride with the park on your left. Go straight through a traffic light at the end of Parque Martí, and turn right on Heredia, the second street after the traffic light, but the first on which you are allowed to turn right. Heredia, though very narrow, is popular with visitors. Among other things, the famous Casa de La Trova is on Heredia. It is eight blocks ahead on the left. Just past it on the right is the entrance to the Hotel Casa Grande, and Parque Céspedes is across the street.

🔟 Three Short Rides from Santiago de Cuba

El Cobre (35 km, 1 day)

This 35-km ride takes you to Cuba's most-visited church, the Iglesia de La Caridad del Cobre, the shrine of Cuba's patron saint. First you'll ride through the industrial outskirts of Santiago de Cuba, then continue into the foothills of the Sierra Maestra. Start Day 1 of the South Coast Loop (Ride 17), but turn left at km 15.5 to El Cobre instead of continuing straight. (See map.) In about 2 km you will reach the village; the church is to the right. Return by backtracking to the city.

El Cristo (35 km, 1 day)

El Cristo is a country town in the hills northeast of Santiago de Cuba. This ride involves a long, steady climb on the Autopista, then a twisting return on quiet country roads. From the traffic circle at the Hotel Las Américas, ride out Avenida General Cebrero onto the Autopista. You will climb gradually but steadily for most of 13 km. At km 15.4, shortly after a PNR control point on the left, turn right off the Autopista. After 1 km, at 16.4 km, turn right again and ride through the center of El Cristo. Enjoy several kilometers of lovely, quiet, downhill riding until you return to the Autopista and head back to the city. (The first 16.4 kilometers of this ride backtracks the end of the Far East Tour, Day 8. See map on page 282.)

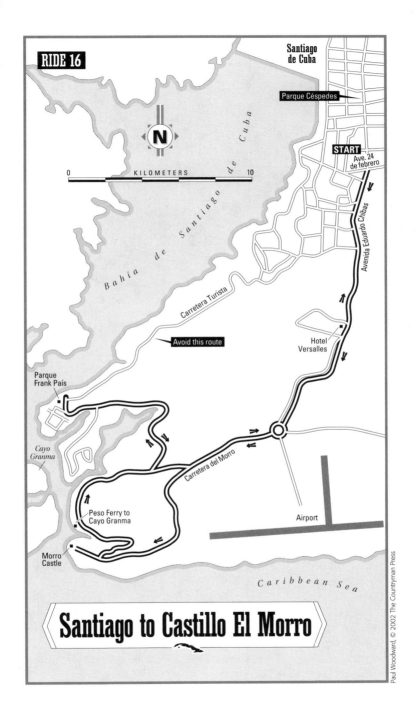

RIDE 16

Santiago
de Cuba

Parque Céspedes

START

Ave. 24
de febrero

Avenida Eduardo Chibas

N

0   KILOMETERS   10

Bahía de Santiago de Cuba

Carretera Turista

Avoid this route

Hotel
Versalles

Parque
Frank País

*Cayo
Granma*

Carretera del Morro

Peso Ferry to
Cayo Granma

Airport

Morro
Castle

C a r i b b e a n   S e a

Santiago to Castillo El Morro

Paul Woodward, © 2002 The Countryman Press

Cayo Granma

El Morro and Cayo Granma (25 km, 1 day)

El Morro is a huge colonial fort guarding the entrance to the bay. It commands fabulous views in every direction. Below the fort, it is possible to catch a *peso* ferry to Cayo Granma, a quiet world away from the bustle of the city. Also, nearby Parque Frank Pais on the mainland is well worth visiting.

Looking at a map, it is tempting to ride a loop to El Morro using the Carretera Turística in one direction. What a horrible misnomer! The memorable feature of this road is a giant cement plant that spews so much grit into the air that we had to ride block after block with our eyes closed some of the time—not the safest practice! It is far better to take Avenida 24 de Febrero and Avenida Eduardo Chibas south from the city center toward the airport. Chibas joins the Carretera El Morro. Then backtrack the way you came rather than using the Carretera Turística.

The ride to Castillo el Morro and back, allowing for a few kilometers of exploration in the hilly, semi-rural areas around the fort, is only 25 km or so. However, El Morro is so interesting, and there are so many possibilities for exploration once you are out that way, that we recommend an early start—especially if you aim to visit Cayo Granma. Otherwise you could get caught riding back through Santiago de Cuba traffic as night falls, an experience that can be just as dangerous and unpleasant as riding past the cement plant with your eyes closed.

If the sound of this ride does not appeal to you, we recommend that you invest in a cab to Castillo del Morro; it is well worth a visit.

⑰ South Coast Loop

500 km, 5 days or more

This is a grand loop through some of the most beautiful scenery in Cuba. Covering nearly 500 km, it can be done in five days, but we recommend a week or more if possible.

The first day, from Santiago de Cuba to Bayamo, is long but exceedingly beautiful, and you will probably finish quite late in the afternoon. Bayamo is one of the most historically important towns in Cuba—the site of Cuba's first revolt against Spain beginning in 1867—and its downtown has been beautifully restored. We recommend two nights in Bayamo to relax in the exceptionally handsome Parque Céspedes and visit some of the historic buildings around it.

The 68-km ride from Bayamo to Manzanillo (Day 2) passes through gently rolling countryside, and it is pleasant and easy. For much of the day, the Sierra Maestra is the backdrop for rich cattle country and bright green fields of cane. Manzanillo does not seem a great destination to us, but this may be a hasty opinion; we have been to the city twice but have never explored it. At any rate, Manzanillo is a convenient layover.

On Day 3, it is possible to ride directly from Manzanillo to Punta de Piedra—about 98 km—or to spend a night at Niquero, which is 73 km from Manzanillo. Like Day 2, this ride also passes through terrain that is either gently rolling or nearly flat; it is pleasantly scenic if not spectacular. There are important historical sites to visit: La Demajagua, the estate where Carlos Manuel de Céspedes freed his slaves and announced the first Cuban struggle for independence; the home of the late Celia Sánchez, a heroine of the revolution and probably the most important person in Fidel Castro's life; and the site where the Granma landed on December 2, 1956, carrying Fidel and Raúl Castro, Che Guevera, and 79 other revolutionaries.

Day 4 takes you 110 km from Niquero to La Mula and is the most spectacular and challenging ride of this tour. Indeed, we believe it is one of the greatest cycling days in Cuba or anywhere else. The route climbs over foothills at the extreme western end of the Sierra Maestra and then follows the shores of the Caribbean. The road is pinched between the sea and the tumbling peaks, occasionally climbing over steep headlands, but offering spectacular views and thrilling downhills as compensation for your hard work.

Day 5, from Campismo La Mula back to Santiago de Cuba, is even longer but not quite as difficult as Day 4, and there are several pleasant beaches. Although we describe the distance from Niquero to Santiago de Cuba in two days of 110 and 115 km, available lodging makes it easy to

Carlos Manuel de Céspedes

"I am the father of all the Cubans who have died for the revolution."

This bas relief appears on the base of a statue of Carlos Manuel de Céspedes in Bayamo's central square. Céspedes was the instigator and leader of Cuba's first revolt against Spain. His son was captured by the Spanish, who told Céspedes that they would spare his son's life if he gave up the struggle for independence. Céspedes refused, and his son was duly executed. These are the father's words about the decision: "Oscar is not my only son. I am the father of all Cubans who have died for the revolution."

break this part of the trip into three or more shorter days. Details follow in the route descriptions.

We describe the loop in a counterclockwise direction. We have done it both ways, and we think that riding counterclockwise minimizes the problem of headwinds, which can be quite severe north of the Sierra Maestra. However, some long-distance cyclists may choose to ride clockwise from Santiago as far as Bayamo and then push on to the west. At the end of the route directions, there are a few notes on riding the loop backwards that will help cyclists who choose this direction.)

Day 1: Santiago de Cuba to Bayamo (124 km)

This day is moderately difficult only because it is the longest on this tour, 124 km. We have looked for practical ways to break the distance into two shorter segments.

The best possibility would be to stop at the Hotel Mirador Valle de

Tallabe, shortly after Palma Soriano, about 48 km from the start. Although the hotel was open in late 2001, the sign had been taken down and it had very few guests. Our fear is that it might not still be in business when you get there.

All things considered, we think it is best to get an early start from Santiago de Cuba and ride all the way to Bayamo in one day. This is not as difficult as it might seem because the only challenging climbs are near the beginning. Then there are moderate, rolling hills part way through the day, and the last third of the ride, after Contramaestra, is extremely easy and fast.

If you start early and reach Palma Soriano by 11 AM (42 km from the start) and Contramaestra by 2 or 2:30 PM (another 33 km), then you should have no problem reaching Bayamo before dark. Most of the 48 km after Contramaestra are nearly flat or imperceptibly downhill. Obviously, fast riders can do these distances in less time.

However you choose to do it, you will find this to be a lovely ride—lush rolling countryside with broad views and the rugged blue peaks of the Sierra Maestra to the south. (If 124 km still seems daunting, or if you are simply pressed for time, you can take the quick, inexpensive Víazul bus from Santiago de Cuba to Bayamo and start the tour from there.)

Food

There are dollar stores and vendors selling street food in Palma Soriano, Contramaestra, Baire, and Santa Rita, and they are all mentioned in the route directions. However, be sure you have plenty of water when you leave Santiago de Cuba, and it is always a good idea to carry some fruit and other snacks.

Lodging

Apart from the Hotel Mirador Valle de Tallabe, the first licensed accommodations that we know of are in Bayamo. There are several *casas particulares* near the center of town. If you haven't noticed the signs on the way in, young men will approach and offer to guide you to casas as soon as you reach Parque Céspedes—or possibly long before then.

Though we usually prefer *casas particulares* to hotels, we have made an exception twice in Bayamo. We really like the Hotel Royalton. It is an old-fashioned place that has been nicely renovated by Islazul. It is right on Parque Céspedes, the best location in town. Also, the Hotel Royalton was relatively inexpensive in late 2001—less than $30 for a double. If you crave a swimming pool, there is the Hotel Sierra Maestra, a big Cubanacán property where bus tours usually stop. It is on the Carretera Central on the way into town.

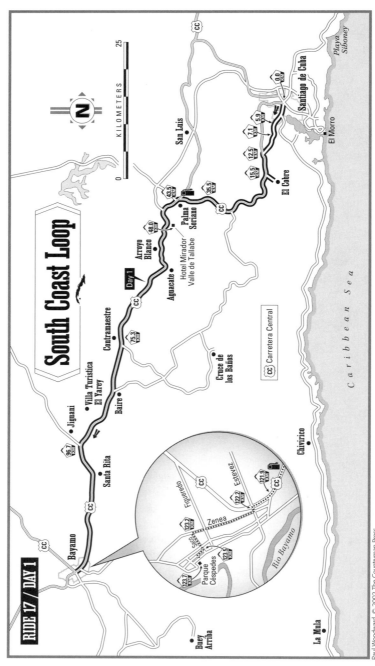

RIDE 17 / DAY 1

South Coast Loop

N

0 KILOMETERS 25

Bayamo

Buey Arriba

La Mula

Santa Rita

Jiguani

Villa Turistica El Yarey

Baire

Contramaestre

96.7 KM

75.3 KM

Cruce de los Baños

Day 1

Arroyo Blanco

Aguacate

Hotel Mirador Valle de Tallabe

Palma Soriano

48.0 KM

43.5 KM

35.5 KM

San Luis

El Cobre

15.5 KM

12.5 KM

7.1 KM

5.9 KM

0.0 KM

Santiago de Cuba

El Morro

Playa Siboney

Chivirico

Caribbean Sea

Carretera Central

Figueredo

Estevez

121.9 KM

122.2 KM

122.2 KM

Zenea

122.5 KM

123.7 KM

Parque Céspedes

Rio Bayamo

Paul Woodward, © 2002 The Countryman Press

Rush hour in Contramaestra

Route Directions

0.0 Start in front of Hotel Las Américas, riding away from the traffic circle on Avenida de las Américas. Almost immediately, pass the Hotel Santiago de Cuba on left.

1.5 Continue straight through the busy intersection with the Circunvalación. The Plaza de la Revolución, with its massive equestrian statue of Antonio Maceo, is on the left.

1.7 Continue straight through the intersection with Avenida de los Libertadores/Carretera Central, following signs toward Sala Polivalente, a sports facility. You will be on a four-lane, divided road.

5.3 After passing numerous identical apartment buildings on the right, the road narrows to two lanes and curves uphill.

5.9 Bear right at a fork. There will now be a couple of stretches, perhaps a kilometer or so altogether, where the pavement disappears. Persist!

7.1 Bear left at a fork.

7.3 The pavement resumes for good. There will be intermittent climbing for several kilometers.

9.7 For about 1 km, ride through a military zone—no photos. The road is climbing into the foothills of the Sierra Maestra. Sleek cattle grazed on grasslands that were rich and green when we rode through in November, not long after the rains. When we were here in March, during a drought, the grass was dry and brown, the cattle thinner.

Antonio Maceo beckons in Santiago's Plaza de la Revolución.

12.5 Turn left at a T-intersection at the top of a climb, following signs toward El Cobre. The right goes back to Santiago de Cuba. The riding will be easy for the next few kilometers. You will probably see vendors along the side of the road who sell flowers for offerings at El Cobre.

15.5 Continue straight, passing a left to the small town of El Cobre and the much-visited Iglesia de la Caridad del Cobre. (It is about 2 km into the village. Our route continues straight to Palma Soriano.)

16.7 There are snacks for sale at a bus stop on the left, shortly before the entrance to the regional hospital, which is ahead on the right.

21.2 Reach the top of a long, very gradual climb and begin a pleasant downhill. There is an army tank on the left that serves as a monument to a victory over Batista's forces in December 1958.

24.3 Enter the *municipio* of Palma Soriano. There is a reservoir below to the left, visible from here to about km 25.

35.5 Bear left, staying on the main road.

38.3 Pass a sign on the right saying BIENVENIDOS A PALMA. It is still over 3 km to the center of town.

41.6 A Cupet gas station on the right has a small dollar store.

41.7 Continue straight in La Palma, following the sign to Contramaestra. In the next few hundred meters, you will pass a Coppelia ice cream park on the left, a dollar store, the main square on the right where street food is available, and a large supermarket on the left.

43.5 Bear left, following the main road.

44.3 Cross a high bridge over Río Cauto.

45.6 Continue straight; the road merging from the right connects to the Autopista.

48.0 The entrance to Hotel Mirador Valle de Tallabe is on the left; the paved lane is nicely landscaped, but there is no sign.

53.8 Pass through the tiny village of Arroyo Blanco. There is a pretty cemetery with a view shortly before the village.

61.3 Enter the *municipio* of Contramaestra.

74.1 Pass beneath an overhead sign for the town of Contramaestra. (Las Américas, to the left, is a sugar *central.)*

75.3 In the town center, there is a small park on the right and a playground on the left. A couple of hundred meters farther, at the Cupet gas station on the left, there is a small dollar store. Continue straight for Bayamo. You will be out of town in another 2 km, and the road is nearly flat. (The left turn at the gas station goes to Cruce de los Baños and El Saltón, high in the mountains.)

84.5 Enter the small town of Baire. *Refrescos,* pizza, and *frituras* should be for sale here. In another 1 km, there is a small park on the right and a dollar store on the left.

89.1 Continue straight, passing a right turn to Villa Turística El Yarey, which is 4 km. (This hotel was open only to prearranged group tours in late 2001.)

90.4 There is a welcome display to Granma Province on the right, and also a sign for the *municipio* of Jiguani. On the left here, a quotation from Castro asks, more or less, How could one write the history of Cuba without the history of Granma?

96.7 Follow the main road as it curves to the left. If you bear right instead, you will reach the center of Jiguani.

104.0 Ride through the small town of Santa Rita. There is a dollar store

The Bayamo Church in which Cuba's national anthem was first sung

on the left as you leave town, and also a *guarapo* stand.

115.8 The *carretera* widens to four lanes, and traffic begins to increase as you enter the outskirts of Bayamo. A large billboard promises a Cupet service center in 6 km.

121.0 On the left is the Hotel Sierra Maestra. (Guidebooks list it as an Islazul property, but it has changed hands and is now operated by Cubanacán.)

121.5 The promised Cupet service center is on the right. There are dollar stores and fast-food places in the next few hundred meters. (The route directions from here to Parque Céspedes and the Hotel Royalton seem complicated, given that the destination is only a couple of kilometers away. This is because of numerous one-way streets, a pedestrian mall, and other minor obstacles. It will be quicker for you to pick your way through these directions than to wander back and forth in this bewildering little city.)

121.9 You must bear right at a fork. Now be on the lookout for a sign on the right indicating that Holguín is straight ahead in 72 km and that Manzanillo and Las Tunas are to the left.

122.2 Turn left, following the sign to Manzanillo and Las Tunas. This is Avenida Estévez. **Then take the very first right, in only 50 meters or so**. This street is Calle Zenea.

123.0 Here, Calle Zenea zigs right and then immediately zags left. Essentially you are continuing straight ahead on Zenea, but the zigzag is a landmark. You will be taking the next left, in about 200 meters.

123.2 Turn left on José Saco.

123.4 Continue straight across José Martí. You will be taking the next right.

123.5 Turn right on Donato Mármol, the next street after José Martí. This turn actually comes less than 100 meters after you cross Jose Martí.

123.6 Turn left into a narrow lane. This turn is less than 100 meters after the turn onto Donato Mármol. Continue on the narrow lane for less than 100 meters and you will reach the southeast corner of Parque Céspedes. Hotel Royalton is at the far end of this lovely park.

Day 2: Bayamo to Manzanillo (68 km)

This ride is easy throughout, either flat or gently rolling all the way, often with views of the Sierra Maestra ahead or to the left. During the first part of the ride, you will cycle through rich cattle country, then you will pass more sugar cane and bananas as you draw nearer to Manzanillo.

Food

Be sure to fill your water bottles before leaving Bayamo. In Veguitas, about 37 km from the start, there is street food and a dollar store where you can top off your water bottles. In another 8 km, in the town of Yara, vendors offer a wide variety of street food.

Lodging

Some guidebooks say that *casas particulares* are not permitted in Manzanillo, but we have found one that is apparently licensed. We once stayed with César Espinoza and his family at Calle Sarinol No. 245, between Saco and Cedina, just three blocks from Parque Máximo Gómez in the center of the city. Although the family was friendly and the food was good, we

Strange bikes attract children in Barranca.

felt that the second-floor rooming arrangement lacked privacy and was inconvenient for cyclists.

If you are simply passing through Manzanillo, it makes more sense to stay at the Hotel Guacanayabo. This big Islazul property is worn around the edges and the food could be better; but when we stayed there, our room was clean, and the friendly staff carried our bikes upstairs and onto our tiny balcony. At $22 to $24 per night for a couple, Hotel Guacanayabo cost little more than Señor Espinoza's *casa*.

Route Directions

0.0 Start in front of the Hotel Royalton. With your back to the hotel, ride left on Maceo, leaving Parque Céspedes behind.

0.1 Turn right at the T-intersection onto Martí. You will pass a much smaller park just before making this turn.

1.2 Turn right onto Avenida Estévez. There is a traffic light at this intersection and a park on the left. On the corner, there is a small brick structure, a reminder of a church that used to stand here, San Juan Evangelista.

2.3 Cross Río Bayamo, hardly more than a stream.

2.9 Turn left, following a sign to Manzanillo, which is in 57 km. The right goes to Las Tunas, and Mabay is straight ahead.

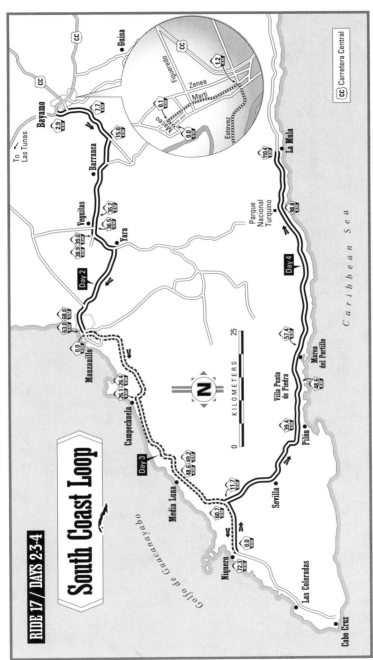

RIDE 17 // DAYS 2-3-4

South Coast Loop

Carretera Central — **CC**

Gilsa

Bayamo

To Las Tunas

2.9 KM

7.7 KM

15.0 KM

Barranca

Veguitas

35.2 KM

36.5 KM

38.9/39.0 KM

Yara

Day 2

Figueredo

CC

1.2 KM

Zenea

Marti

0.1 KM

Maceo

Estevez

0.0 KM

Manzanillo

0.0 KM

63.0/68.0 KM

26.1/26.4 KM

Campechuela

Day 3

48.6/49.2 KM

Media Luna

60.7 KM

Niquero

0.0 KM

72.3 KM

Las Coloradas

Cabo Cruz

Sevilla

11.7 KM

39.4 KM

Pilón

48.6 KM

Marea del Portillo

Villa Punta de Piedra

57.4 KM

Parque Nacional Turquino

98.8 KM

Day 4

110.4 KM

La Mula

Caribbean Sea

Golfo de Guacanayabo

N

KILOMETERS

0   25

7.7 Bear right, staying on the main road. So far, the road has been absolutely flat. Soon there will be gently rolling countryside, but the riding remains easy.

15.0 Bear right at a fork toward Barranca.

21.4 Continue straight through an intersection. There is a tiny park on the left and a couple of basic cafeterias. This place is Entronque de Bueycito.

25.8 Pass through the little town of Barranca. There is no dollar store, and there are only a couple of roadside vendors. Both times we have been here, we have been struck by the number of cheerful, nicely dressed children attending the big elementary school on the left.

27.5 Enter the *municipio* of Yara.

35.2 Bear right at a fork, staying on the main road.

36.5 Turn right at a T-intersection as you enter Veguitas, a one street town with a few basic cafeterias and street vendors. There is a TRD Caribe dollar store at km 37.2 on the right, and a tiny park immediately after it.

38.9 Stay on the main road as it curves 90 degrees to the left.

39.0 Bear right, staying on the main road. Land use is changing from cattle country to sugar cane. In another kilometer or so, a sign warns VÍA EN MAL ESTADO (the road is in bad shape). However, the conditions present no problem for cyclists.

43.6 Cross diagonal railroad tracks and enter the Yara city limits.

45.0 In the center of Yara there are many vendors selling pizza, other snacks, and *batidos*. There is quite a good selection, but we found no dollar store for bottled water. From here to Manzanillo, the road is mostly flat and rather boring. The Sierra Maestra, mountains that made much of this ride so beautiful, are no longer in sight.

59.2 Continue straight. (There is a major right turn here for Río Cauto.) From here into Manzanillo, a bike lane is demarcated by speed bumps. Use it!

62.6 Pass the Manzanillo bus terminal on the left.

63.0 Turn left onto a four-lane road with a divider. This is the Circunvalación. (Downtown Manzanillo is straight ahead.)

67.0 Continue straight through a crossroad. There is a small Cupet gas station on the right. (The right turn leads back into downtown Manzanillo. The left goes to Pilón and Niquero, and you will be coming back to this road the next day.)

67.3 Note the medical school on the left. This school draws students from all over Latin America and the Caribbean. Soon there will be a grand view of the sea below.

68.0 Turn right into the driveway of the Hotel Guacanayabo.

Riding is easy from Manzanillo to Niquero.

Day 3: Manzanillo to Niquero or Punta de Piedra (72 km)

The 73-km ride from Manzanillo to Niquero is easy throughout, level to gently rolling, with no difficult hills. It is also pleasantly scenic, with pretty views of distant mountains during the first half.

If you choose to go only as far as Niquero, you will have time to visit La Demajagua and the home of Celia Sánchez. You can even ride 20 km beyond Niquero to reach Playa Los Colorados, where there is a Cubamar campismo. Nearby are the exact spot where the *Granma* landed and the entrance to the Parque Nacional Desembarcadero del Granma. If you choose to stay at Playa Los Colorados rather than Niquero, plan on riding only as far as Punta de Piedra the next day.

If time is short, you can skip Niquero and cycle directly from Manzanillo to Punta de Piedra. This distance is 98 km instead of 73. It involves climbing over some moderately difficult foothills, with a spectacular downhill run to the Caribbean as a reward. (If you go to Niquero or beyond, you will come back to climb these hills the next day.)

Food

Places to buy food and bottled water are nicely spaced along the route. There are dollar stores and street food vendors at Campechuela, only 27 km from the start, and at Media Luna, about 21 km farther. In another 24 km you will be in Niquero, where there are a number of options, including peso snacks, a dollar store, and the hotel restaurant.

If you ride directly to Punta de Piedra, skipping Niquero, it will be almost 40 km from Media Luna to the next food and bottled water at a convenience store in Pilón. Top off your water bottles and carry some snacks when you leave Media Luna.

Lodging

If you are going to spend the night in Niquero, plan on staying at the Hotel Niquero, a property that has been nicely renovated by Islazul. Our inexpensive room—$22 in late 2001—was large and pleasantly decorated. It had a clean private bath with hot shower and a balcony overlooking the main street. One warning: When we ate in the hotel restaurant, there was no printed menu. We had become so accustomed to Islazul restaurants that we did not ask the price of the pork we ordered. Big mistake! If there is no menu, be sure to ask what things cost before you place your order.

Beyond Niquero there is a *campismo* at Playa Los Colorados. If you plan to stay there, it is wise to book in advance at the Campismos Populares office in Bayamo.

If you ride directly to Punta de Piedra, you will find Villa Turística Punta de Piedra on the right. It is a pleasant, moderately priced place with a dining room and bar. When we stayed there, our room was spacious, with a surprisingly quiet air conditioner. Though the motel is nicely situated near the water, the adjacent beach is dark, weedy, and unappealing.

The well-heeled cyclist might push on to Marea del Portillo, where there are two expensive, all-inclusive resorts. One of our correspondents did so and found it well worth the price. As far as we have been able to learn, there are no licensed *casas particulares* in Niquero, Pilón, or Marea del Portillo.

Route Directions

0.0 This day's ride starts from Hotel Guacanayabo in Manzanillo. At end of the driveway, turn left and climb a moderate hill—the hardest of the day!

1.2 Turn right at the crossroad. There is a small Cupet gas station here. (You reached this intersection at km 67 of yesterday's ride.) Almost immediately, the terrain is gently rolling. The road surface is rough here and there—not the potholes into which compact cars vanish without a trace, just rough pavement.

8.2 Pass the entrance to a crocodile farm on the left. (The entrance lane is dirt, badly rutted, and almost impassable. You would have to *love* crocodiles more than we do to try it.)

11.7 On the right is the entrance to Parque Nacional la Demajagua. A billboard says HERE WAS BORN THE CUBAN REVOLUTION. It is a couple of kilome-

Statue of Celia Sánchez in Media Luna

ters to the remains of the estate of Carlos Manuel de Céspedes, the father of the Cuba's 19th-century independence struggle. There is a museum.

15.7 Enter Calicito, a tiny village. Note the display for a sugar *central,* CAI La Demajagua, complete with bell. The bell is a reference to the one Céspedes rang when he freed his slaves and declared rebellion against Spain.

16.9 Enter the *municipio* Campechuela.

26.1 Turn right. There is a prominent welcome sign at this turn.

26.4 Follow the main road as it turns 90 degrees to the left.

26.8 The route continues straight through the busy center of Campechuela. (If you look down the side streets to your right, you should easily spot a couple of dollar stores. If you turn right to shop, you can continue to a modest waterfront park. It's run down, but there is usually a cool breeze. Back on the route, there is also a dollar kiosk on the left that was well stocked with bottled water last time we stopped.)

36.0 Pass through the tiny village of San Ramón. Just past the village, there is a sign on the right for Media Luna, Niquero, and Las Coloradas.

42.2 Enter the *municipio* of Media Luna.

48.6 Turn left at a T-intersection in Media Luna. (If, instead of turning left, you first ride 100 meters to the right, you will come to a park with a statue of Celia Sánchez sitting with her shoes off by the side of a fountain. Near the park there is a dollar store, and vendors sell *batidos* and *frituras*. After visiting the park, backtrack to the T-intersection and continue straight.)

49.2 Bear right directly in front of a large sugar *central*. Then bear right again onto the main street of town, a boulevard.

49.7 The birthplace of Celia Sánchez is on the left. It is a modest wooden house painted green, now an interesting museum. Entrance fee is $1 (U.S.) per person.

49.8 There is another Tienda Panamericanas on the right. Ride straight through the intersection that follows, passing a small, triangular park on the right.

58.7 Enter the *municipio* of Niquero.

60.7 Continue straight past Entronque Pilón, a major intersection. (If you want to go directly to Punta de Piedra—a few kilometers before Marea del Portillo—turn left here instead of going straight. This turn is km 11.7 of tomorrow's ride. It is 37 km from here to Villa Punta de Piedra.)

71.5 In Niquero, pass the bus terminal on the right and then a small park on the left.

72.3 The Hotel Niquero, in the center of town, is on a corner on the left.

Day 4: Niquero or Punta de Piedra to Campismo La Mula (110 km)

This lonely, 110-km ride is the most spectacular of the tour and also the most challenging. There is almost no traffic on the beautiful south coast. The road climbs over headlands, then drops precipitously to the sea far below. The thrill of working your way up the difficult hills and then flying back down them is unforgettable. Keep your speed under control!

If you are not in a hurry, you can make the day much shorter by stopping at Punta de Piedra or Marea del Portillo for a night. On the other hand, if you intend to cycle the whole way from Niquero to Campismo La Mula in a single day, leave Niquero as early as possible—preferably at dawn.

Cycling toward La Mula

Food

On this ride, there are long distances from one source of food and bottled water to the next. When you set out from Niquero, be sure to top off your water bottles. You need three big ones at least. Plan ahead and buy some fruit and *turrón de maní* or other sweets—anything for energy—the night before you leave. If you brought energy bars from home, use some on this day.

At Pilón, km 39.4, top off your water bottles again and have some ice cream. Buy fast food, cookies, or anything else that's available to carry you through. There is a bar and restaurant at Villa Turística Punta de Piedra just a few kilometers farther, but food is served during limited hours; and apart from the all-inclusive tourist hotels that are inconveniently located off the main road, you can't count on buying more food or water until Campismo La Mula, about 70 km farther.

Don't be intimidated by the food issue. We have survived this jaunt twice in good spirits. The food at Campismo La Mula, while certainly tolerable, will seem better if you arrive half-starved!

Lodging

Fortunately accommodations are no problem. Villa Turística Punta de Piedra at km 48 is the first place along the way; and 4km farther, at Marea

Pico Turquino towers over the coast.

del Portillo, you could splurge at one of two all-inclusive resorts—Hotel Farallón or Hotel Marea del Portillo.

The full-length ride ends at Campismo La Mula. This is a holiday camp catering mainly to Cubans but it is also popular with budget travelers, as well as those who wish to climb Pico Turquino. Plain, bare rooms have cold showers, but they are clean. There is a thatched restaurant with drinks and simple meals. Rooms in 2001–2002 were $18 for two people, basic breakfast included. This is the kind of place where you will want to have mosquito repellent, but we enjoyed it. Both times when we planned to stop at Campismo La Mula for a single night, we were given a friendly welcome by assistant manager Maribel Ruiz Picez and ended up staying for two or three. There is swimming in the clean, cold waters of Río Turquino right at the *campismo*, and tiny pocket beaches along the Caribbean can be found just a short bike ride away in the shadow of Pico Turquino.

Route Directions

0.0 Backtrack through Niquero on the main street, just as you came in.

11.7 Turn right at Entronque Pilón, km 60.7 in yesterday's ride. So far today's ride has been close to flat; there will be more intermittent climbing as you work your way into the foothills. The highest point in this part of the ride comes a few kilometers after Sevilla.

21.9 Enter the *municipio* of Pilón.

25.3 Pass through the village of Sevilla.

31.5 Reach the top of the steepest climb so far.

32.0 Begin the long downhill run to the sea. In 1 km, the downhill becomes steep, with a vista of the Caribbean below. Use your brakes and make it last; the road is rough. This downhill continues steeply for over 3 km, and then the ride is level or gently downhill the rest of the way to Pilón.

39.4 Stop for a cold drink and fill your water bottles at a new gas station, dollar store, and ServiSoda (fast-food place) at the intersection. Then continue straight toward Marea del Portillo. (The right goes to the center of Pilón.)

48.6 Villa Turística Punta de Piedra is on the right.

52.3 Pass a sign for the Cubanacán Club Amigo. The Hotel Farallón and the Hotel Marea del Portillo are both down the entrance lane on the right in another 100 meters.

55.3 Ride through Marea del Portillo. There are no services for travelers in this small village.

57.4 Bear right—essentially continuing straight ahead. (There is a wider, better-paved road here that angles off to the left. It looks like the main road, but it ends in a kilometer or two at the tiny settlements of Mota Una and Mota Dos.)

60.8 The road runs beside the rocky shore—the first of many places like this, and a good spot for a break. For the next 30 km there will be several major climbs as the road crosses headlands and sweeps back down to the sea. One of the two most difficult climbs begins at around km 70, with the steepest part lasting over 1 km. The reward is one of the most spectacular downhill rides of the day, almost 3 km of stunning views. Also, along this stretch of road, there are a few short sections with no pavement. Rock slides or washouts have occurred at these spots, and the route has been cleared with bulldozers. On a bike, these short, unpaved sections are no problem.

94.9 Pass a sign indicating that Chivirico is 46 km and Uvero is 24 km.

98.8 Pass the entrance on the left for Parque Nacional Turquino. Guides are required for climbs of Pico Turquino, Cuba's highest mountain. To reach the summit and get back down in one arduous day, you must arrange in advance to meet your guide and start before dawn.

104.6 Cross a bridge and notice below, to the right, a small golden sandy beach, popular with people vacationing at La Mula. You can easily ride back here if you stay more than one night at Campismo La Mula.

105.7 Pass through the tiny village of Ocujal.

106.1 A sign on the right indicate that Uvero is 19 km and Santiago de Cuba is 109 km.

107.5 A badly faded sign says EL MUERTO. What a great name for a place to live! Then there is a Ministry of the Interior Frontier Guard Post on the right, followed by a bridge. Look from the bridge below and to the right, and you will see our favorite beach in this area. It is much smaller than the one before Ocujal, more private, and prettier. There are rocks just off the beach, and when there is surf, they can be dangerous. At the far left end of the beach, however, there is a lovely sheltered spot where you can cool off even when the surf is heavy. This is a great place to spend an afternoon.

110.4 Turn right into the first entrance to Campismo La Mula. This entrance, which is the most convenient, has no sign. It is the first paved road of any sort to the right after the beach described under km 107.5. It slants gently down to the right. If you miss this turn, there is a clearly marked entrance on the right a few hundred meters farther, just past a bridge over Río Turquino. One warning: This road into Campismo La Mula crosses the shallow river, and water sometimes flows over it. If the concrete road surface is wet, it is very slippery, so get off your bike and walk.

Day 5: Campismo La Mula to Santiago de Cuba (115 km)

This day is not quite as challenging as Day 4, but it is still extraordinary. Again, you will ride near the sea, with occasional climbs, exciting downhill runs, and spectacular views of the Caribbean. There are a few very short, unpaved sections, which are in reasonable shape and should pose no problems for cyclists. There are beaches for a swim here and there along the route.

Food

Snacks are available in Uvero, about 19 km from La Mula; and there is a greater variety in Chivirico, and a dollar store for bottled water at 40 km. From El Francés (km 63) to the end of the ride, there are occasional public beaches where soda and beer are available, possibly bottled water. Food may be offered at private homes as well, but you should buy enough in Chivirico to last until Santiago de Cuba.

Lodging

There are two also all-inclusive hotels along the route; these accommodations are mentioned in the route directions. See page 203 for suggestions on lodging in Santiago de Cuba.

If you wish to shorten the ride, there are inexpensive accommodations at Motel Guama, a few kilometers past Chivirico.

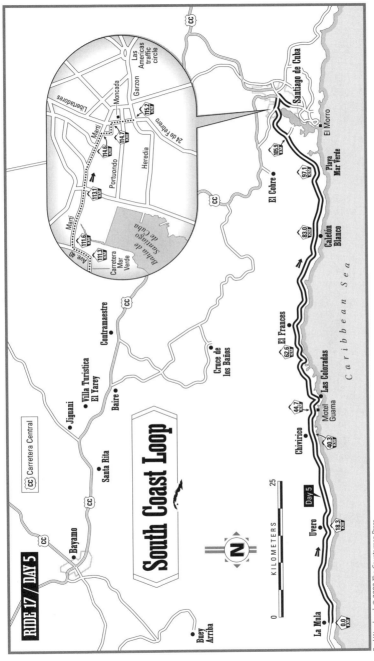

RIDE 17 / DAY 5

South Coast Loop

Caribbean Sea

Santiago de Cuba

El Cobre

El Frances 62.6 KM

Chivirico 40.3 KM

Uvero 18.3 KM

La Mula 0.0 KM

Caletón Blanco 83.0 KM

97.1 KM

105.9 KM

El Morro

Playa Mar Verde

Las Coloradas

Motel Guama 44.7 KM

Bayamo

Jiguani

Villa Turística El Yarey

Baire

Santa Rita

Cruce de los Baños

Contramaestre

Buey Arriba

N

KILOMETERS

0   25

Day 5

CC Carretera Central

Las Americas traffic circle

Libertadores

Marti

Moncada

Garzon

Portuondo

Heredia

24 de Febrero

Marti

Ave 40

Carretera Mar Verde

bahía de Santiago de Cuba

115.2 KM

114.7 KM

114.6 KM

113.7 KM

111.6 KM

111.3 KM

Route Directions

0.0 Start at the bridge over Río Turquino, just outside Campismo La Mula. Ride east, with the sea to your right.

3.0 After a gradual rise and a short, exhilarating downhill, there is a very steep climb—fortunately short, only about 0.3 km. There will be a number of climbs up and over headlands on this ride, most of them after Uvero, but none quite as difficult as yesterday's.

18.8 In Uvero, there is a park with some benches and shade on the left. Just a little farther, in the center of town, there are a few vendors and a small *peso* cafeteria, but no dollar store. Uvero is a site of some importance in Cuban history. Here, on May 28, 1957, Castro and 80 rebels attacked an army base and defeated the Batista forces. It was the revolution's first victory in battle.

30.0 For the next 7 km, the road repeatedly crosses headlands, providing more challenging climbs and fast descents.

39.4 Watch for a smooth, brown sandy beach close to the road. It's a lovely place for a quick swim or just to wade and cool off. You are about to enter Chivirico.

40.4 In the center of Chivirico there are dollar kiosks on the right, and there are a few vendors and *peso* cafeterias. There is also a shady park. Chivirico is an appealing little town right on the sea, and there always seems to be a light breeze. The Hotel Los Galeones sits on a hill just outside town.

43.1 Pass a sign for Cubanacán Nautica restaurant. It is on a small island—Cayo Dama—a couple of hundred meters offshore to the right. This place is patronized mainly by tour groups on excursions from the all-inclusive resorts.

44.7 The entry to Motel Guama is on the right, just after a small sign. We have talked to cyclists who say this place was a bargain.

46.3 A short climb over a headland is followed by a downhill with a spectacular view of the Hotel Sierra Mar, across the bay. Hotel Sierra Mar is an all-inclusive resort.

51.4 The entrance to Hotel Sierra Mar (now sporting a freshly painted sign and a slightly new name, Brisas Sierra Mar) is on the right.

55.6 In the tiny village of Las Coloradas, there is a small cafeteria, which probably doesn't offer much, but it's open.

62.6 Enter El Francés. What looks like a fancy resort hotel on the left is actually a rest-and-recreation center reserved for the Cuban Army. Just past the hotel there is a public beach on the right. Cold drinks are usually available here, but not much else.

80.2 A sign warns of danger, but this refers to potholes that could be

Our favorite beach near La Mula

deadly for motorists traveling at high speeds. There is also a short, unpaved section of road, but it shouldn't present a problem for cyclists.

83.0 Pass another public beach on the right in Caletón Blanca. As in El Francés, cold drinks are likely to be available, but not much else unless a local offers to fix you a meal. There is a sheltered swimming area. There are *cabañas* here, but on both occasions when we stopped, the booking office was closed—and we're not sure if it is ever open. Perhaps in the middle of summer.

91.6 A challenging 1-km climb is followed by a great downhill.

95.0 A road on the right goes to a small public beach that is less attractive than the beaches at El Francés and Caletón Blanca.

96.3 A sign on the right announces that you are entering the *municipio* of Santiago, the Heroic City.

97.1 Playa Mar Verde is on the right. This is Santiago's closest public beach on the west side. Like El Francés and Caletón Blanca, it has run-down facilities and a cafeteria that may offer cold drinks. If you swim here, watch for *erizos del mar* (sea urchins). It was safest at the left end of the beach when we were there, but look to see where Cubans are swimming.

98.2 Pass a sign indicating that Refinería is 8 km and Santiago de Cuba is 15 km.

104.6 On the right is Escuela Tec Canina, Zona Oriental. This is a cen-

Meeting a mule train on the road

ter for training police dogs and their handlers; there is a statue of a dog on the hillside in front of the facility.

105.9 Bear left, following the sign to Santiago de Cuba. (The oil refinery is 1 km to the right.)

111.3 Turn left. This turn comes a couple of hundred meters after a sign indicating left to Avenida Jesús Menéndez. Be on the lookout for this sign! It is easy to miss. Immediately after turning, climb a short, steep hill and cross a bridge over railroad tracks.

111.6 Turn right onto a busy, multilane road.

112.5 Pass a Mercedes distributor on the left.

113.1 Proceed carefully straight across the busy intersection with Avenida Jesús Menéndez. The modern railway station is on the right just before the intersection. The Carretera Mar Verde becomes Paseo Martí.

114.3 Begin climbing a steep hill on Paseo Martí. Note a large wall mural on the left.

114.6 Bear right at the top of the hill, about 100 meters before a set of traffic lights. (You want to turn right onto Avenida de los Libertadores, the busy road at the traffic lights ahead. To accomplish this, bear right here, then continue straight past another small road on the immediate right, until you reach Libertadores.)

Sunbathers on the beach at Guardalavaca

114.7 Turn right onto Avenida de los Libertadores. You will soon pass the Moncada garrison on the left, then Parque Abel Santamaría on the right, and finally the Palace of Justice on the left.

115.2 Reach the intersection with Avenida Garzón. To return to the start of the loop, turn left and proceed to the traffic circle at the Hotel Las Américas. To go downtown toward Parque Céspedes, turn right.

Riding the South Coast Loop Backwards

Most of the route should be fairly easy to follow backwards. Here are tips for leaving Santiago and getting onto the coast road.

If you are coming from the eastern side of the city, head downtown (west) on Avenida Garzón, turn right on Libertadores, and then left on Paseo Martí shortly after the Moncada garrison. Cross Avenida Jesús Menéndez and head straight out of town. (After you cross Menéndez, the railroad station will be on your left.)

If you are starting from the older part of the city, near Parque Céspedes, ride downhill toward the harbor on any of the streets going that way, and turn right on Avenida Jesús Menéndez; this is the broad street that parallels the waterfront. Then turn left onto Paseo Martí/Carretera Mar Verde. There are traffic lights at this major intersection, and the railroad station will be on the left.

In either case, once you have passed the railroad station, you will be traveling on a wide boulevard through a light industrial area on the outskirts of town. **Follow signs to the refinery**, first taking a left, then a right.

About 8 km from town, **watch for a sign to Mar Verde; turn right** here. Straight ahead is the refinery. You are now on the coast road through Mar Verde, heading toward Chivirico. **On the coast road**, at La Plata, about 17 km after La Mula, **bear right** on the main road and climb a long hill.

When you reach Bayamo, coming from the southwest instead of the northeast, our directions for finding Parque Céspedes and the Hotel Royalton do not work. This is because of the frustrating pattern of one-way streets. You should enter the downtown from the southwest on Avenida Estevez; Parque Céspedes will be about eight blocks to the left. If you don't see signs, ask.

Holguín and the Far East of Cuba

Holguín Province is one of the best areas in Cuba for bicycle touring, but relatively few cyclists travel this way. This section begins with short rides in Holguín City followed by a trip to Gibara, a scenic and pleasantly dilapidated town on the coast that was once bigger and more important than Holguín.

The rest of the rides in this section can be combined to make a long, challenging tour of eastern Cuba, as far as Baracoa. We are calling this the Far East Tour and somewhat arbitrarily dividing it into eight days. To enjoy all its possibilities, you should allow several extra days for stopovers— preferably two weeks altogether.

Cycling in and near Holguín City

The capital of Holguín Province is a busy industrial city with a downtown centered on the attractive Plaza Calixto García. Holguín is sometimes called the City of Parks; and if you do Ride 18, Holguín Miradores, you will see why.

Though the city of Holguín is largely flat, it is surrounded by hills, two of which at opposite ends of town are topped by *miradores* with panoramic views of the surrounding countryside. It is worthwhile to spend a day exploring the city and riding out to the *miradores*. From Holguín City, you can also ride to Gibara on the north coast and return in a day, or you may enjoy spending a night in Gibara.

Much of the tourist traffic in Holguín consists of people on their way to Guardalavaca and other beach resorts on the north coast. We joined the throng on two visits, and we learned that Holguín Province is a wonderful area for cycle touring. The coast is indented with bays and blessed with

Mules carry coffee beans down from the mountains.

some gorgeous beaches. Inland, rich, rolling fields are punctuated by *mogotes* reminiscent of those in western Cuba. Just south of the coast between Guardalavaca and Banes, the lush hills of the Grupo de Maniabón make for splendid cycling. Farther east, the Sierra Cristal is more imposing and challenging for cyclists who venture that way.

Food and Lodging in Holguín City

There are a few restaurants in Holguín City identified in the general guidebooks, but chances are that you will eat in your hotel or casa particular. A special treat in Holguín is *maní* (peanuts) sold on the street. Vendors keep their paper cones full of roasted, salted peanuts in insulated boxes so that you can buy them while they are still warm. Delicious! Holguín is the only city in Cuba where we found hot peanuts served this way.

The best tourist hotel in town is El Bosque. It is near the Plaza de la Revolución. Islazul's hotel at Mirador de Mayabe is less convenient to the city, but the views, the large pool, and the beautifully situated outdoor restaurant make the ride worthwhile.

We stayed several nights in a *casa particular* that we liked very much and recommend highly. It is the home of Antonio Ochoa. He and his wife, Amada Pacheco, are a gracious older couple, and their home is in the Colonial style, with rooms ranged around an interior courtyard that is open to the sky. Meals at their *casa* are less expensive than average but very good.

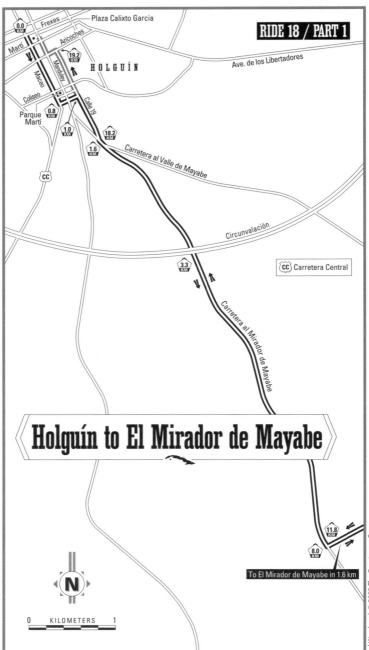

RIDE 18 / PART 1

Plaza Calixto Garcia

Frexes

Martí

Aricoches

Mandulay

HOLGUÍN

Ave. de los Libertadores

0.0 KM

19.2 KM

Macco

Coliseo

Calle 19

Parque Martí

0.8 KM

1.0 KM

18.2 KM

1.6 KM

Carretera al Valle de Mayabe

CC

Circunvalación

3.3 KM

CC Carretera Central

Carretera al Mirador de Mayabe

Holguín to El Mirador de Mayabe

11.8 KM

8.0 KM

To El Mirador de Mayabe in 1.6 km

N

0   KILOMETERS   1

The address is Morales Lemus No. 199, between Martí and Frexes, just a couple of blocks from Plaza Calixto García. The telephone number is 42-3659.

⑱ Holguín Miradores

29 km, 1 day

This is a pair of short rides, both of which can easily be done in a day with time in between for relaxing or sight-seeing. It would be fun to ride in the morning to Mirador de Mayabe and perhaps have lunch and a swim in the pool. Later in the afternoon you could ride back through town and up to the Mirador de Holguín. Late afternoon light highlights the contours of the vast landscape below, and you could quickly return to the city at dusk. Food and drink are available at both *miradores* and noted in the directions.

Route Directions to Mirador de Mayabe (see map for Ride 18, Part 1)

0.0 Start on Plaza Calixto García in front of the restaurant La Begonia. Ride along Maceo, first with the plaza to your left, then leaving the plaza behind. (Maceo is one-way.)

0.2 Pass Plaza Julio Graves de Peralta, a small, shady park on the left. When we were there in late 2001, a lovely new bandstand had just been built; check for outdoor concerts.

0.7 Pass Parque José Martí on the left.

0.8 Turn left on the second street after the park. There is a basic restaurant on this corner called El Daiquiri. After you make the turn, Holguín's small railroad station will be on your right. Continue straight ahead until you must turn at a T-intersection.

1.0 Turn right at the T-intersection. You will be on Calle 19, a two-lane road busy with horses, cycles, and occasional cars.

1.6 Bear just to the right of straight ahead at a complicated intersection, following the overhead sign to Hotel Mayabe—the Islazul hotel at Mirador de Mayabe. (The left at this fork goes to Valle de Mayabe.) You will be riding on the Carretera del Mirador al Mayabe.

3.3 Continue straight across the Circunvalación. The route will now pass through more rural areas.

8.0 Make a sharp left at the entrance to the *mirador.* This turn is clearly marked. Soon you will begin some serious climbing. The hill to the *mirador* is not long, but it is steep.

9.6 Partway up the steepest part of the hill, there is a right to Finca Mayabe. The sign says it is 500 meters, but in fact it is less than that. Finca Mayabe is an elaborate tourist draw, an outdoor restaurant and bar sur-

Statue of Calixto García in Holguín

rounded by the trappings of a peasant farm home, complete with many animals. If you continue straight a few hundred meters farther instead of turning for Finca Mayabe, you will reach the top of the hill and enter the parking area of the Hotel Mirador de Mayabe. You can have lunch at the hotel's open-air dining room (great views), buy a sandwich by a pool perched on the edge of the hill, or have a meal at Finca Mayabe.

To return, backtrack until you are in the center of town, where one-way streets require a slightly different route. (The following distances in the route directions may not match yours; it will depend on how much riding you did around the hotel and Finca Mayabe.)

11.8 At the bottom of the steep lane from Finca Mayabe or Mirador de Mayabe, **make a sharp right** onto the Carretera al Mirador de Mayabe, following a sign to Holguín.

16.5 Continue straight across the Circunvalación, and begin riding through a residential neighborhood.

18.2 Reach the complicated intersection described at km 1.6. There is a waiting zone for horse-drawn carriages on the right. Simply follow the sign, more or less straight ahead, for Centro de Ciudad. You will be riding once again on Calle 19. (In about 0.5 km you will pass the road on which you came from the railroad station, but continue straight.)

18.8 Continue straight across the intersection with Coliseo. Calle 19 changes to Morales Lemus.

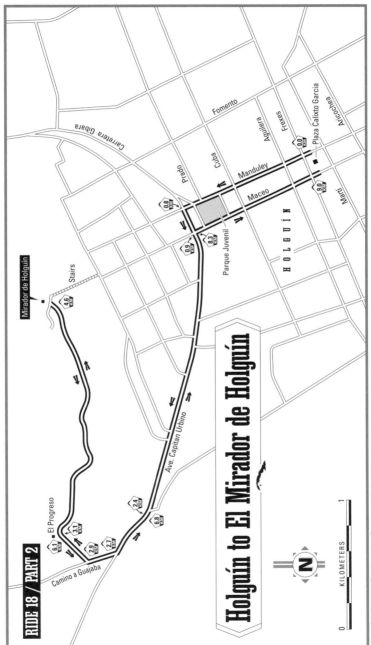

RIDE 18 / PART 2

Mirador de Holguín

Stairs

El Progreso

Camino a Guajaba

Ave. Capitán Urbino

Carretera Gibara

Fomento

Prado

Cuba

Aguilera

Frexes

Plaza Calixto Garcia

Aricochea

Manduley

Maceo

Martí

Parque Juvenil

H O L G U Í N

0.0 KM

9.0 KM

0.8 KM

0.9 KM

8.3 KM

4.6 KM

6.1 KM

3.1 KM

2.9 KM

2.7 KM

2.4 KM

6.8 KM

Holguín to El Mirador de Holguín

N

KILOMETERS

0   1

Paul Woodward, © 2002 The Countryman Press

19.2 Turn left at a traffic blinker. This is Aricoches. In two very short blocks, you will arrive at Plaza Julio Graves de Peralta, the small park with the bandstand, where you will be turning.

19.3 Turn right at the plaza. You will be on Manduley, also called Libertadores—somewhat confusing because there is an Avenida de los Libertadores heading east from downtown as well.

19.5 Reach Plaza Calixto García, where the ride began.

Route Directions to Mirador de Holguín

0.0 This ride begins on Plaza Calixto García where the first *mirador* ride ended. Start on Manduley, just opposite the statue of Calixto García and just before Casa Azul, a prominent store on the plaza. Ride on Manduley (also called Libertadores), heading north.

0.3 Pass Plaza San José on the left; this shady park is surrounded by an old, Colonial church.

0.6 Reach Parque Juvenil, a large playground on the left. You will be taking the second left after this park.

0.8 Turn left on the *second* street after the park. This is Avenida Capitán Urbino.

0.9 Stop at a five-way intersection. There is a fork directly ahead. **Bear right at this fork.** In the next few kilometers the route passes through neighborhoods that are poor but lively. There is a lot of traffic on Avenida Capitán Urbino, but it will consist of horse carts, bicycles, the occasional motorcycle or truck, and very few cars. Many people sell sweets and snacks at small stands along the road.

1.2 Pass a school and an adjoining sports stadium on the left.

2.4 Bear right as Avenida Capitán Urbino merges with a road coming from the left. Urbino now becomes somewhat rougher and narrower.

2.7 Bear right again.

2.9 Bear right in order to stay on the pavement—straight ahead is dirt.

3.1 Bear right yet again as you pass the entrance to El Progreso, Communidad de Nuevo Tipo. This is a small and attractive cluster of workers' housing. Soon, the difficult part of the climb to the *mirador* begins.

4.1 Reach the top of the climb. Above to the left are thatched buildings including a bar and a popular *peso* restaurant. It is worthwhile to continue past this facility and its parking lot for another 0.5 km.

4.6 After passing tall transmission towers on the left, reach the end of the road. A circular paved platform with benches and columns offers a grand view of almost 360 degrees. A long stairway from the city rises to this point. You will probably see a jogger or two pounding up the steps. There is a small thatched bar for cold drinks.

The only differences on the return ride occur in town because of one-way streets. To return, ride downhill. There is a great view, so maintain a safe speed and enjoy it.

6.1 Bear left at the entrance to El Progreso, the small housing development, and continue bearing left until you are back on Avenida Capitán Urbino.

6.8 Bear left at a fork, staying on Capitán Urbino.

8.0 Pass the school and sports stadium on the right.

8.3 You must turn right onto Maceo; straight ahead is one-way in the wrong direction. In one block you pass the Parque Juvenil on the left. Continue straight along Maceo.

8.7 Pass Plaza San José, with its antique church, on the left.

9.0 Arrive at Plaza Calixto García, the starting point of this ride.

⑲ Holguín to Gibara

66 km, 1–2 days

The 33-km ride from Holguín to Gibara is easy and delightfully scenic, passing through rolling countryside with views of *mogotes* and a pair of sensuously rounded hills that locals compare to breasts.

Today Gibara is only a modest, somewhat ramshackle fishing port, fronting a broad bay and extending into the rugged hillsides beyond. In the 19th-century, however, it was wealthy and important, and faint traces of former affluence are still discernible here and there. In the center of town there is an attractive park, Plaza de la Iglesia, and the badly battered Malecón is still a wonderful place to watch surf crash on the pitted limestone shore. There are a couple of museums and a cigar factory to visit.

In many ways Gibara is reminiscent of Baracoa, though it is smaller and has far fewer tourists. There are even flat-topped mountains outside both towns—Silla de Gibara near Gibara, El Yunque near Baracoa. This resemblance between the two mountains is at the center of an ongoing controversy. Christopher Columbus described a flat-topped mountain near the site of his first landing in the New World. Citizens of both Gibara and Baracoa claim that their own mountain is the one Columbus meant.

Food

On the way to Gibara, there is a good selection of street food and a small dollar store in Floro Pérez. In Gibara, there is a *paladar* (La Mina), which is on Joaquín Aguero No. 13. We did not try it, however. We bought delicious

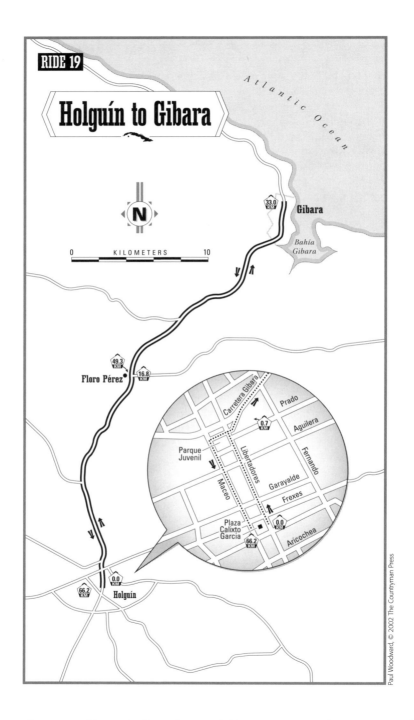

RIDE 19

Holguín to Gibara

Atlantic Ocean

Gibara

Bahía Gibara

33.0 KM

N

KILOMETERS
0   10

49.3 KM

Floro Pérez

16.8 KM

Carretera Gibara

Prado

0.7 KM

Aguilera

Parque Juvenil

Libertadores

Fernando

Maceo

Garayalde

Frexes

0.0 KM

Plaza Calixto Garcia

66.2 KM

Aricochea

0.0 KM

66.2 KM

Holguín

pork sandwiches for a few *pesos* from a street vendor just outside the dollar store near the park.

Lodging

Gibara has licensed *casas particulares* if you wish to stay for a night—and it is a relaxing town. We inspected Casa La Fortuna at Martí No. 22 between Independencia and Sartorio, right on the park. On their business card, hosts José and Antonio Gonzales modestly describe their place as the best *casa* renting rooms in Cuba. This is an overstatement, but the *casa* is pleasant. You could also try the guest rooms at La Mina, and there are a couple of other choices as well.

Route Directions

0.0 Start at Plaza Calixto García on Manduley where Ride 18, Mirador de Holguín, also began. Ride along Manduley, past the square and away from it. (Manduley, also called Libertadores, is one-way.)

0.3 Plaza San José is on the left.

0.7 Turn right at the end of Parque Juvenil, the large playground on your left. You will be on the Carretera Gibara. For the next few kilometers this road will be quite busy with cars, cycles, and horse carts, but traffic will gradually diminish until the *carretera* is just a quiet country road.

2.3 On the right, note the Fábrica de Órganos, the only organ factory in Cuba. Other instruments are also made and repaired here. It is well worth a visit.

13.0 Leave the *municipio* of Holguín and enter the *municipio* of Gibara. The next town will be Floro Pérez.

14.0 There are *mogotes* in the distance off to the right—limestone monoliths that erupt from the rolling landscape.

16.8 Reach a park on the right in the center of Floro Pérez. Snacks and drinks—pizzas, *bocaditos,* ice cream, *guarapo,* and *batidos*—can be found in the immediate area, and there is a small TRD Caribe dollar store on the left. (You may notice a major road heading northeast from Floro Pérez. We were tempted to use it on a couple of occasions, but we were warned that its condition is very bad, and much of it is dirt—nearly impassable if you get caught in the rain. It is best for mountain bikers only.)

27.4 Cross a bridge over Río Cacoyugüín. This river will be on your right from here until it flows into the Bahía Gibara.

33.0 Pass under an archway marking the entrance to the town of Gibara. To explore the town, ride along the bay, watching on your right for a display featuring a swordfish and a slogan exhorting revolutionaries never to lie or betray their principles. If you turn left here, you will reach the center of town in a few blocks. There are dollar stores, a cigar factory on the park to the right, and a couple of museums. Continuing through town, you will reach the Malecón, the waterfront boulevard that faces the ocean rather than the bay. Because we do not know how much you will ride around in Gibara, distances on the return route are calculated from the archway under which you rode at km 33. Simply retrace the route to Holguín.

33.0 Exit town through archway.

38.7 Re-cross bridge over Río Cacoyugüín.

49.3 Pass the park in the center of Floro Pérez.

53.2 Enter the *municipio* of Holguín.

65.3 Back in Holguín, bear left at a fork, continuing on the main road.

65.4 Reach the Parque Juvenil. Continue riding with the park on your left.

65.6 Turn left at the end of the park. This is Maceo.

65.9 Pass Plaza San José on the left.

66.2 Return to Plaza Calixto García, the end of this ride.

⑳ The Far East Tour

561 km, 8 days or more

On **Day 1,** the tour leaves Holguín City for the great beaches around Guardalavaca. This 57-km ride is easy. If you love the beach, you might never get any farther than this!

Day 2 continues through the rolling hills of Grupo de Maniabón to Banes. It is a little hillier than Day 1, but at 34 km this ride is so short that it is the easiest of the tour. (You might be tempted to go farther, but it is wise to start Day 3 from Banes because of the distance to the next accommodations.)

On **Day 3** the route heads south and then east from Banes to a basic *campismo* at Río Cabonico, beyond Mayarí. Though no single part of this ride is particularly difficult, the distance is 84 km, a fairly long day.

Continuing farther east on **Day 4,** the tour leaves Holguín Province and enters Guantánamo Province, ending at Moa. This section has many hills; and though it is only 70 km, it is challenging.

On **Day 5,** the 75-km ride from Moa to Baracoa is harder still. It is beautiful, but the hills are steeper than on Day 4, and the road is in bad shape much of the way.

On **Day 6,** the route swings south and climbs over the easternmost mountains of Cuba on a road named La Farola (the Beacon) but sometimes called the Roller Coaster—for obvious reasons. This 79-km day is the most challenging of the tour and also the most spectacular. The day ends at an exceptionally well-appointed *campismo* with a good beach.

On **Day 7,** the 74-km ride west along the coast of Guantánamo Province is spectacularly beautiful in its own austere way: The blue of the Caribbean meets arid hills along a coast lined with cactus and flowers. Heat may be the biggest challenge you face because there are few difficult hills. The day ends in Guantánamo City. We cheerfully skip the U.S. naval base.

On **Day 8,** after a stop in Guantánamo City, the tour heads to Santiago de Cuba. As on Day 7, heat can be the biggest challenge on this 89-km ride. You could complete a 700-km loop around eastern Cuba by continuing from Santiago de Cuba City back to Holguín. Also, from Baracoa, we briefly describe a lovely outing to Río Yumurí. It is certainly worth an extra day, and Baracoa is a favorite of many visitors to Cuba.

In summary, the first two days, from Holguín as far as Banes, are easy and would be fine for almost any cyclist. However, the rides along the north coast to Baracoa and over the mountains to the south coast of Guantánamo are the most challenging in this book. Though the daily distances are not as great as the Far West Tour or the South Coast Loop, this tour is more difficult overall. It is for experienced cyclists who want a challenge.

We have corresponded with several cyclists who visited Baracoa but did not have time for such a long loop. Some of them started in Santiago de Cuba, biked the south coast of Guantánamo, rode north over La Farola to Baracoa, and then returned by bus or truck. If you also want to visit Baracoa but prefer a shorter tour, we urge you to do it differently. Instead of jumping on your bike in Santiago and heading east, take a Víazul bus to Baracoa. Then ride over La Farola from north to south and continue west along the coast. La Farola is a major challenge no matter how you do it, but it is far steeper from south to north. You might as well do it the easier way—and remember that *easier* does not mean *easy!*

Day 1: Holguín City to Guardalavaca (57 km)

We're going to the beach! Guardalavaca, the end point of this ride, is eastern Cuba's most popular beach resort, deservedly so. It has all the features of the quintessential tropical paradise: dazzling white sand; clear, blue water shading from turquoise to deep indigo; and palms and sea grapes for shade along the shore, all framed by distant hills and mountains. We also like Guardalavaca because, even though it is entirely devoted to tourism, there is a public beach open to ordinary Cubans. There is excellent cycling in the immediate area.

There are other beaches and resorts before Guardalavaca where you

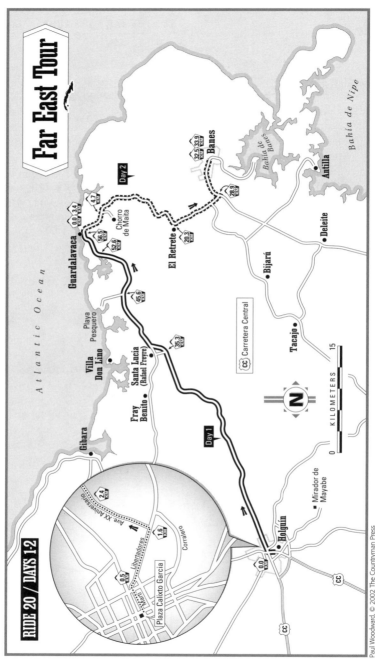

RIDE 20 / DAYS 1-2

Far East Tour

Atlantic Ocean

Bahía de Nipe

Gibara

Villa Don Lino

Playa Pesquero

Santa Lucia (Rafael Freyre)

Fray Benito

Guardalavaca

Chorro de Maita

0.0 KM 3.4 KM

4.7 KM

56.7 KM

52.6 KM

45.6 KM

35.3 KM

Day 2

El Retrete

20.3 KM

28.9 KM

32.5 33.9 KM KM Banes

Bahía de Banes

Antilla

Deleite

Bijarú

Tacajo

Day 1

Mirador de Mayabe

Holguín

0.0 KM

CC Carretera Central

N

KILOMETERS

0   15

CC

CC

Ave XX Aniversario

2.4 KM

1.6 KM

Corralero

Libertadores

0.5 KM

Martí

Plaza Calixto García

Paul Woodward, © 2002 The Countryman Press

may choose to stop. The first is Playa Blanca, north of Santa Lucía (Rafael Freyre.) This is a quiet spot with only one hotel. Playa Pesquero, a few kilometers farther, is a different matter. It is booming. Two new luxury hotels were open in late 2001, a Club Med was receiving the final touches, and still more construction was underway. The beach at Playa Pesquero is beautiful, but it is still not our favorite. That honor goes to the small, crescent beach at Playa Esmeralda, just a few kilometers before Guardalavaca.

Also along the way to Guardalavaca is Parque Natural Bahía de Naranjo. In the bay there is an island with an open water aquarium. Trained dolphins perform here daily, and it is possible to swim with them for a price. We know that some people are appalled by the confinement of these intelligent animals; but at this place the dolphins are in huge, open water areas separated from the bay and sea only by a wall of netting. When a pair of dolphins took Barbara for a high-speed ride, she found it impossible to believe that they were not having almost as much fun as she was. Even if you don't care for the beach (unbelievable!), you can still enjoy this route. The road north and east from Holguín rolls through lovely countryside. It is surprisingly easy for a ride with such fine scenery.

Food

There is a Rumbos cafeteria only a few kilometers outside of Holguín, and there may be vendors selling snacks at km 35.3, the turn for Rafael Freyre; otherwise, you would have to turn north into Rafael Freyre for food. But this ride is only 57 km, and it is easy, so you could do it between breakfast and lunch; and of course, you may be stopping even before Guardalavaca. Just bring plenty of water and a snack, and enjoy yourself.

At Playa Blanca, Playa Pesquero, and Playa Esmeralda, the only places to eat are the hotels. In Guardalavaca, a couple of small restaurants are noted in general guidebooks, but we have heard complaints that they are overpriced. Most people are here for the beach and eat in the hotels. If you want to cycle in the surrounding countryside, which is quite beautiful, you can raid a buffet table for needed supplies. A small dollar store in Guardalavaca is noted in the directions.

Lodging

The first possibility is Hotel Don Lino at Playa Blanca. We have not been there, but cycling friends loved it. Don Lino is a small hotel, and one correspondent rode there only to discover that all 36 rooms were booked. Call before you trek north from the main route.

Two luxury hotels were open at Playa Pesquero in 2001. We waited out

Packing bikes in the lobby of Superclub Brisas Costa Verde

a hurricane at Brisas Costa Verde, a luxury, all-inclusive hotel run by the Jamaica-based Superclub chain. It was the kind of place where we lost track of the bars, restaurants, and swimming pools. The price was not unreasonable considering the unending stream of free food and drink and the free sailing, scuba diving and so on. Well, free after you have paid between $120 and $200 per night for two people, depending on the season. Another big, all-inclusive hotel run by the German chain LTI International is next door, and a Club Med was about to open when we were there.

At Playa Esmeralda there are three hotels, all operated by Spain's Meliá Group: Río de Mares, Río de Luna (next door), and beyond that, Meliá de Oro. We once stayed at Río de Mares and visited the others. Meliá de Oro is the newest and most expensive of the bunch, and Río de Mares is the least expensive—though certainly not cheap. Actually, we liked its design and landscaping the best of the three.

Other than Playa Blanca with its single small hotel, Guardalavaca proper is the only place with hotels that carry less than four stars and prices to match. There are at least five hotels here, the biggest and best of which is the high-rise Hotel Las Brisas. Cyclists on a budget may prefer Villas Cabañas, back from the beach and at the opposite end of the price spectrum. We inspected one of the units at this modest place in 2001, and it was adequate for a night or two. There was an inexpensive, thatched restaurant. Villas Cabañas was the only place in town with a room under $30 per couple. There are no licensed *casas particulares* in Guardalavaca or at any of the other beach resorts in this area.

Route Directions

0.0 Start in Holguín on Plaza Calixto García, in front of Teatro Comandante Eddy Sunol on Martí. The theater is a large and distinctive art deco building on the south side of the Plaza. Ride on Martí—it is one-way—leaving the plaza behind. (If you are staying at the hotels Pernik or Bosque, you can more easily pick up the route at km 1.8.)

0.5 Bear right, following a sign to Guardalavaca and Mayarí. This is Avenida de los Libertadores. Soon you will begin passing a series of small monuments to Latin American liberators.

1.6 Turn left, following large overhead signs to Guardalavaca and Santa Lucía.

1.8 Pass the sports stadium, Estadio Calixto García, on the left. Also continue straight past a turn to the right for the hotels Pernik and Bosque.

2.3 The Plaza de la Revolución is on your right. Notice the reviewing stand's bas-relief backdrop depicting revolutionary heroes. To your left is a large building with a red star—headquarters of the Provincial Committee of the Communist Party.

2.4 Enter a rotary and follow the sign for Guardalavaca.

2.7 Pass Universidad de Holguín on the right.

3.6 Enter another rotary—this time without the benefit of any signs. Simply continue straight by riding about halfway around the rotary and then bearing right. In another kilometer you will enjoy a long, straight, gentle downhill, with small mountains, some of which are shaped like miniature volcanoes, erupting from the gently rolling landscape. In a couple more kilometers there is a Rumbos cafeteria on the right.

18.0 Leave the *municipio* of Holguín and soon enter the *municipio* of Rafael Freyre.

27.0 As you glide on a long, gentle downhill, catch a first glimpse of the sea ahead.

35.3 A road to the left goes to the Hotel Don Lino. This is the first good option along this route for spending the night. **Otherwise, continue straight toward Guardalavaca.**

42.0 Pass a sign for Marina Internacional Puerto Vita.

45.6 A road to the left goes to Playa Pesquero, where there are accommodations at upscale, all-inclusive hotels, some of which were open in 2001, while others were still under construction. **Otherwise, continue straight toward Guardalavaca.**

52.6 Pass the turn on the left for Parque Natural Bahía Naranjo and the aquarium. If you stay in this area for a day or two, a swim with the dolphins can be a great experience. It is cheaper to go to the park on your own by bike than to take one of the tours offered by the hotels.

53.9 Another left goes through a guarded gate to the three Meliá Group hotels on Playa Esmeralda, not easily accessible to Cubans.

55.9 Pass a gas station on the left with a small dollar store.

56.5 Exit to the right for Guardalavaca and the beach. The exit ramp crosses over the main road and then heads toward the beach. You will see some of the hotels ahead to the right. The farthest and most prominent of them is Hotel Las Brisas. In just over 0.5 km, there is a fork. The right goes to Hotel Las Brisas and most of the other hotels. The left goes to the small town center, the public beach, a dollar store, an international clinic and pharmacy, and Villas Cabañas, the only budget accommodations in town.

Day 2: Guardalavaca to Banes (34 km)

This short route winds through the lush hills of Maniabón, past peasant farms and through tiny villages. It is one of the most picturesque rides in Holguín Province.

Along the way you may opt for a side trip to the Museo de Chorro de Maita, high on a hill with memorable views. This museum is built around a burial ground once used by the Taíno Indians, inhabitants of the region before the conquest by Spain. The museum also features a reconstructed Taíno village, complete with life-sized figures of Indians going about the activities of daily life. There is a handsome restaurant at the site.

Banes is a small, quiet town, notable mainly for the Museo Indocubano, Cuba's most important museum of pre-Columbian history, and for the church in which Fidel Castro was first married.

Food

Other than the restaurant at Museo de Chorro de Maita, the only food available along the route will be from roadside vendors, if that's even the case.

This should not be a problem, however, because the ride is so short. Once you reach Banes, there are any number of *peso* joints selling pizzas and *bocaditos,* and also a couple of *paladares.* The best food, we believe, is at the *casa particular* we recommend under the section about lodging.

Lodging

There are not many choices in Banes. Before you reach town, you will notice a sign for Motel Brisas de Banes, which is up a long dirt lane. We have not been there, but we know it is a very small, basic place that may no longer be open. Also, it may not accept foreigners, and it is so far out of town that you would not want to stay there.

On the outskirts of Banes you will pass the Motel El Oasis on the right. This used to be the only place catering to tourists, and it was adequate. In 2001, however, it closed because of water problems. There is a *peso* hotel in town that is unlikely to accept foreigners. That leaves only *casas particulares.*

When we last visited Banes, we found one *casa* that was closed and another that was full. Luckily we landed at a third that was probably the best in town. Casa Evelyn Feria had three rooms upstairs with a roof-top terrace. Evelyn and her husband are big, hearty, people who obviously enjoy their own excellent food. The address is Calle Bruno Merino No. 341, between Delfín Pupo and Heredia. Information about how to get to this *casa* is included in the route directions under km 33.9. If you arrive at Evelyn's and it is full, just ask for help finding other accommodations.

Route Directions

0.0 Start from Guardalavaca in front of Hotel Las Brisas and ride away from the center of town. Immediately past the hotel, the road turns 90 degrees to the left, then again to the right, after which it crosses a bridge over a small inlet with fishing boats at anchor. Continue along this narrow, lightly traveled road, with the sea to your left.

1.0 Bear left as you merge with the main road from Holguín to Banes. (Holguín is 55 km to the right and Banes is 33 km ahead.)

3.4 Follow the main road as it forks to the left. Ahead and to the right are roads that immediately turn to dirt.

4.7 On the right is the turn for a detour to Chorro de Maita, a museum and re-creation of an Indian village. There is a tourist restaurant there as well. It is a steep climb of almost 2.5 km, but the views are wonderful. On the way back down, you must use your brakes because the road is rough with frequent potholes. (If you make the detour, turn right on the road to

Banes when you get back to the bottom of the hill, and add 5 km to subsequent distances.)

7.8 A sign indicates that you are entering Canadon. You will be riding through hilly countryside past small farms and homesteads for many kilometers.

20.3 Turn left following the paved road. This is the small village of El Retrete. There are no services other than a very basic cafeteria on the right.

21.9 From the top of a difficult hill, you can see over the lowlands ahead and as far as the Bahía de Banes. Then you will enjoy another great downhill, almost 2 km long.

25.4 Pass a left to Motel Brisas de Banes.

27.3 Continue straight, passing an unmarked road to the right. It goes to Tacajo and Baguano. (It should be possible to return to Holguín this way, a distance of about 75 km. We have heard that there is food and a dollar store in Baguano but no licensed accommodations for tourists. The road to Baguano and the one from there to Holguín are designated as *principal highways* on some maps so they are probably paved all the way, but you should ask before trying it.)

28.9 Continue straight past a road on the right to Mayarí. (If you're continuing east after Banes, you'll return to this point and turn left tomorrow.)

31.8 Enter Banes.

32.5 Note a new, modern surgical hospital on the right, followed shortly by the Motel El Oasis, closed in 2001.

33.9 Turn right at a T-intersection, following a sign to Centro Ciudad. This T-intersection is the point from which we will start on the next day's ride to Río Cabonico. The center of town is only blocks away. To reach Casa Evelyn Feria in Banes, **turn right at the T-intersection** and **turn left at the next intersection**. Continue several blocks, watching for the large Centro Telefónico on the left. At this intersection, **turn right**. **Turn right again** at the next intersection (there is a park on the left), **and then make the first left** onto Calle Bruno Merino. The *casa* will be halfway down the block on the left.

Day 3: Banes to Río Cabonico (84 km)

This 84-km ride first leads south from Banes on a pleasant, nearly level road that passes through fields of sugar cane. If the cane is not too high, there will be expansive views of the Sierra Cristal in the distance. When the route turns east toward Mayarí, it becomes even prettier, with a lovely valley view, rolling hills, rich grasslands dotted with Royal Palms, and the Sierra Cristal still in the background.

Between Banes and Río Cabonico

Mayarí is the only town of consequence on this route. It has an attractive valley setting, but accommodations can be a problem, so it is important mainly as a place to buy food and water.

Beyond Maryarí, there are more rolling hills, and eventually the road draws near the coast, with occasional views over the bays of Nicaro and Cabonico. The route ends at a *campismo* tucked in a wooded valley on the shores of Río Cabonico. This pretty little river is a good spot to cool off at the end of the day.

Food

The only reliable sources of food and water are 57 km along the route in Mayarí, where you can buy sandwiches, ice cream, snacks, and bottled water. Fortunately the riding is not difficult, but be sure to leave Banes with full water bottles and a snack.

In Mayarí, be sure to top off your water bottles again and eat something because the next chance of food is a basic cafeteria that is 25 km farther, and it may have nothing but rum and cigarettes. There is a dollar kiosk for bottled water just a couple of kilometers after that, near the *campismo*. The only place on the route for an evening meal is the *campismo* at the end of the ride.

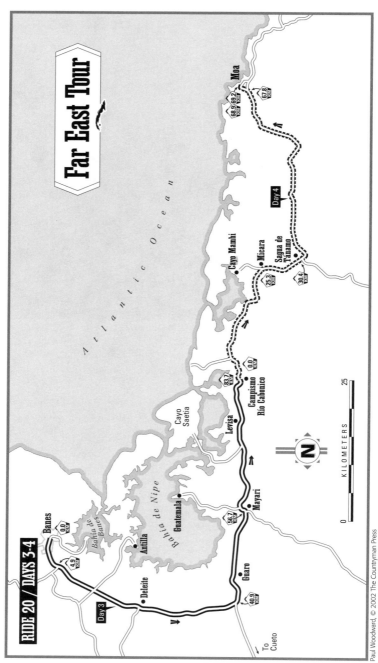

Far East Tour

RIDE 20 / DAYS 3-4

Banes
0.0 V.K.M

4.9 V.K.M

Day 3

To Cueto

Deleite

Antilla

Bahía de Banes

Bahía de Nipe

Guatemala

Guaro

40.9 V.K.M

Mayari

56.7 V.K.M

Cayo Saetia

Levisa

Campismo Río Cabonico

83.7 V.K.M

0.0 V.K.M

Cayo Mambi

Micara

25.3 V.K.M

Sagua de Tánamo

30.4 V.K.M

Day 4

Moa

68.9 69.2 V.K.M V.K.M

67.8 V.K.M

Atlantic Ocean

N

0   KILOMETERS   25

Paul Woodward, © 2002 The Countryman Press

Lodging

We have found no licensed *casas particulares* anywhere on the route. Other choices are limited. The first two possibilities are Motel Bitiri, a dilapidated place in Mayarí that may not give you a room, and Villa Cayo Saetia, a good hotel on an island game park that is expensive and inconveniently located for cyclists. The remaining possibility—we think the best— is the Campismo Río Cabonico. Even if you are able to get a room at Motel Bitiri or can afford one at Villa Cayo Saetia, you should still stop the next night at Campismo Río Cabonico. Otherwise, the ride all the way to Moa would be too difficult for all but the strongest and most masochistic cyclists.

Campismo Río Cabonico is basic, but it is not a bad choice, especially for the flexible cyclist on a budget. When we stopped there, it was a rainy weekday evening in the off-season, and the staff obviously did not expect foreign guests. Nevertheless, a room was soon prepared for us—bunk beds with thin foam mattresses on plywood, clean sheets and towels but no soap or toilet paper, cold shower, and a fan, all for $5 per person. The friendly staff even managed a fine little dinner for us: fried chicken, fried bananas, and a lovely, ripe avocado for $1 per person not counting beer and *refrescos!*

Route Directions

0.0 Begin in Banes at km 33.9 of yesterday's ride. From the T-intersection, ride back the way you came, toward Guardalavaca.

1.1 Pass the Motel El Oasis on the left and then the surgical hospital.

4.9 Turn left to Mayarí. The turn is unmarked from this direction, but it is easy to spot because this is a major road. If in doubt, just ask "Mayarí?" There are always people around.

13.5 Continue straight through a crossroad, probably with many people waiting for rides. Be careful here; when we rode through, there was a surprisingly deep rut across the road. Los Negritos is to the left, and Antilla beyond it, but no town or facilities can be seen from the main road. Also, by the way, the *Guía de Carreteras* shows a town farther along this route named Deleite, but neither the town nor any services are noticeable from the road.

14.2 Cross railroad tracks. There will be many more railroad crossings along this route, all clearly marked with signs. Some of the tracks are dangerous; approach all of them with caution. (The diagonal lines on the signs indicate the distance to the tracks—100 meters per line.)

16.0 From this point to the end of the ride, you can see the Sierra Cristal ahead to the left; views will be increasingly dramatic as you draw closer to the mountains.

Signs warn of railroad crossings—100 meters for each diagonal stripe.

19.0 You will soon come to occasional, short sections of badly broken pavement, but most of the road is good.

31.9 Continue straight past a turn to the left. Herrera is shown on the map here, but there are no services on the main road.

38.6 Pass a secondary school on the left.

40.9 Turn left at an intersection following a battered sign to Baracoa, Cayo Saetia, and Mayarí. The road to the right goes to Cueto. There may be a couple of vendors selling snacks at this intersection, but don't expect much.

47.3 Continue straight, passing a right turn at Guaro.

52.7 Pass a small dirt road on the left leading to Playa Juan Vicente. Soon, the terrain will become more rolling as you approach Mayarí.

55.4 Pass a welcome sign on the right for Mayarí. You can see the town below in the distance.

56.3 Enter the town limits.

56.7 Note a road to the left with a sign to Moa. This is the road to follow, but first you should visit Mayarí to buy water and food. Ride downhill toward the center of town. In about 0.5 km you will pass a tree-shaded area on the right with benches and vendors selling *bocaditos,* ice cream, and other snacks. You can buy water and cold drinks at the small dollar store attached to a Cupet gas station farther into the town. To find it, keep going straight a few hundred meters until you reach the Motel Bitiri, which is on a Y-intersection. Ride to the right of the motel and continue for two blocks. Turn left, and left again at the next major street. The gas station will be on your right. The attached dollar store is a very small one. Then simply continue past the gas station until you reach the Y-intersection and return to the main road on which you entered town. As you ride back out of Mayarí, watch on the right for the major turn with signs to Moa, Levisa, and Cayo Saetia. This is where the route resumes. **Turn right.**

59.1 Continue straight, passing a turn to the right that leads back to Mayarí.

66.1 Continue straight, passing a turn on the left to Felton. (This left also leads to Cayo Saetia. (Note: *The Guía de Carreteras* and some other maps show a second turn 5 km farther along our route, leading directly to Cayo Saetia. However, Moon's *Cuba Handbook* reports that this second road does not exist, and indeed we never saw it. Therefore, if you want to leave this route and visit Cayo Saetia, make this left to Felton.)

75.6 Continue straight through a major crossroad in Levisa. Street food is available from vendors at this intersection.

76.1 Continue straight, passing a turn on the left to Nicaro.

76.2 A sign on the right says BIENVENIDOS A CONSEJO POPULAR CABONICO, which indicates you are approaching your destination; there are 7 more km to go.

80.8 Pass a turn on the left to Prisión Dos Bahías. People here smiled and reassured us that, yes, the *campismo* was still ahead.

81.6 Note a very basic cafeteria on the left. They don't offer much, but the sign claims that whatever there is, is available 24 hours per day. The turn to the *campismo* will be in 2 km.

83.7 Watch for a dollar kiosk on the left, and turn right on the

dirt road opposite it. When we were here, the sign for the *campismo* had been taken down even though it was still very much in business, so the turn was hard to identify. The landmark kiosk is a typical metal building selling cold beer, soda, soap, and so on, but with a thatched awning for shade. In fact, this is the only dollar store of any sort that we saw between Mayarí and Moa, so if you aim to get an early start the next morning, buy bottled water and anything else you need before going into the *campismo*. The cluster of houses through which you pass on the way to the *campismo* is called Pueblo Nuevo. As you ride 0.75 km on the rutted dirt road, you may find it hard to believe it is going anywhere at all. However, after a steep, rocky downhill, you will arrive at the *campismo* on the banks of Río Cabonico.

Day 4: Río Cabonico to Moa (69 km)

This is the ride about which one Cuban warned us, "Muchas lomas!" but when cycling it, we decided it's not that there are *many* hills, this road is *all* hills! It seemed that we were always climbing a hill or rushing down the other side. And because climbing a hill took many times longer than coasting back down, we seemed to be climbing nearly all the time. The only substantial area of flat riding was a few kilometers in the valley around Sagua de Tanamo. On the plus side, the many hills give the area its visual appeal, and most of them are not terribly steep. This is a great ride.

As beautiful as much of this day's ride may be, it ends in ugliness. Moa is the center of Cuba's nickel mining and smelting industry. Hillsides have been stripped, spoil banks are distributed all over the area, and dark, noxious smoke pours from the stacks of the huge Fábrica Ernesto Che Guevara east of town. Taking photographs near this smelter is forbidden, perhaps because the Cuban government is embarrassed by the environmental devastation, but you will not need photographs to remember it. (Las Camariocas, a newer smelter built by a Canadian corporation, is not as dirty an operation. It is a few kilometers farther east.)

We have heard from visitors to Cuba who are genuinely horrified by the environmental damage around Moa, and it should not be minimized. Nevertheless, we remember what the New Jersey Meadowlands across the Hudson River from New York were like not too many years ago. We have not been lucky enough to visit the strip-mined hills of Southern Appalachia or the wastelands around Sudbury, Ontario, but we doubt the environmental destruction near Moa is worse than what has been done in many industrialized countries.

A visitor sees Moa, possibly learns from it, and leaves the next day. Many Cuban families make their lives here. They find jobs in Moa in the mines and

Nickel smelters pour smoke into the sky near Moa.

smelters, their children study at the university, and their work generates needed foreign currency. For the time being, Moa may be a necessary evil.

Food

At the very beginning of this ride there is a dollar kiosk. If you get an early start, however, it will be closed. That is why we suggest buying water when you arrived at Río Cabonico in the afternoon.

The next reliable source of food and bottled water is in 30 km at Sagua de Tanamo. There are street vendors, a couple of dollar stores, and a Rápido-style cafeteria in town. Top off your water bottles, eat something, and buy extra snacks or fruit to carry with you because there may not be another opportunity until you are almost in Moa, and there are a few long hills before you get there. In Moa, you will probably have dinner at the hotel.

Lodging

Islazul's Hotel Miraflores is the only realistic possibility in Moa. It is nothing special, but it is adequate and cheap—less than $25 when we were there. Also, the staff was incredibly helpful to us, with four people helping us carry our awkward bikes and equipment to our room and onto our tiny balcony. (Typically, the elevators were out of order and probably had been for years.) There was a great deal of noise from the empty swimming pool below our

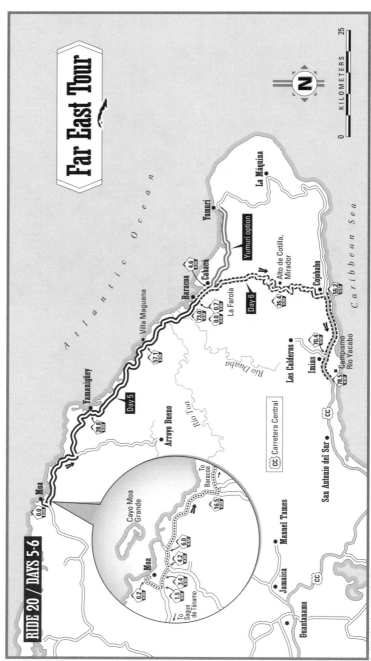

Far East Tour

RIDE 20 / DAYS 5-6

Paul Woodward, © 2002 The Countryman Press

room. Despite the lack of water, the poolside is still a popular place for young Cubans to hang out, drink, and dance to loud music. We faded before the music did.

Dinner in the hotel restaurant was reasonably good and the service was surprisingly efficient. Payback came in the morning, when it took 45 minutes to get one egg, coffee, and juice—in that order.

Route Directions

0.0 When you leave Campismo Río Cabonico, you may have to walk your bikes up the steepest part of the dirt lane back to the main road. **Turn right on the main road toward Moa**.

5.5 A sign indicates that Corinthia is to the left and Sagua de Tanamo and Moa are straight ahead.

12.5 To the left there are pretty views of Bahía de Sagua de Tanamo. Soon the road will pass quite close to the bay.

15.6 Cross railroad tracks carefully; they are hazardous. There is also a bus shelter here.

21.6 Pass CAI Frank País. The sugar *central* is farther down the road.

25.3 Bear right. The road merging from the left leads to Cayo Mambí. Soon you will enjoy views across a broad valley with low hills and mountains in the background. The area around Sagua de Tanamo is the prettiest part of this day's ride. The valley is lush, with banana trees, palms, and more cultivated fields than in the areas before and after it.

25.8 Pass a welcoming billboard on the right to Sagua de Tanamo. There is another one in less than 2 km.

29.6 A small sign indicates that you are entering the town proper. Shortly after this sign we found pork sandwiches and *batidos* at a little stand on the left—it didn't look inviting, but we were hungry enough to enjoy it thoroughly.

30.4 Bear left at a Y-intersection, following the main road. There is a monument at the Y-intersection.

31.8 Just after a shady park on the right, there is a small dollar store and cafeteria. A few meters farther on the left is another, somewhat larger, dollar store. You will now ride through an attractive residential area, but it lasts only a few blocks. Then there is a steep downhill, a bridge, and you are suddenly back in the country. It is almost as if the town never existed!

33.9 Continue straight where a road merges from the right.

40.0 A sign indicates that Moa is 36 km and Baracoa is 103 km. After you leave the valley of Sagua de Tanamo, there will be long, challenging climbs ahead.

54.2 A sign says MUNICIPIO DE MOA. The sign is near the top of a long climb—not terribly steep, but wearying!

56.0 You may begin noticing that the tops of hills ahead and to the right have been stripped for nickel mining. This is the first indication of the environmental damage that you will see around Moa.

60.0 Pass a small cafeteria on the right.

65.3 From here on there are low banks of spoil on either side of the road. Soon, there will also be pipes on the left that leak some kind of effluent.

67.0 Pass under an archway of modernist design and enter Moa proper.

67.8 Turn left following signs that say UNIVERSIDAD and REPARTO LAS COLORADAS.

68.9 Start around a traffic circle. You can see the Hotel Miraflores ahead to the left. Go three-quarters of the way around the rotary and bear off on the third exit.

69.2 Turn right into the Hotel Miraflores driveway.

Day 5: Moa to Baracoa (75 km)

Today's ride, and the ride over the mountains on La Farola on Day 6, are the two most challenging parts of this tour.

Leaving Moa, you must ride first through the blighted area around the two nickel smelters. By the time you are 20 km from the city, environmental damage is no longer obvious. However, the hilly landscape is not as lush as it was on previous days. Most of the vegetation is scrub, with occasional small pines and very few palms. There is little or no cultivation for many kilometers, and few people live in the area. The landscape gradually becomes more lush and green, and the countryside more heavily populated, about halfway to Baracoa.

There are only half a dozen notable hills on this ride, but they are long and sometimes very steep. The pavement on one of the hills was so badly broken that we could not maintain momentum and had to walk for a while—the only occasion in thousands of kilometers when we were forced to do this. Sometimes the arrays of potholes are so intricate that negotiating them is a distinctive sport, rather like mogul skiing except that you are going uphill as often as down.

The goal that sustains you through this difficult ride is Baracoa. When you arrive, the locals you meet will repeatedly say things like, "Isn't this a beautiful city? This is the best place in Cuba!" They mean it, but we disagree even though this makes us part of a very small, grouchy minority. Perhaps we were disappointed on our visit because of sky-high expectations based on rave reviews from friends and guidebooks.

Busy outdoor market in Baracoa

The setting is certainly beautiful. Baracoa is on the shore of a huge bay surrounded by lush hills and mountains. El Yunque is a flat-topped mountain that locals believe was spied by Christopher Columbus when he first landed on the Cuban coast. (Residents of Gibara claim the same honor for Silla de Gibara.) Unspoiled beaches are close at hand. The setting makes Baracoa an unsurpassed base for hiking and cycling.

However, the city itself left us cold when we there for several days. Literally cold, that is. Baracoa is certainly the rainiest city in Cuba and possibly the windiest too. We had gray skies, frequent showers, and high winds every day of our visit. Baracoa is known for its distinctive cuisine, but we

Walking our bikes up a hill near Baracoa

had the bad luck to find perhaps the only *casa particular* in Cuba where the hosts, nice as they were, simply could not cook.

Of course the weather might have just as easily been beautiful, and almost any other *casa* would have had better food. But we have two more complaints about Baracoa. It is tragically dilapidated—not the worst in Cuba by any means, but as the oldest city in the Western Hemisphere in one of the loveliest settings, Baracoa deserves more restoration than has yet been accomplished. Our other issue with Baracoa is the *jineteros*. We have cautioned against overreacting to these hustlers, but the *jineteros* in Baracoa seemed more persistent, and for the size of the place, more numerous than anywhere else we have visited.

Now that we have gotten everything off our chests, go to Baracoa. The weather *will* be perfect, you *will* find a good *casa* or enjoy one of the pleas-

Baracoa's malecón

ant hotels, and you *will* enjoy the cycling and the magnificent setting. You may love the town. Most visitors do.

Food

Pickings are slim along the ride. There is a convenience store at a gas station about 10 km after Moa. Buy extra water there and anything else available—we stocked up on packaged cookies from Argentina. The next chance to buy food—but not water—is 30 hilly km farther at a *guarapo* stand where passenger trucks regularly stop. Heavy, sweet *pan de maíz* (corn bread)— really more like pudding than bread—will probably be available. We ate it gratefully when we arrived. There is nothing else until you are almost in Moa. Because this is a very challenging ride, it would be another good time to use some of those energy bars from home.

Lodging

We have already mentioned our bad luck with our casa *particular* in Baracoa so we can't recommend it. Fortunately there are scores of other *casas*—and any number of young men who want to take you to them.

There are also four hotels from which to choose. About 16 km before Baracoa there is Villa Maguana. Cyclists from Switzerland spoke highly of this small Gaviota property, which has its own lovely beach. Hotel El Castillo is on a hilltop in the city. It is known for its charm and is very popular. Reservations are advisable. Hotel La Rusa, a less expensive Islazul property, is nicely located on the Malecón, while Hotel Porto Santo, across the river from town, is less convenient. Check any of the general guidebooks for details on these hotels.

Route Directions

0.0. Start at the Hotel Miraflores in Moa. Turn left at the end of the driveway.

0.2 Bear right at the rotary.

1.5 Turn left on the main road from Holguín to Baracoa. This is a broad, four-lane road with the bay and the town center below to the left.

3.4 Bear left at a fork; a sign here points the way to Baracoa.

4.2 Turn left at a T-intersection; Moa's small airport is on the left.

6.0 Bear right at a fork, following a sign pointing to Fábrica Ernesto Che Guevara and Camarioca.

6.4 A sign almost hidden in the greenery indicates that Baracoa is 67 km. The Che Guevara smelter is straight ahead in the distance. It is like a William Blake nightmare of the industrial revolution—a dark, satanic mill. When you actually pass the smelter, notice the large, bronze statue of Che Guevara in front of the administration building on the right, close to the road.

10.0 There is a Cupet gas station on the right with bottled water. If you haven't stocked up, this will be your last chance to do so for a very long while.

16.0 The newer Las Camariocas smelter is on the left.

16.5 Bear left, staying on the main road.

17.4 Pick your way through a minefield of potholes.

27.8 As you cross a small river, you may see people using horse carts and handcarts to haul large containers of water up the hill to a village ahead. People may be washing clothes in the river as well. This sort of thing is not commonly seen in Cuba these days except here in the Oriente.

28.2 Bear right at the fork, following the main road. To the left is the small village of Yamaniguey.

34.8 Enter the *municipio* of Baracoa.

38.2 Cross a bridge over a small river. There is a small school and village here, and the vegetation is becoming more lush and tropical, with some cultivation and many more palms. Soon the road will deteriorate badly, and it will remain very bad indeed for several kilometers.

40.8 Just after a bridge over another small river, there is a stand that sells cold *guarapo*—it absolutely hit the spot—and *pan de maíz*. It is nothing like the corn bread with which you are familiar. It is something between bread and a thick, sweet pudding. It is certainly filling.

42.4 Climb a tough hill, not the longest or steepest of this ride by any means, but the broken, blasted road surface multiplies the difficulty.

51.9 Pass through a small settlement, followed by a bridge over a tidal inlet. In 1 km there is a tiny beach on the left where local people fish and swim. You may want to join them.

57.1 Continue straight past the rough, unpaved road on the left to Villa Maguana, a small beach hotel.

Baracoa to Yumurí

The ride from Baracoa east to Yumurí is an exceptionally lovely day trip—about 40 km round trip. Some of it is quite hilly and includes wonderful views. It is a pleasure to stop on one of several beaches for a swim and have lunch prepared by a local family. This was our best time in Baracoa—perhaps because there were a couple of hours of sunshine! Few directions are necessary.

Start on the Malecón in front of Hotel La Rusa and follow the route directions to La Farola on Day 6 of the Far East Tour as far as km 4.6. Then turn left toward Punta Maisí. (The road to Guantánamo continues straight.) Climb a moderate hill for a couple of kilometers and then enjoy a great downhill to St. Luis. After St. Luis, there is another climb and another downhill.

At km 12.4, enter the town of Jamal; and after 0.2 km, turn left in the center of town, following a sign to Punto Maisí. Shortly after the turn, you will pass a small dollar store on the right.

From here to the end of the ride, watch for opportunities to visit a beach. About 5 km from Jamal, there is a straight concrete lane on the left with no sign that takes you to the shore of Bahía de Mata. It is scenic, but the swimming is better farther along. Watch for Manglito and Arenas Blancas, where there are some almost-white sandy beaches. There is a coral reef not far offshore where the snorkeling can be good if the water is calm. After Arenas Blancas and Manglito, the beaches are dark, coarse sand, but there are a number of them.

Before you get to Yumurí, you will ride along a particularly striking stretch where there are rugged limestone cliffs on the right, and the sea is below to the left. There is even a place, shortly before Yumurí, where you ride through a natural tunnel in a limestone cliff.

About 20 km from the start, you will reach Yumurí, where the river flows between sheer cliffs, in a sort of a canyon, before it empties into the sea. It is a lovely spot. There is a small cafeteria with cold beer and soft drinks, and many of the families who live along the beach are eager to cook seafood meals for you. Women sell sweets, skin oil, and varicolored snail shells. Don't buy the shells—they are from an endangered species. You may also be offered a boat ride up the river.

The ride back is straightforward, also with hills and some spectacular views. Just reverse the route directions; ride 15 km to the T-intersection in Jamal and turn right. Bear right again when you reach the main road between Baracoa and Guantánamo.

La Farola twists up the mountains

67.5 Cross a bridge over Río Toa.

71.0 Cross a bridge over Río Duaba.

71.6 Continue straight past a right turn Finca Duaba, a fruit farm with a thatched restaurant.

72.0 There is a chocolate factory on the left on the outskirts of Baracoa. You can tell by the smell.

73.0 A sign welcomes you to Baracoa and gives distances to the hotels Porto Santo and El Castillo, 1 and 2 km, respectively. If you continue straight ahead, you will be on Primero de Abril, which takes you downtown in less than 2 km.

Day 6: Baracoa to Yacabo Abajo via La Farola (79 km)

This ride is the most challenging on the Far East Tour. It leads from Baracoa over La Farola, the most impressive mountain road in Cuba. In the first 15 km, you will cycle through landscape that is tropically lush and nearly level. Then you reach La Farola and a 20-km climb with only a few breaks. The vegetation and climate gradually change from tropical abundance to cool pine woods. Riding down the steeper south side of La Farola, you'll find sharp turns cantilevered out from the sheer hillsides. You will frequently use both your brakes and your camera.

By the time you reach the bottom, passing hillsides where coffee is

Cucurucho, a sweet treat wrapped in banana leaves

grown, the climate and landscape have changed dramatically. The country-side is hot and arid. The ride along the shores of the Caribbean, especially in late afternoon light, is incomparable.

Food

Once you leave Baracoa, do not count on finding bottled water or a cold drink until you reach the top of La Farola at km 35.4. It is a good idea to pick up something for lunch before you leave Baracoa. If you have not already done so, stock up with bottled water at the convenience store on the way out of town, km 0.8.

"La Farola—a fraud in the past, a revolutionary reality today"

Riding up La Farola, you will see hawkers selling oranges or other fruit if the season is right. They will almost certainly have *cucurucho* and coffee beans as well. *Cucurucho* may be overly sweet for your taste, but it certainly helps power you up and over the hills. Cold drinks and bottled water are available at the top of La Farola. Also, a few families live up there, and it is possible to buy lunch in a local home.

There is a small village (Cajobabo) at the bottom of La Farola on the coast, but we pushed through without noticing any dollar stores or food vendors. No matter, it is only 15 easy km to Imias, a pleasant town with a good dollar store. We each bought two servings of ice cream along with cold water and soda. There are also street vendors in Imias, but they may have shut down by midafternoon when you are likely to arrive. Campismo Río Yacabo, where you should be able to have dinner, is only a few kilometers farther.

Lodging

We recommend that you ride to Campismo Río Yacabo, 79 km from Baracoa, even though there are a couple of options somewhat sooner. The first of the less agreeable possibilities is a small *campismo* outside Cajobabo. It is only open on weekends at best and there is unlikely to be food when you arrive. There is also a basic *campismo* outside Imias, but it is only 7 km from the bigger, newer Campismo Río Yacabo.

Campismo Río Yacabo is one of the better *campismos* that we have visited. Although the rooms are still basic, they are in handsome, two-story stone buildings that were erected in 1999. There is an attractive outdoor restaurant and a good beach with coarse sand just meters away.

The only problem—and it is important for your planning—is that Campismo Río Yacabo is *officially* open Wednesday through Sunday. If you arrive on Monday or Tuesday, as we did, there may be one or two staff around, or at least a watchman, but you will have to beg and plead for a room, as we did. For a while, it seemed that we might not succeed. Finally, a nice guy came up with a room key just before dark and also found us two beers, but we couldn't get any soap, towels, sheets, toilet paper, or food. Be smarter than we were and make reservations before leaving Baracoa, at the Campismos Populares office on Martí, No. 225, between Galano and Reyes.

Route Directions

0.0 Start on the Malecón at Hotel La Rusa and ride east, with the sea on your left.

0.7 Turn right near the end of the Malecón, just before a little park with a statue of Columbus that looks as if it were made of red mud. **Then immediately bear left** at a triangle and **turn left again.** You will be on the main road to Guantánamo.

0.8 Pass a Cupet gas station on the right with a small dollar store and El Rápido cafeteria.

2.3 A sign on the right indicates that Guantánamo is 148 km and Imías is 65 km.

2.8 Cross a bridge over Río Miel.

4.6 Continue straight, following the sign to Guantánamo. (The left goes to Yumurí.)

6.1 Pass the zoo on the left.

12.3 Enter the small town of Sabanilla. There is a church on the left, Torre Fuerte (Strong Tower) Church of God in Christ.

14.7 A sign announces that you are starting up the Viaducto La Farola. Batista promised to build a road connecting isolated Baracoa with the rest of the nation, but it didn't happen until Fidel Castro did the job. This is why the sign also says, more or less, "Yesterday a fraud (a false promise), but today a reality because of the Revolution. "You will be climbing now for most of the next 20 km. The first brief respite is at km 18.0, and at km 19.4 there is a small cafeteria. There is not much available, but hawkers may be selling fruit and *cucurucho* here or farther along the route.

20.5 An elevated wooden trough by the side of the road dispenses a strong flow of spring water—a great spot to cool off.

21.4 There is a wooden lookout tower above the road on the left. It is worth walking up for the view.

22.9 Ride through the tiny village of Palma Clara. From here to the top, there will be some level sections and downhills, including one that is 4 km long and *very* steep in places. However, there is more intense climbing before the top.

32.6 After the 4-km downhill, cross a bridge and resume climbing. The uphill is more or less continuous, with a few extremely difficult sections, for almost 3 km.

35.4 At the top, there are two cafeterias on the left, a simple *peso* place and a dollar bar for cold beer and soft drinks. You should pay the 50-cent fee to walk up a nearby path and climb the rickety steps of a wooden tower. The views are spectacular, and if it is clear enough you can see both the north and south coasts of Cuba. From here to the Caribbean, the ride is mostly downhill, and some of it is terribly steep and absolutely thrilling. However, you can't quite coast all the way to the coast.

45.5 Shortly after Communidad Veguita del Sur, climb a steep, short hill. From here on, the generally downhill trend will be interrupted only by some moderate climbs.

52.4 Enter the small town of Cajobabas.

54.5 Continue straight. There is a left in the center of the tiny village that goes to the basic *campismo,* but you can't count on it being open.

55.2 Cross Río Cajobabo, and in less than 0.5 km, the Caribbean miraculously appears below to your left. You have made it from sea to shining sea. From here to the end of the ride, cacti grow by the sea, and tiers of rocky bluffs on the right obscure the higher peaks beyond.

68.0 Ride through the outskirts of Imias.

70.4 In the center of Imias there is a well-stocked dollar store, a dollar kiosk, a video club for youth, and the Casa de La Cultura. A few hundred meters farther, vendors sell street food, including *batidos,* though they may be closed if you arrive late in the afternoon. There is a pleasant park as well. Imias is a neat, attractive little town and would be a nice place to stay for a few days. Unfortunately there were no licensed *casas particulares* in 2001, though this could change. It is only another 7 easy km to Campismo Río Yacabo.

71.4 Leaving Imias, pass a sign indicating that Guantánamo is 85 km and San Antonio del Sur is 20 km.

75.5 Enter Yacabo Abajo.

Wally's favorite statue of José Martí

78.5 Cross a bridge over Río Yacabo. **The entrance to the *campismo* is on the left about 300 meters after the bridge,** almost at the top of a modest hill.

Day 7: Campismo Río Yacabo to Guantánamo (74 km)

This 75-km ride, mostly along the dry coast, is scenic and not difficult. The main challenge is likely to be the heat; this part of Cuba is known for it. Rest when you find shade, especially in the afternoon, and drink plenty of liquids.

The first several kilometers are flat with wonderful views. Be sure to look behind you where mountains tumble to the sea. After 6 or 7 km, the terrain begins to roll, but there are only one or two difficult hills starting at km 43, after the road has turned inland. Even here, the main problem is likely to be the heat, not the grade. The road will sweep back to the coast, and the last 20 km are mostly flat.

Guantánamo does not get good reviews in general guidebooks, but we liked it. The *casa* we recommend is only a block from Parque Martí, the very center of town. There is a pretty old church in the park, Iglesia Parroquia de Santa Catalina, and Wally's favorite statue of José Martí.

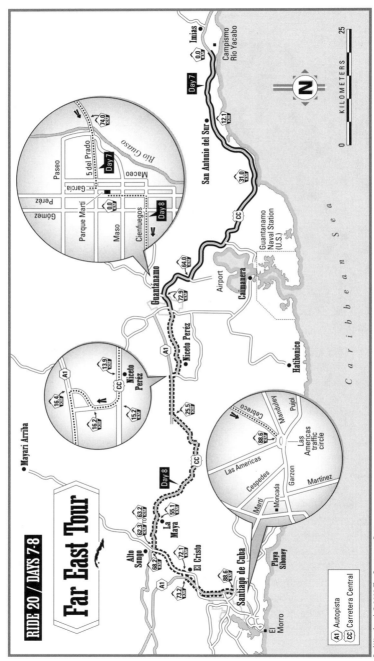

RIDE 20 / DAYS 7-8
Far East Tour

A1 Autopista
CC Carretera Central

Paul Woodward, © 2002 The Countryman Press

Food

About 12 km after Campismo Río Yacabo, you will reach the pleasant town of San Antonio del Sur. There are a couple of dollar stores, and vendors sell pizza and other goodies. Buy some food to carry with you, and be sure to top off your water bottles. It is also a good idea to buy a large extra bottle of water and stuff it in a pannier. There may be no more bottled water until you are in the outskirts of Guantánamo, 60 km from here.

Past the hamlet of Tortuguilla, 32 km from the start, there is an open-air, thatch *peso* restaurant with cold drinks and simple meals. Bottled water will probably not be available. We each drank a couple of cold *peso* colas to conserve our water supply.

Lodging

Hotel Guantánamo, the principal tourist hotel in town, received dreadful reviews from several cyclists to whom we spoke along the road. There are other accommodations mentioned in the general guidebooks, but we headed directly for a *casa particular,* and we liked it very much.

The *casa* of Elsye Castillo is not impressive from the outside, but beyond the battered doorway is a roomy, rambling home, part of which is Colonial and filled with antiques. There is a sunny, enclosed patio where you can have a cold drink. Elsye and her family are friendly and the food is great. The address is Calixto García Norte No. 766, between the Prado and Jesús del Sol. The telephone number is 32-3787, and directions for finding the place are included at the end of the route directions under km 74.

Route Directions

0.0 From Campismo Río Yacabo, ride west along the coast, with the sea to your left.

1.2 Enter the *municipio* of San Antonio del Sur.

9.5 Enter and quickly pass through the small town of Acopio.

12.1 Enter San Antonio del Sur. There is a park in 0.5 km in the center of town, a dollar store on the left, and another dollar store farther down the street on the right. Vendors offer a variety of snacks. This is pleasant spot for a break.

19.9 A sign indicates that Guantánamo is 55 km and Santiago de Cuba is 139 km. You will be riding close to the sea for several kilometers, and it is blue and tantalizing. However, the shores are rough, pitted limestone. You need foot protection if you want get into the water. Or wait until km 29.2, where there is a small, rocky beach on the left with easier access.

31.0 Enter Tortuguilla. In less than 2 km, there is an attractive, open-air

Traffic in a village near Guantánamo

peso restaurant on the left.

33.8 Playa Yateritas is a defunct holiday camp on the left, and it is an easy place to get into the warm water for a swim.

36.6 Around the small settlement of Yateritas, commercial banana groves line the road for over 1 km. This is a good place to buy several bananas for a *peso*.

47.5 A sign warns of a dangerous downhill ahead, tallying 26 accidents and 65 deaths! (There must have been a bus crash to generate numbers like that.) However, on a bicycle this 2-km run back to the sea is merely pleasant. Just use your brakes occasionally to stay under control.

51.3 Enter Glorieta. The terrain is relatively flat. You will ride through some grazing land; and then in a few kilometers, fields of sugar cane begin lining the road.

64.0 Bear right on the main road, passing an unmarked left turn that goes to the airport. There is a striking billboard here opposing the blockade.

72.9 Enter a rotary and follow the sign to the left for Ciudad. This rotary comes immediately after a military zone on the right, in the outskirts of Guantánamo City.

74.0 Bear right at another rotary; when you are less than halfway around, bear left at a fork. This street is the Prado, and it will take you directly to the center of the city. The *casa* of Elsye Castillo is on Calixto

García Norte, a major crossroad on the first block to the right of the Prado. García is one-way to the left, however. You should walk your bikes to the right. The *casa* is across García partway down the block.

Day 8: Guantánamo to Santiago de Cuba (89 km)

If you ask people in Guantánamo to point the way to Santiago de Cuba, they will send you straight to the Autopista. However, we start this ride going west on the old Carretera Central. Then, shortly after Niceto Pérez, the Carretera Central merges with the Autopista for 5 km, at which point this short section of the Autopista ends, and you return to riding on the Carretera Central.

This day of the tour offers beautiful scenery, passing through rolling countryside and brushing the northern foothills of the Sierra de la Gran Piedra. The only challenging climbs are midway along the route, between km 30 and 50. They are made difficult by the heat more than by the grades. In fact, the principal challenges of this ride are likely to be the heat and the distance from Guantánamo to the next reliable source of bottled water and food. The last 15 km of the route are gently downhill or level, an easy finish as you arrive at Santiago de Cuba, the end of this tour.

Food

It is absolutely necessary on this ride to carry plenty of water and some snacks or fruit as well. Even if you have three big water bottles per person, it is wise to buy an extra 1.5-liter bottle and find a place to stow it on your bike.

After Guantánamo, the first reliable source of food and water is the town of La Maya, 55 km from the start. In this town, you will find a dollar store, street food, and a basic cafeteria. We got an early start, bought a lot of water in La Maya, and made it to Santiago de Cuba for a late lunch.

Lodging

The ride ends in Santiago de Cuba, where there are any number of places to stay. For more information, see the section entitled Food and Lodging in Santiago de Cuba at the beginning of Part IV.

Route Directions

0.0 The ride begins at Parque Martí on Pedro Pérez, directly opposite the park in front of the Casa de la Cultura. Ride south—this puts the Casa de la Cultura on your right and the park on your left as you begin.

0.5 Turn right on Avenida Camilo Cienfuegos, a broad boulevard.

2.1 Turn left onto the Carretera Central, following overhead signs for Santiago de Cuba and Niceto Pérez.

3.5 Pass the interprovincial bus terminal on the left.

4.5 Enter the *municipio* of Niceto Pérez. At this point, the Carretera Central has already turned into a quiet country road with little or no traffic, better-than-average paving, and increasingly lovely scenery for the next several kilometers. First you will pass through rough grassland with grazing cattle, then more cultivated areas with bananas, *malanga*, and maize. Mountains are hazy blue in the distance ahead and to the left.

13.9 Continue straight, passing a left to Niceto Pérez.

15.2 Bear right, following the main road; do not go straight.

15.8 Pass Campamento Provincial Recreativo Daniel Llosas Pavel on the right.

16.2 Stay on the main road as it turns 90 degrees to the right.

16.4 Turn left at a T-intersection onto the Autopista. Though much wider, this highway will be almost as quiet and scenic as the Carretera Central.

16.8 A sign on the Autopista gives distances to Yerbaguinea, La Maya, Songo, and Santiago de Cuba.

25.5 The Autopista ends. Bear left and continue on the old Carretera Central.

30.7 Enter the province of Santiago de Cuba. The terrain here is rolling, closer to the foothills of the mountains, so the grades become longer and steeper.

38.9 Continue straight, passing a left to Ramón de las Yaguas. There is a sign indicating that it is 16 km to La Maya. You are in the center of a small village, Yerba de Guinea. You *may* be able to buy food here. There are a couple of stands, but when we passed through in late morning, none of them were operating. Don't count on buying water either.

43.2 Note a sign on the right for Perseverancia! In the heat and rolling terrain, perseverance is just what you need.

54.1 A faded sign welcomes visitors to La Maya. On the left, a coffee grove is shaded by beautiful trees hung with epiphytes; it looks almost like a park.

55.1 Follow the main road as it bears right at a fork. You are now in La Maya.

55.8 There is a tiny convenience store in the Cupet gas station on the left. We bought all the water we could drink and then more to refill our bottles. There are a couple of basic *peso* cafeterias in town, but La Maya is a rather dreary place, and you may want to press on to Santiago de Cuba for a late lunch.

56.3 Pass another dollar store on the left.

56.4 Continue straight as a road merges from the right. At this busy intersection, there are many hawkers selling goods—but not food—on the sidewalk to the left. It is something like a flea market.

62.3 Turn right, following a sign indicating that Santiago is another 26 km. Do not go straight toward Songo. You will now ride downhill for almost 1 km.

63.2 Turn left at a major intersection; there are no signs here! In another 0.5 km you will ride through a long tunnel.

67.2 Continue straight past a turn on the left to Loma del Gato, a tiny settlement at the top of a long, difficult hill.

68.2 Bear left, staying on the main road. On the right is the entrance to a hospital.

70.8 Pass a sign on the right for Santiago de Cuba, the Heroic City. You are entering the *municipio;* the city proper is still 10 km away. You will also pass the Lenin Polytechnic on the right.

72.1 Go straight through a small crossroad. (Note: The *Guía de Carreteras* is misleading here. It indicates that the road you are on passes directly through the center of El Cristo, with a small connection to the right for the Autopista. In fact, the main road goes directly to the Autopista, and the center of El Cristo is a few hundred meters to the left at this intersection.)

73.2 Stop at a T-intersection at the Autopista. Cross carefully and ride to the left. In a few hundred meters you will pass a PNR control point and then begin a long downhill. In fact, it is downhill most of the way to the city.

82.9 A sign on the right indicates you should continue straight to Avenida Victoriano Garzón. There are exits to Villa Panamericanas and Sala Polivalente. **You should continue straight, ignoring any turns or exits,** to the very end of the Autopista.

85.1 Continue straight, passing a right to Hotel Las Américas and Hotel Santiago de Cuba. (It is simpler to go straight even if you are staying at one of these hotels.)

88.0 Continue straight, carefully, through a busy intersection. The Autopista ends at this point and becomes Avenida General Cebreco. Continue on Cebreco through several more intersections.

88.6 Arrive at the traffic circle at Hotel Las Américas. The hotel is on your right. If you bear right and then turn right immediately, you will see the Hotel Santiago de Cuba ahead. If instead you continue around the circle, you will end up on Avenida Garzón, the main road west to the older, historic part of the city.

Part V:
Connecting the Regions of Cuba

This section is for the cyclist who would like to connect the regions we have described, perhaps riding the entire length of the island. The most important advice we can give to anyone planning such a trip is this: *Cycle from east to west.* If you arrive in Havana or Varadero, please don't plan to bike to the Oriente. Here's why:

Between central Cuba and the Oriente lie the great, mostly open plains of Ciego de Ávila, Camagüey, and Las Tunas provinces. The distance between Sancti Spiritus and Bayamo or Holguín is nearly 400 km. The principal difficulty of this ride is the prevailing wind from the east or the northeast. Starting midmorning, the wind is usually constant, and it can be very strong. If your flight arrives in Havana or Varadero, use a domestic flight or a Víazul bus to travel east, and then cycle west.

With the wind at your back, the ride across the plains can be reasonably pleasant, if monotonous, and you can easily cover long distances in a day. Against the wind, every kilometer is a struggle. Therefore our suggestions for riding across the plains begin in Bayamo or Holguín and end in Sancti Spiritus.

The flat plains of Las Tunas

From Sancti Spiritus, we recommend using part of the Central Cuba Tour (Ride 11) and cycling to Trinidad, Cienfuegos, and Playa Girón. We will make suggestions for a route past Playa Larga, through Ciénaga Zapata, and on to Matanzas City. Routes in and out of Havana and Pinar del Río (Part I and II) can be combined for a ride all the way to the west end of Cuba.

㉑ Cycling Cuba's Great Plains

400 km, 4 days or more

This 400-km ride across the plains west from Holguín or Bayamo is best skipped if your time is limited. However, if you want to cycle all of Cuba, you can do this ride and perhaps even enjoy it. It can be exhilarating to roll up the impressive daily distances that are possible when the trade wind pushes you along.

There is no need for kilometer-by-kilometer directions across Cuba because there are almost no turns except inside the major cities. Here is some helpful information based on our experience.

Use the Carretera Central. It is possible to ride from east to west along a route that is sometimes called the Circuito Norte, roughly parallel to the north coast but well inland. However, we fear it could be difficult to find enough accommodations, food, and water along the way. Even on the Carretera Central, there is little outside the major cities.

Bayamo to Las Tunas (82 kilometers)

The first leg of the route across the plains is 82 km from Bayamo to Las Tunas. (If you are starting from Holguín instead, the distance to Las Tunas is exactly the same.) From Bayamo, the road is level. A few kilometers outside town, there are huge rice fields irrigated with water from Río Cauto, Cuba's longest river. There are fields of cane as well.

About 30 km from Bayamo, go straight past the turn to Río Cauto. There should be *refrescos* and snacks for sale at this major intersection. In another 16 km, in Vado del Yeso, you can get sandwiches and bottled drinks at Rápido las Brisas, which is on the left.

When we did this ride, we left Bayamo at 7 AM in the morning. In the cool morning air, with level roads, we made the 82-km trip to Las Tunas very quickly (for us) and arrived in time for lunch. Then we made our first big mistake.

In the afternoon we decided to push on as far as Guaimaro, another 48 km to the west. The problem was the accommodations at the Hotel Guaimaro, the only licensed accommodations we could find. The staff was friendly and the little restaurant was not too bad, but the night was spoiled by a smelly, noisy room, rife with mosquitoes. Wally slept with the aid of rum, but Barbara was less willing to sedate herself and had a miserable night. Things may have improved since then, but we recommend that you stay overnight in Las Tunas and get an early start the next morning for Camagüey.

Las Tunas to Camagüey (120 kilometers)

The distance from Las Tunas to Camagüey is over 120 km, but should not be difficult if you start near dawn. Those lovely trade winds will push you along. Las Tunas Province continues to be flat; but about the time you enter Camagüey Province, the landscape begins to roll gently. Closer to Camagüey City, some of these *rolls* might even be called *hills,* but none of the cycling is difficult. This is cattle country. The road is lined with white-washed fence posts and barbed wire, kilometer after kilometer. The Sierra Maestra is just visible on the southern horizon.

We did not notice food or water stops between Las Tunas and Guaimaro, but as long as you set out with plenty of water and something to nibble on, the first 48 km go by very quickly. Guaimaro is a fair-sized town with cafeterias and a dollar store, as well as the hotel's basic restaurant.

The first town after Guaimaro is Martí, but we did not stop until Carrosco, which is about 22 km from Guaimaro and 70 km from Las Tunas. There is a Tiendas Panamericanas dollar store on the right, near the far side of town, but it is inconspicuous. If you come to a small triangular park, also on the right, you have missed the dollar store by a couple hundred meters.

Only 8 km beyond Cascorro is Sibanicú, the biggest town on the route. It has a hotel that you could check out, but it may be no better than the one in Guaimaro. From Sibanicú it is less than 50 km to Camagüey.

A possible alternative to riding the rest of the way to Camagüey is to stop at Campismo La Barbacoa, a Cubamar *campismo* near Sibanicú. The address is Carretera Central, Alvaro Mora, Sibanicú, and the telephone number is 3-8709. We have not been there, but the brochure is attractive and you could ask about it.

We spent the night at the Hotel Camagüey, a big, nondescript Horizontes establishment where we were deeply grateful for the swimming pool and our clean room. The hotel is on the east side so you will reach it before the city proper. We were able to get breakfast fairly early—7 AM—and we remember the excellent yogurt.

On our ride across the plains, we stayed in hotels even though there were *casas particulares* in every city. We did this because the hotels were convenient, right on the Carretera Central, and we simply wanted a swim, dinner, and an early start the next day. Other hotels besides those we mention are described in the general guidebooks. If you are interested in staying in a *casa particular* and spending time in one of the cities along this route, we recommend Camagüey; it is by far the biggest and most attractive, with many squares and parks, museums, and other attractions.

Camagüey to Ciego de Ávila (108 kilometers)

Camagüey is a big, sprawling city, and after leaving the hotel on the east side, it seems to take forever to reach the other side of town. There were even minor bicycle traffic jams when we rode through! West of Camagüey, the first part of this 108-km ride seems to be gently downhill. We weren't sure if this was an optical illusion, but the cycling was certainly easy.

The best town for a break is Florida, about 40 km from the start. This place is distinctive because you enter town through a green tunnel of shade trees that completely arches over the Carretera Central. There is a Tiendas Panamericanas dollar store and a small park on the right.

Near the border of Ciego de Ávila Province, hawkers along the Carretera Central sell a treat that we enjoy—slightly tangy, fresh farmers cheese and blocks of *guayaba*. Together on crackers, a taste sensation! The only problem is that they sell the stuff in such huge blocks that you need big zip-lock bags for the leftovers.

About 43 km past Florida, there is a Rumbos cafeteria on the left. A few kilometers farther, on the right, is Finca Oasis, an outdoor restaurant. It is only 19 km farther to Ciego de Ávila.

In the city, we stayed at the Hotel Ciego de Ávila, another Horizontes hotel, concrete poured into the same mold as the one in Camagüey. The staff was friendly and amused when Wally cleverly lost his room key in the bottom of the deep swimming pool. The lobby and bar of this hotel were attractive, and the rooms were satisfactory.

Ciego de Ávila to Sancti Spiritus (76 kilometers)

After an overnight in Ciego de Ávila, the ride to Sancti Spiritus is an easy 76 km. About 28 km from the hotel in Ciego de Ávila, there is a crossroad on the Carretera Central near Majagua. There is a gas station with a dollar store and a small restaurant.

About 40 km from Ciego de Ávila, you can catch glimpses of the Sierra del Escambray in the distance. Nearer Sancti Spiritus, the terrain is slightly more varied, just enough to be interesting, and the vegetation is more diverse. The mountains gradually draw closer.

Rather than ride into the city, we stayed at Hotel Zaza. The left for the hotel, about 5 km before Sancti Spiritus, is marked by a kiosk. This hotel is on the shore of Embalse Zaza, Cuba's biggest reservoir—a place that is popular with fishermen. The hotel itself is slightly run-down, but it has a good pool and beautiful views over the vast expanse of shallow water. Alternatively, you can continue straight to town. In either case, it is easy to pick up the Central Cuba Tour from here.

㉒ Playa Girón to Matanzas City

152 kilometers, 2 days

Assuming that you use the Central Cuba Tour as far as Playa Girón, you will need to connect Playa Girón to Matanzas City—152 km, 2 days. On Day 1, the route follows the shore of the Bahía de Cochinos to Playa Larga and then north to lodging at Australia. The Day 2 ride is 91 km to Matanzas City. Fortunately the ride is not difficult because the terrain is gently rolling

Entering Florida

or flat. On Day 2, the heat is likely to be the biggest challenge, so get a very early start from Australia.

On Day 1, you will ride from Playa Girón to Australia. Only 16 km northwest of Playa Girón is Cueva de los Peces on the right. For $1 you get the opportunity to swim in the clear waters of a deep, natural limestone pool inhabited by colorful fish. Presumably you will arrive too early for lunch, but there should be time to stop if you wish.

About 10 km farther, Campismo Victoriana Girón is on the left, and foreigners are accepted. We have heard the food is poor. Presumably you will ride much farther. About 30 km from Playa Girón, there is a beach at Caleta del Rosario.

Playa Larga is the first town along the route, 34 km from Playa Girón. There is a Horizontes hotel, but it was closed at the end of 2001. We hope it will reopen because it is a pleasant, inexpensive place. There are also *casas particulares* in Playa Larga.

The next likely stop is the so-called Tahitian Village at Guama, 47 km from the start. The parking lot is usually full of tour buses. There are thatched gift shops, a restaurant, dollar store, ceramics factory, and crocodile farm. Also part of this tourism complex is a hotel where guests are housed in thatched cottages, many on stilts, built on an island in Laguna del Tesoro. We talked to cyclists who stayed and enjoyed it. However, it costs $10 per person just to get to the hotel by boat, plus a room, plus meals. Two people should plan on $100 or more per night.

Guama is only 17 km from Batey de Don Pedro, the accommodation we recommend. It is comfortable and picturesque for half the cost of Guama. Guest rooms at Batey de Don Pedro are in separate wooden buildings, each built with a high, thatched roof in the style of a *bohío* (peasant hut). But these rooms are not huts; they have air-conditioning, dark tile floors, excellent baths, and even satellite television if you care. There is a restaurant; and next door to Batey de Don Pedro is Finca Fiesta Campesina, which has another restaurant and café and a scattering of farm animals about.

To find Batey de Don Pedro, turn right in Australia and then left, following signs to Jaguey Grande and the Autopista. Batey de Don Pedro is on the left, a couple of hundred meters past the huge *central*.

On to Matanzas City

The easiest route from Batey de Don Pedro to Matanzas City is north through San José de Marcos and La Isabel to Jovellanos, then northwest on the Carretera Central. As you pass kilometer after kilometer of flat citrus fields, the challenges will be heat and monotony. You can largely deal with the heat by starting at dawn or even a little before. Because the route is easy, you can arrive in Matanzas for a late lunch. At least we did, and we are slow cyclists. We don't have advice for dealing with the monotony!

Get an early start. The café at Finca Fiesta Campesina is supposed to be open 24 hours, though we did not try it and are not sure what would actually be available at dawn.

Turn left when you leave Batey de Don Pedro, and in a few hundred meters you will reach the Autopista. This is Entronque Jaguey. Head west (left) and you will immediately pass a large complex on the left—a service station, convenience store, and Rumbos restaurant. Some of this is open 24 hours as well, another slim chance for a cup of coffee or something to eat. At least be sure your water bottles are filled. The next reliable source is 38 km away in Jovellanos.

Ride on the Autopista 6 km and turn north. In another 2 km, proceed straight through a crossroad—the right goes into Jaguey Grande. From here it is a straight, mostly flat ride to Jovellanos.

Jovellanos is a big, shabby town, but there are plenty of places to buy pizza and *bocaditos*, and there is a dollar store. Jovellanos also has the Hotel Moderno, which is anything but modern. We tried for a room there once, but foreigners were not accepted. It was probably just as well.

From Jovellanos, head northwest on the Carretera Central. Some of the terrain will be rolling, even moderately hilly. There is a dollar kiosk for water and cold drinks in Coliseo, 17 km past Jovellanos and 24 km from Matan-

On the road near Unión de Reyes, Matanzas

zas. There is probably food and water in Limonar as well, but we have never tried stopping there.

In Matanzas, you could stay at one of the few *casas particulares* or at the Hotel Louvre. Better yet, push on to the Casa del Valle de Yumurí. Once we made it from Batey de Don Pedro all the way to Playa Jibacoa, but we were beat when we got there.

We have also cycled a longer and more complicated route from Australia to Matanzas. It passes through several small towns that add variety and also provide more opportunities for drinks and food. The route goes through Bolondrón, Unión de Reyes, and Cidra. The problems: it is longer, it has complicated twists and turns through the towns, and it begins with 37 monotonous km on the Autopista. All things considered, the more direct route through Jovellanos is better.

Once you reach Matanzas or Valle de Yumurí, you can take the Vía Blanca to Havana (essentially doing Ride 3, Havana to Playas del Este and Matanzas, backwards) and then continue west into Pinar del Río.

¡Buen viaje!

Appendixes

Spanish for Cyclists

Here we have listed a few cycling-related words and phrases that are useful when touring in Cuba. For pronunciation and more extensive vocabulary lists, pack a good phrase book and/or English-Spanish dictionary.

Questions for when your bike breaks down

Is there someone nearby who fixes bikes?
¿Hay alguien por acá que puede arreglar la bicicleta?

Is there someone nearby who fixes flat tires?
¿Hay alguien por acá que coja ponches o puede arreglar la goma ponchada?

My brake (derailleur) cable is broken.
El cable del freno (de la torre) está roto.

Can you help me fix it?
¿Puede ayudarme a arreglarlo?

Do you know where I can buy another ____?
¿Sabe usted dónde puedo comprar otro ____?

Where is the bus station? (For when things get really desperate.)
¿Dónde está la estación de guaguas?

Can I get a ride to Havana? (Another option for when things get desperate.)
¿Me puede llevar a Havana?

Bike parts most likely to break or need adjustment
wheel—*la rueda*
rim—*la llanta*
spoke—*el rayo*
tire—*la goma*
tube—*la cámara de aire*
flat tire—*la goma ponchada*
tire repair shop—*la ponchera*
chain—*la cadena*
brake—*el freno*
brakeset—*el sistema de freno*
cable—*el cable*
derailleur—*la torre*
crank—*el cigueñal*
shift lever—*la manilla de cambios*
free wheel—*piñonera*
front hub—*el centro delantero*
rear freehub—*el centro trasero*
frame—*el caballo*
fork—*el tenedor*
handlebars—*el manubrio*
helmet—*el casco*
saddle—*el sillín*
pedals—*los pedales*

The most basic tools
tire pump—*la bomba*
socket wrench—*la llave de ojo*
open wrench—*la llave española*
flat screwdriver—*el destornillador plano*
Phillips screwdriver—*el destornillador de estrías*
pliers—*los alicates*
knife—*el cuchillo*
tire patch and glue—*ponche en frío*

Questions (and some sample answers) when you are lost or need directions

How far is it to Trinidad?
¿A cuántos kilómetros queda Trinidad?

It is two kilometers to Trinidad.
Trinidad queda a dos kilómetros.

Trinidad is not far.
Trinidad no queda lejos.

It is nearby.
Está cerca.

How do I get to Trinidad?
¿Cómo llego a Trinidad?

Turn right.
Doble a la derecha.

At the next corner.
En la próxima esquina.

In three blocks.
En tres cuadros.

In four kilometers.
En cuatro kilómetros.

Turn left.
Doble a la izquierda.

Keep going straight ahead.
Sigue derecho (or *recto*).

What is the name of this road?
¿Qué carretera es ésta?

What is the name of this town?
¿Cómo se llama este pueblo?

Does this road go to Baracoa?
¿Es éste el camino a Baracoa?

Where does this road go?
¿Dónde va este camino?

Is the road hilly?
¿Hay muchas lomas en este camino?

Are there many potholes?
¿Hay muchos baches?

Is this road paved?
¿Es este camino pavimentado?

Is the road o.k. for bikes?
¿Este camino sirve para bicicletas?
¿Pueden pasar las bicicletas por este camino?

Other useful questions
Where can I keep my bike?
¿Donde puerdo guarda mi bicicleta?

Will it be safe?
¿Estara segura?

Can I bring my bike on the bus/train/airplane?
¿Puedo llevar mi bicicleta en el ómnibus/tren/avión?

Other means of transportation
truck—*el camión*
car—*el carro*
rental car—*carro de alquiler*
bus—*la guagua, el omnibus*
bus station—*la estación de guaguas*
train—*el tren*
plane—*el avión*
airport—*el aeropuerto*
ticket office—*la taquilla*
boat or ferry—*la lancha, el transbordador*

Spanish words used in directions
el norte—*north*
este—*east (direction)*
el oriente—*east (place)*
el oeste—*west*
el sud—*south*
la guía—*guide*
cerca de—*near*
lejos de—*far*
próximo—*next*
el último—*last*
a la izquierda—*to the left*
a la derecha—*to the right*

el recto/derecho—*straight ahead*
adelante—*ahead, forward*
aquí/allí—*here/there*
desde—*from, since*
hasta—*as far as, until*

Warnings and road signs

el punto de control—*control point, a police checkpoint*
el semáfaro—*traffic light*
peligroso—*danger*
cuidado—*caution*
las curvas—*curves*
los pendientes—*steep slopes*
ceder—*yield*
pare—*stop*
vía en mal estado—*bad road conditions*
los baches—*potholes*

Maps and geographical features

el mapa—*map*
el mirador—*lookout, viewpoint*
el embalse—*dam, reservoir*
el lago—*lake*
la bahía—*bay*
la playa—*beach*
el cayo—*key*
la isla—*island*
las alturas—*highlands*
la loma—*hill*
la montaña—*mountain*
la sierra—*mountain range*
las cuchillas—*ridges*
el mogote—*knoll, humplike mountain*
la cueva—*cave*

Roads and streets

la calle—*street*
la avenida—*avenue*
la carretera—*road*
la autopista—*highway*

el camino—*road*
el sendero—*path*
la vía—*roadway, way*
el malecón—*waterfront boulevard*
la circunvalación—*ring-road, bypass*
el entronque—*junction*
la esquina—*corner*
la cuadra—*block*

Cities and towns
la ciudad—*city*
el pueblo—*town*
la aldea—*village, hamlet*
el municipio—*municipality, municipal jurisdiction*
el barrio— *district, suburb*
el reparto—*zone*
la vecindad—*neighborhood*

Rural features
la finca—*farm, ranch*
la vega—*meadow, tobacco farm*
la central—*sugar mill*
el organopónico—*organic garden*
el jardín—*garden*
el bohío—*hut, peasant cottage*

Common abbreviations on signs
PCC—*Partido Comunista de Cuba*
PNR—*Policía Nacional Revolucionaria*
CDR—*Comité de Defensa de la Revolución*
UJC—*Unión de Juventud Comunista (Union of Communist Youth)*
CAI—*Complejo Agroindustrial (Agro-industrial complex—primarily for sugar production)*
UBPC—*Unidad Basica de Produccion Cooperativa (This and the next two are types of farm cooperatives—see the sidebar entitled* Alphabet Soup *on page 104.)*
CPA—*Cooperativa de Producción Agrícola*
CCS—*Cooperativa de Créditos y Servicios*

Reading List

What follows is a list of four of the best general guidebooks, some good cycle touring and repair books, and our very favorite books about Cuba. Christopher Baker's *Cuba Handbook* has the most extensive bibliography that we have seen in general guidebooks on Cuba. Be sure to get the latest edition available when purchasing a general guidebook. Also, both of the books on bicycle repair and maintenance are well illustrated and useful for learning basic skills before you leave on tour, but they are much too bulky to carry with you in a pannier.

General Guidebooks

▶ Baker, Christopher. *Cuba Handbook*. Emeryville, CA: Moon Travel Handbooks from Avalon Travel Publications, 2000.

▶ McAuslan, Fiona and Matthew Norman. *The Rough Guide to Cuba*. London: Rough Guides (Penguin Group), 2000.

▶ Stanley, David. *Cuba*. Melbourne: Lonely Planet Publications, 2000.

▶ Aeberhard, Danny et al, editors. *Cuba*. London: Insight Guides, 2000.

Bicycle Touring and Repairs

▶ Lovett, Richard A. *The Essential Touring Cyclist*. Camden, Maine: Ragged Mountain Press/McGraw Hill, 2001.

Currently the best book available that we have seen on cycle touring.

▶ Forester, John. *Effective Cycling*. Cambridge: MIT Press, 1993.

A classic on all aspects of cycling, with substantial chapters on repairs and touring. Could use more illustrations to help visualize repair jobs.

▶ Bicycling Magazine's *Complete Guide to Bicycle Maintenance and Repair*. Emmaus: Rodale Press, 1994.

▶ Henderson, Bob. *The Haynes Bicycle Book—Step by Step Repair and Maintenance*. Haynes North America Inc., 2001.

Our Favorite Books on Cuba

▶ Anderson, John Lee. *Che Guevara: A Revolutionary Life*. New York,: Grove Press, 1997.

An extraordinarily detailed biography that gives an intimate sense of the man, the causes for which he fought, and his central role in the Cuban revolution.

▶ Benjamin, Medea, Joseph Collins, and Michael Scott. *No Free Lunch: Food and Revolution in Cuba*. San Francisco: Institute for Food and Development Policy, 1984.

A fascinating history and analysis of developments in Cuban agriculture in the first 25 years after the revolution. It is best read along with a 2001 report from OXFAM entitled *Cuba: Going Against the Grain* by Minor Sinclair and Martha Thompson. At press time, a new book on Cuban agriculture had just been published by the Institute for Food and Development Policy, *Sustainable Agriculture and Resistance: Transforming Food Production in Cuba*. See the next section on Internet resources for web sites for OXFAM and the Institute.

▶ Carmer, Mark. *Culture Shock! Cuba, A Guide to Customs and Etiquette*. Portland, Oregon: Graphic Arts Publishing Center, 1998.

Information on contemporary attitudes and customs in Cuba with sensible advice for the visitor about what to expect and how to behave.

▶ Pérez, Louis A. *Cuba and the United States: Ties of Singular Intimacy*. Athens, Georgia: University of Georgia Press, 1997.

A distinguished Cuban scholar told us that Louis Pérez is the best historian of Cuba writing in English. We found this book to be a tremendous eye opener. Several other books by Pérez are also available.

▶ Ripley, C. Peter. *Conversations with Cuba*. Athens, Georgia: University of Georgia Press, 1999.

Ripley repeatedly traveled from the U.S. to Cuba during the 1990s, the years of the Special Period; and in this book he keeps track of the friends he made and how they coped during those difficult years.

▶ Smith, Wayne. *The Closest of Enemies: A Personal & Diplomatic History of the Castro Years*. New York: W. W. Norton, 1987.

Wayne Smith is a retired U.S. diplomat who gives an insider's view of U.S.-Cuban relations from the revolution through the Reagan years. This book should be required reading for any American going to Cuba. Unfortunately it is out of print, but it is still available through Amazon.com and in many public libraries.

▶ Szulc, Tad. *Fidel: A Critical Portrait*. New York: Morrow, 1986.

Whatever one thinks of Castro and his government, he is one of the most fascinating leaders of our age, and Szulc's book is well balanced and highly readable.

Internet Resources

The Internet is now perhaps the best way to find current information on Cuba. However, because so many people have strong feelings about Cuba, some information on the web—especially of a political nature—is unreliable.

This Guidebook

▶ www.bicyclingcuba.com
e-mail: wbsmith@valley.net

General

▶ http://afrocubaweb.com
An extensive list of cultural and informational sites.

Cuba In-Country Links

▶ www.cuba.cu/cubainternet/cubainternetes.html
This site is in Spanish but it offers a comprehensive list of sites in Cuba, and some are in English.
▶ www.geocities.com/vedadohavana/lalala.html
Helpful sites from Raul Sarmiento in Havana.
▶ hometown.aol.com/merengue123/cubaeng.html
An interesting explanation of the day-to-day economy by a Cuban.

News

▶ www.cubadaily.com
A sampling of news on Cuba from across the ideological spectrum.
▶ www.granma.cu/ingles/index.html
Cuba's official government newspaper, the country's only daily, with a weekly Internet edition.
▶ cubanet.org/cubanews.html
The Miami exile version of events.

Travel

▶ cubalinda.com
Internet travel service based in Havana.
▶ www.culturecuba.com/E/cuba/biking.html
Travel from Montreal.
▶ www.infotur.cu/eng/index.html
Helpful information in Havana.
▶ www.cubaclimbing.com
A great deal of good information for general travelers as well as climbers
▶ www.cubatravel.cu/en

Bus

▶ www.viazul.cu/home_eng.htm
Complete schedules and service for Víazul.

Airlines

▶ www.airtransat.com

Air Transat

▶ grupotaca.com

Grupo Taca, the Airline of Costa Rica

▶ www.cubana.cu

Cubana Airlines

Bike Boxes

▶ www.deltacases.com

▶ www.crateworks.com

▶ www.performance.com

Cuba Bicycle Tours

▶ www.macqueens.com

MacQueen's Bicycle Tours

▶ www.ibike.org/cuba/index.htm

International Bicycle Fund

▶ globalexchange.org/tours/cuba/BicycleAdventures.html

Global Exchange

▶ www.horizontes.cu/naturaleza/programas/ingprogramas_de_ciclo-turismo.htm

Horizontes bike tours.

Casas Particulares

▶ www.geocities.com/cubanexchange/index.html

▶ www.casaparticular.com

▶ users.pandora.be/casaparticular

Money/Debit Card

▶ www.transcardinter.com

The Transcard, useful if you have only American credit cards and are staying a month or more

Agriculture and Development

▶ www.oxfamamerica.org/art1164.html

Report: *Cuba, Going Against the Grain.*

▶ www.foodfirst.org/cuba/

Information on *Sustainable Agriculture and Resistance,* a new book from the Institute for Food and Development Policy.

U.S. Legal Issues, the Embargo, and Licences

▶ www.ccr.ny.org
The Center for Constitutional Rights; see The Cuba Travel Project.
▶ www.lawg.org/cuba.htm
The Latin America Working Group, a coalition of over 60 religious, human rights, and policy and development organizations that strives to influence U.S. policy toward Latin America and the Caribbean in order to promote peace, justice, and sustainable development.
▶ www.treas.gov/offices/enforcement/ofac/sanctions/tiicubapdf
Official U.S. documents about U.S. embargo.

International Reports on Human Rights in Cuba

▶ www.web.amnesty.org/web/ar2001.nsf/webamrcountries/
CUBA?OpenDocument
Amnesty International 2001 report on Cuba.
▶ www.hrw.org
Human Rights Watch has a report on Cuba.

Cuban Solidarity Groups

▶ www.ifconews.org/cuba.html
Pastors for Peace
▶ www.cubasolidarity.com
▶ www.witnessforpeace.org
▶ www.cubasolidarity.net
▶ www.letcubalive.org
▶ www.ciponline.org/cuba
Center for International Policy—Cuba Project.

Cuban Recipes

▶ www.cuba.cu/recetas.php
In Spanish.

Books

▶ www.ibike.org/bibliography/cuba-books.htm
Extensive bibliography from the International Bicycle Fund.

Organized Cycling Tours

The number of companies and organizations offering bicycle tours in Cuba is growing at an astonishing rate. Be cautious in selecting a tour company. Experience counts, and we mean experience running tours in Cuba.

MacQueen's Bicycle Tours

Gordon MacQueen, who founded this company, is an old friend from Prince Edward Island, Canada. His tours in Cuba are run by his son, Danny, and daughters Kristin and Kelly together with congenial Cuban guides.

MacQueen's has invested years of time and effort in Cuba, often operating at a loss, to develop the routes, locate the accommodations, and make the contacts needed for successful, smoothly run tours. Now business is booming, and of all the companies operating in Cuba, MacQueen's has the most experience and probably comes closest to providing the kind of professional, van-supported, inn-to-inn tour that cyclists enjoy in North America and Europe. MacQueen's tours are relatively expensive, but by all accounts, well worth it. Check out their web site at www.macqueens.com/tours.html, or call 1-800-WOW-CUBA.

Global Exchange

Global Exchange is a politically progressive, nonprofit organization based in Berkeley, California. For years they have organized *reality* tours in many countries. These are, first and foremost, educational programs that aim to open participants' eyes to political and economic conditions in the developing world. Global Exchange has offered this type of tour in Cuba for years, including bicycle tours.

Global Exchange is licensed by the U.S. State Department to conduct educational tours in Cuba, so U.S. citizens who go with Global Exchange will not be breaking any U.S. laws. You may be interested in their informative web site at www.globalexchange.org.

International Bicycle Fund (IBF)

This is another U.S.-based, nonprofit organization with years of experience in Cuba. IBF tours are the least expensive of those listed here. They are *people-to-people* tours; and whenever it is practical, guests stay in private homes with Cuban families. They also stay in moderately priced hotels and *campismos*. We have asked IBF guests, in the midst of their Cuba experiences, how things were going. They were uniformly enthusiastic. We have also met and talked with Pedro Curbelo, who leads most of IBF's tours in Cuba. He is an enthusiastic, competent tour leader.

At press time, IBF still did not have a license from the U.S. State Department, so American guests on these tours, as with the Canadian companies, are violating the Trading with the Enemy Act. Check out information concerning this on www.ibike.org.

Other cycle touring companies based in North America and in Europe are listed in the general guidebooks. We have described only those of which we have firsthand knowledge. If you are considering other companies, be sure to ask how long they have been offering cycle tours in Cuba, and just as important, how many tours they have successfully conducted. It is also a good idea to ask for references, past riders that you can contact about their trips. If you don't get satisfactory answers, look elsewhere.

Airline Regulations

The following is information about the air routes most commonly used by North Americans. These are rates and rules that prevailed at press time. *Check with your travel agent for current regulations before purchasing a ticket.*

From Canada

Cubana de Aviación, Cuba's national airline, runs frequent flights from major Canadian cities. Cubana accepts bikes on the same terms as other baggage. That is, bikes count toward your weight allowance, but there is no special charge for them.

Cubana allows 30 kilograms per person. With most bikes weighing 12 or 13 kilograms, this leaves 17 kilograms for all your equipment and clothing. We have found that this is enough for everything we really need.

Grupo Taca, the airline of Costa Rica, offers flights from Canada to Cuba. Grupo Taca provides a generous weight allowance—two large pieces of luggage at 32 kilograms each—and a boxed bike can count as one of them. Grupo Taca tickets were a bargain at press time, but Canadian flights departed only from Toronto and Montreal, and Havana was Grupo Taca's only Cuban destination.

If you plan to stay in Cuba for two weeks or less, a popular choice from Canada is AirTransat. This Montreal-based charter company runs frequent night flights from many Canadian cities to several Cuban destinations, but not to Havana. Air-only tickets are a bargain, and bikes do not count against your 20-kilogram weight allowance—they are carried free of charge.

It is possible to fly Air Canada to Jamaica and continue to Havana from there. Air Canada treats bikes as part of a 70-pound weight allowance; so by packing light you can easily bring your bike without incurring an extra charge.

From Jamaica

On flights to Havana, Air Jamaica allows one carryon and two pieces of checked baggage, and your bike is simply counted as one of the checked pieces. As with Air Canada, the bike counts against a 70-pound weight allowance, and there is no additional charge.

From Mexico

From Mexico City, Mexicana Airways charges an extra $50 each way for bikes on its flights to Havana. Bikes are allowed on AeroCaribe's flights from Cancun to Havana on the same terms.

Boxing Bikes

Cubana will carry bikes either boxed or unboxed. *All the other airlines mentioned in this book require that bikes be boxed.* We have shipped bikes both ways. If a bicycle is in a box, it is presumably safer. However, when a bike is unboxed, baggage attendants know just what it is, and they will usually handle and stow it appropriately. We would not ship expensive, ultra-light road bikes this way, but we would not bring such bikes to Cuba.

If you want or need to ship your bike in a box, there are several ways to do this. High quality, hard-shell cases of ABS plastic or polyethylene can cost $300 or more, but they do a good job. Besides being expensive, these cases can also weigh 30 pounds or more. For examples of this product, see www.deltacases.com, or contact Performance Bicycle (www.performance.com; 1-800-727-2453). Padded, soft cases for bicycles are also available from www.deltacases.com and elsewhere. They can be equally expensive and do not offer quite as much protection as hard cases, but they weigh less and can be easily folded and stored.

A cheaper alternative is provided by Crateworks Transport Systems. They make bike boxes of either polystyrene or sturdy cardboard with internal padding and tie-downs. Even the cardboard models, which cost under $100, are reusable many times. The polystyrene boxes cost between $130 and $150, and they will last indefinitely. They also weigh less than the premium hard-shell cases. The polystyrene boxes have another significant advantage over the alternatives: They are designed to fold flat so they can be stored under a bed or in a closet—an important consideration if you must find a place to leave your storage box during your tour. For more information about Crateworks, go to their web site at www.crateworks.com, or call 1-800-934-5214.

Note: For the cheapest alternative, you can ask a local bike shop for an empty bike box and some packing materials.

Storing your bike box can be a minor problem while you are on tour. If you are based at a resort hotel during a short visit, there will probably be a storage room available. If you are traveling, try staying at a *casa particular* for the first night or two and ask your host to help with arrangements. When we have done this, we have been offered storage space for free. Obviously it is easier for your host to grant such a request if your bike box folds flat like those made by Crateworks.

Bicycle Tools and Spares

Flats are the most common mishap of all, so you must bring the following:
- ▶ Tube patch kit
- ▶ Tire levers
- ▶ Good quality pump
- ▶ Spare tube and tire boot (for rides of a week or more)
- ▶ Spare tire (for extended tours)

Chain and spoke problems are next in frequency. If your bike uses a Shimano chain, consider switching to a Sachs/SRAM chain or other quality chain of the correct width. This is because of the special pins required for repairing Shimano chains. If you lose the little Shimano pins while you are in Cuba, replacements may be impossible to find. For chains, carry these tools and spares:
- ▶ Chain link quick connector (recommended: SRAM Powerlink or Missing Link)
- ▶ Chain tool (recommended: Park's Compact Chain Tool)
- ▶ Extra chain links

You should also carry spare spokes and the tools needed to change them. Remember that there may be spokes of three or even four different lengths on your bike. It is wise to take your wheels to a local bike shop and ask them to cut or select a set of two or three spare spokes (with nipples) of each length. To replace a spoke, you need your tire levers for removing the tire, plus a screwdriver and a spoke wrench of the correct size.

If a spoke breaks on the drive train side of the rear wheel, you must remove the gear cluster, so an additional tool is needed. For older-style freewheels, carry a small freewheel removal tool for your specific brand. For wheels with newer freehub-cassette combinations, carry a lockring removal tool. In fact, still more tools are needed. For freewheel removal, a big wrench or bench vise is necessary; for removing the cassette lockring, a chain whip is needed. However, you can just carry the small, specialized removal tool and trust in the ingenuity of Cuban *poncheras* to help you change a broken right rear spoke. Add these items to your list:

- ▶ Spare spokes with nipples
- ▶ Spoke wrench
- ▶ Screwdriver (Phillips and flat)
- ▶ Cassette lockring or freewheel removal tool

Fortunately, we are already at the end of the most frequent emergency repairs. Very rarely, a derailleur or brake cable will snap. Spare cables are light and take up almost no space, so you might as well carry one of each type. Other tools and spares are needed for occasional maintenance on a long tour. For adjusting brakes, tightening mounting bolts, changing brake pads and cables, and various other small jobs:

- ▶ 8, 9, and 10 mm box wrenches and/or 6-inch adjustable wrench
- ▶ Allen wrench set (metric)
- ▶ Needle-nosed pliers

You should bring a few more items for maintenance, including lubricant. For long tours, we recommend good old Tri-Flow, or the equivalent, rather than the newer lubes like White Lightning or ProLink. This is because a little Tri-Flow goes a lot farther and lasts longer. Here is the rest of our list:

- ▶ Spare brake and derailleur cables
- ▶ Spare brake pads
- ▶ Lubricant
- ▶ Small tube or plastic jar of hand cleaner
- ▶ A few rags

Many combination tools are on the market and can be substituted for several of the tools listed above. Some are useful, but others are junky toys. None are quite as versatile as a collection of individual tools, but the better ones include the Topeak Alien and the CoolTool. Multi-tools made by Leatherman and Gerber are not designed for work on bikes, but they are so useful in other ways that we keep one in our kit.

Note: It is possible to carry all the tools and spares listed, except for the spokes, rags, hand cleaner, and pump, in a good-sized wedge pack that goes under your seat.

Personal Items

General considerations about clothing were covered in the text, and our complete list of everything we carry on cycle tours in Cuba appears after this section. Here we address a few additional items you need to consider when you plan your packing.

If you aim to spend a good deal of time in the water, especially on undeveloped beaches or on the south shore, it is a good idea to pack a pair of water shoes. Lightweight nylon slip-ons with thin rubber bottoms will give you the protection you need when walking on coral, and they help keep you safe from sea urchins.

It is important to bring some sort of hat because of the hot sun. A cotton bandana is handy for wiping sweat, and you can soak it in water and wear it on your head for a good cool-down. Sunglasses or other protective eyewear are essential when you are on your bike, and sunscreen is a must. We bring insect repellent too, but in winter when the weather is generally dry, we do not often use it. Nail clippers are hard to find. If you will be staying long enough to need them, bring them.

Face soap, laundry detergent, shampoo, and toothpaste are available in dollar stores everywhere in Cuba. We recommend bringing toothpaste and one bar of soap (or a small, plastic bottle of liquid soap) to get you started. Shops in the hotels, if not all dollar stores, carry skin creams, cosmetics, razors, and shaving cream. However, if you have special needs or tastes in these items, it is best to bring your own. Barbara, for example, wants special soap and creams because of Cuba's heat and sun, so she brings quite a selection, despite Wally's grumbling.

Though most *campismos* and all *casas particulares* and hotels provide towels, we each bring a small, chamois-type camp towel. Washcloths are rarely available, so bring them as well. Because we are beach nuts, we also carry beach towels—far too bulky, but we do it anyway.

We bring sleep sheets, which we use as extra, lightweight blankets and emergency sleeping bags, or when we are unhappy with the cleanliness of the sheets provided at a hotel or *campismo*. We also bring a water filtering pump. These are other items that we have found to be necessary or useful:

- ▶ First-aid kit
- ▶ Kleenex and/or toilet paper
- ▶ Refreshing wipes in foil packets
- ▶ Zip-lock bags in various sizes
- ▶ Assortment of zip ties

▶ Tape (Some cyclists carry duct tape, but we think that packing tape reinforced with threads of fiberglass is more useful.)

▶ Flashlight or headlamp and batteries

▶ Pens, pencils, and pads or small notebooks

▶ English-Spanish dictionary, and books, as many books as we can carry. (Any book will be a much-appreciated gift when you have finished it.)

The Complete List
Bicycle tools, spares, and accessories
tube patch kit
tire levers
good quality pump
spare tube
tire boot
spare tire
chain link quick connector
chain tool
extra chain links
spare spokes with nipples
spoke wrench
cassette lockring or freewheel removal tool
screwdriver (Phillips and flat)
8, 9, 10 mm box wrenches and/or 6-inch adjustable wrench
metric Allen wrench set
needle-nosed pliers
multi-tool
spare brake pads
spare brake and derailleur cables
lubricant
small tube or plastic jar of hand cleaner
a few rags
racks, panniers, and handlebar bag
cable lock
cycle computer
bell

Clothing
sun hat or cap (1)
sunglasses (1)
cotton bandana (1)

cotton T-shirts (2)
cycling jersey (2)
long-sleeved polypro layering garment (1)
lightweight windbreaker or rain jacket (1)
cycling gloves
bicycle helmet
belt (1)
bike shorts (2)
tropical shorts (1 or 2)
tropical slacks (1)
skirt (1)
blouse or polo shirt (1)
bras or sport bras (2)
underwear (3)
biking sandals (1 pair)
walking sandals or casual shoes (1 pair)
water shoes (1 pair)
padded socks (1 pair)

Toiletries
soap and container
toothbrush
toothpaste
hair brush or comb
shampoo
sunscreen
lip balm
eye drops
insect repellent
skin creams
razor and blades
shaving cream (in a tube is best)
towels (beach towel and camp towel)
washcloth
nail clippers
ibuprofen
vitamins

Other Items

first-aid kit
water filtering pump
sleep sheet
matches
knife-fork-spoon set
drinking cup
zip-lock bags (strong, various sizes)
assortment of twist ties
tape
flashlight and batteries
headlight
pens and pencils
pads or small notebooks
Cuba guidebook
English-Spanish dictionary
Spanish phrase book (preferably Cuban Spanish, but at least Latin American)
books
camera and accessories
tape recorder
laptop computer and accessories

Index